Perennials for the Southwest

Perennials for the
SOUTHWEST

Plants That Flourish in Arid Gardens

MARY IRISH

With Photographs by
GARY IRISH

TIMBER PRESS
OCM 60931429

Published in 2006 by
Timber Press, Inc.
The Haseltine Building
133 S.W. Second Avenue, Suite 450
Portland, Oregon 97204-3527, U.S.A.

www.timberpress.com

For contact information regarding editorial, marketing, sales, and distribution in the
United Kingdom, see www.timberpress.co.uk.

Printed through Colorcraft Ltd., Hong Kong

Library of Congress Cataloging-in-Publication Data

Irish, Mary, 1949-
  Perennials for the Southwest : plants that flourish in arid gardens /
Mary Irish ; with photographs by Gary Irish.
      p. cm.
  Includes bibliographical references.
  ISBN-13: 978-0-88192-761-0
  ISBN-10: 0-88192-761-9
  1. Perennials--Southwest, New. 2. Arid regions plants--Southwest,
New. I. Title.
  SB434.I75 2006
  635.9'32'0979--dc22   2005019890

A catalog record for this book is also available from the British Library.

For Neal Maillet, who helped me and countless others become the author they only glimpsed inside them.

Many thanks.

CONTENTS

ACKNOWLEDGMENTS

I would like to offer my deep thanks to the following people who were so generous with their knowledge and their time: Wynn Anderson, Tony Avent, Wendy Hodgson, George Hull, Glenn Huntington, Melodie Lewis, Sarah and Paul McCombs, Pat McNeal, Judy Mielke, Jill Nokes, Bart O'Brien, Scott Ogden, Janet Rademacher, Wade Roitsch, Carl Schoenfeld, Sallye Schumacher, Greg Starr, Dennis Swartzell, and Tera Vessels. My greatest fear is that I have forgotten someone and, if I did, let me know and I will make it up to you.

I visited many public gardens during the writing of this book and would like to acknowledge both their collections and their staffs for the wonderful plantings that helped me learn so much about these plants. These gardens are worth a long visit anytime you are in the area. They are Arizona-Sonora Desert Museum in Tucson, Arizona; Austin Garden Center in Austin, Texas; Boyce Thompson Southwest Arboretum in Superior, Arizona; Desert Botanical Garden in Phoenix, Arizona; Fredericksburg Herb Farm in Fredericksburg, Texas; Kerrville Nature Center in Kerrville, Texas; Lady Bird Johnson Wildflower Center in Austin, Texas; Living Desert Museum in Palm Desert, California; Rancho Santa Ana Botanic Garden in Claremont, California; San Antonio Botanical Gardens in San Antonio, Texas; Tohono Chul Park in Tucson, Arizona; and Tucson Botanical Garden in Tucson, Arizona.

On the home front no one will have better support for a book project than what I had from my dear husband, Gary. Thanks is much too inadequate for all you have done.

CHAPTER 1

Introduction

PERENNIALS HAVE BEEN THE STARS of the gardening world since the first gaudy, linear planting in a Victorian estate was replaced with the luscious, casual overflow of a perennial border. As a class of plants they have few rivals for the beauty and flair they bring into our gardens. Gardeners, designers, and growers all over the country have responded with an immense outpouring of species, selections, and cultivars to meet the increasing demand for perennials. Yet when you look through plant catalogs, you discover that species designed to match the formidable conditions of the American Southwest are unaccountably missing.

That glaring omission was one of the principal reasons I began this book. While this is not an encyclopedia of all perennial species suitable for the region, it is a beginning for gardeners in this fast-growing area.

I have lived and gardened in the Sonoran Desert of Arizona for 20 years. During that time I have watched as plants from deserts around the world have become more and more commonly available and a part of the gardening lingua. As I have traveled around the Southwest from California to Texas visiting numerous gardens both public and private, I have noticed an increasing awareness of what these species—some locally native, others just beautifully adaptable—offer to a garden. Native desert and arid-adapted perennials bring all the excitement, long-lasting structure, and thrilling bloom to Southwestern gardens without needing relentless soil amendment, time-consuming cultivation, or exorbitant irrigation. These species learned to live in arid regions long before we did, and Southwestern gardeners are wise to learn from them.

Like all reckless gardeners I have dragged home untold numbers of plants, many of them perennials, to see how they do in the demanding conditions of the low desert. I have watched while many thrived for a few years, declining later as old age or my mistakes took them out. Others settled into their new home and are still thriving today. Some so completely resisted my garden that they did not make it through a single season. All that trial and error is part of why I love gardening: you never can tell when the right combination of luck or skill is going to make a glorious showpiece in your garden. While I have injected much of that experience into this book, the effort has been greatly enriched by the gardening life of numerous other gardeners throughout the region.

I am continuously astounded by the resilience and beauty of arid species, and delight not only in their captivating beauty but also in their generous grace in the face of such extreme growing conditions. It is my sincere hope that you will find the same thrills in experimenting with these grand perennials that I have found.

Purpose of the Book

The American Southwest is new territory for numerous gardeners who live there; they find it a daunting and difficult place when they first begin to plant. I find that the key to successful gardening anywhere, but especially in harsh or exacting places such as the dry and often excruciatingly hot climates of the Southwest, is to understand the conditions under which you garden and to find species that will accommodate to them with ease. I believe that the species described in this book will satisfy the second requirement for gardeners in arid and semiarid areas.

Many of the species I describe are native to the region; some are immune to anything a desert climate has to offer but move into more benign areas or growing conditions with equal ease. They tolerate dry soils, and many in fact demand such soils. These species grow without effort in alkaline soils. While few of them will grow on natural rainfall alone in the driest parts of the region, all grow well with low to minimal supplemental irrigation. Perhaps the most telling trait they all share is that they will tolerate and thrive in the astounding summer heat that occurs throughout most of the region.

Species from deserts or other arid regions that have long periods without rainfall, such as semiarid shrub lands or the dry hills of the Mediterranean, are often described as being drought tolerant. It is more than that; they not only put up with drought as tolerance suggests, but they also are superbly adapted to it. Some require dry spells, shutting down in the heat, while others are completely at home with an extended interval, often weeks, between waterings.

In a gardening situation, *drought tolerance* can be a tricky and sometimes misleading term. For me, species that will live in a given area either on natural rainfall or on supplemental watering no more than three times a month in summer exhibit high drought tolerance. From there it is a continuum; if a species tolerates even less watering than that, it certainly qualifies as extremely drought tolerant, and if it needs a bit more than that, then it is only moderately drought tolerant.

The drought tolerance of the species in this book varies widely depending on where plants are growing. Grow a particular species in the cities of Southern California outside the Coachella Valley and most display extraordinary drought tolerance because the climate is so mild and conditions are close to ideal. If, however, you move that same species to Palm Springs, Yuma, or Las Vegas, its apparent drought tolerance is quite different. In those extremely dry and hot parts of the region without any summer rainfall to speak of, growing plants on natural rainfall limits things immensely and is rarely practical. In those areas almost anything will need summer watering at least two or three times a month and that is considered excellent drought tolerance.

I have included a few species from the canyons and riverside areas of the region, and they will not be especially drought tolerant. They are, however, well tuned to the extreme heat of most of the region. These species offer an opportunity to use regional natives that are at home near a pond or other area with abundant water.

Regardless of the details of drought tolerance, when you consider the twin perils of continuous population growth and migration into the region and an increasing reliance on diminishing water supplies, choosing garden plants that use as little water as possible makes great sense. Only so much water is available to go around, and it is incumbent on all of us who live and garden in the arid Southwest to use species that create the glorious gardens we all want without forcing an unbearable strain on our surrounding environment. Such gardens can be done with flair and style. I have seen many of them, and the species profiled in this book were chosen because they can help all of us achieve those gardens.

Just What Is a Perennial?

Although the term *perennial* has a strict and useful meaning in the language of botany, it has been confiscated and, some argue, corrupted by gardeners. A perennial is any species that lives out its life cycle over more than one year, although plants in a subset known as biennial complete their life cycle in precisely two growing seasons. By this definition, trees, shrubs, cacti, and almost all succulents, agaves, yuccas, and all their kin are perennial as are bulbs.

In the gardening world, however, the term describes species that not only live for more than two seasons, but also are not succulent, woody, or bulbs and chiefly grow less than 4 ft. (1.2 m) tall. It is a shame really that the term came to have these dual meanings; it always causes confusion. But there it is, and probably there it stays.

In this book I have taken up the gardening definition, and the species included herein are herbaceous, although many have a semiwoody base, are not succulent, do not arise from a bulb, and grow to 4 ft. (1.2 m) or less. It is also implied, but not stated, that these species reliably bloom with showy flowers from year to year under routine care. Of course, there are exceptions. Mexican sunflower (*Tithonia fruticosa*), a species that meets all these conditions but grows much larger, is included as are species like mugwort (*Artemisia ludoviciana*) that are grown for their beautiful foliage, not their blooms. Also included are some species that simply defy categorization, such as desert milkweed (*Asclepias subulata*). Although I stuck to the criteria most of the time, if I really thought a certain species worthwhile, I included it.

The Region

The American Southwest is a large and variable region that extends roughly from central and western Texas through all or part of New Mexico, Arizona, Utah, Nevada, and California. This book, however, covers only the warmer parts of the region, areas that are below 4000 ft. (1200 m) in elevation, that have moderate to warm winters and long, hot summers, and that are arid with low annual rainfall which comes in seasons rather than uniformly through the year.

I have further divided this portion of the region into three zones (see the map, facing): the low-elevation (or hottest) deserts, the mid-elevation deserts, and the milder areas. While the geography and climates of the region do not fall neatly into these categories, it is helpful when assessing plant performance to draw some distinction, particularly regarding an area's heat and cold extremes.

LOW-ELEVATION DESERTS

These are the hottest deserts and occur in a long band from the Coachella Valley of California east to the Phoenix metropolitan area in Arizona. The area includes the cities of Palm Springs and Palm Desert in California and their associate cities, Yuma in Arizona and the smaller cities along the Colorado River, and the Phoenix metropolitan area. The entire area is below 2000 ft. (600 m), and some of it is at or near sea level.

In the California parts of this area the soils are sandy and without significant amounts of nitrogen. Wind can be continuous and, in some places, moves sand around in impressive dunes. Winters are mild, often frost free, averaging 57°F (14°C), and rarely below 35°F (2°C). Summers are long and ferocious; the July

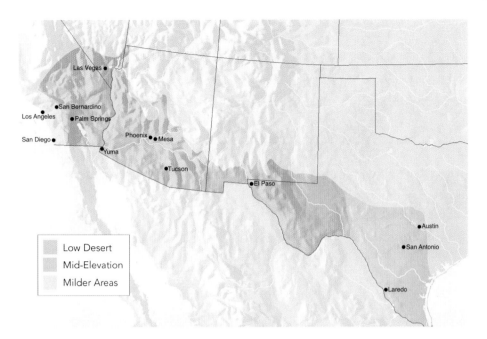

Low Desert
Mid-Elevation
Milder Areas

average is 108°F (42°C), and days over 110°F (43°C) are common and numerous. Rainfall averages 5 in. (125 mm) per year and almost all of it falls in the winter.

The Phoenix metropolitan area is more complex owing both to its complicated interplay of hills and valleys as well as the effect of the great urban mass. Soils can be clay, loam, or mineral and rocky, and are often punctuated by extensive caliche outcrops. Caliche is that impenetrable layer of calcium carbonate left over as water evaporated from these alkaline soils during the change from wetter to drier climates. Neither water nor roots penetrate it, and thick layers near the surface are a gardening problem where they occur. Winters are mild with the January average at 43°F (6°C). While freezing temperatures may occur in some locations, they are of short duration, rarely over three or four hours. Rainfall averages 8 in. (200 mm) a year with about a third in the winter and the rest in the summer.

Mid-Elevation Deserts
The hottest deserts are enclosed by a roughly U-shaped area that is still extremely arid but is milder in the summer and colder in the winter. This arc extends through the Mojave Desert, the cities of Lancaster and Palmdale in California, and Las Vegas in Nevada. This desert zone lines the southern boundary of the

Perovskia atriplicifolia

hottest deserts in and around the city of Tucson, Arizona, and continues east in an interrupted pattern with the cities of Las Cruces in New Mexico and El Paso in Texas squarely within its bounds.

Elevation is important in understanding these deserts because rainfall patterns and temperature ranges are greatly affected by the interruption of higher hills and mountains that define this area. All the deserts in this zone are below 4000 ft. (1200 m) in elevation and receive 12 to 15 in. (300 to 380 mm) or less of average annual rainfall. As in the hottest deserts, soils in the mid-elevation deserts vary widely from place to place, from tight clays to gravelly mineral soils with caliche outcrops.

In the California and Nevada parts of the region, winters are considerably colder than in the hottest deserts, with January highs averaging 33°F (1°C) and at least a few freezes lasting overnight. Summers, however, are hot, with July averaging 106°F (41°C) in Las Vegas and a bit less in the California areas, but they are up to a month shorter than in the hottest deserts. Rainfall averages a scant 5 to 6 in. (125 to 150 mm) annually with wide variations from year to year; most of it falls in the winter.

Tucson and the northernmost suburbs of Phoenix have somewhat cooler winters and milder summers than the hottest deserts. The January average for Tucson is 39°F (4°C). A few freezing nights are expected every year; however, freezes are of short duration. The July average for Tucson is 104°F (40°C), and days over 108°F (42°C) are rare, with the summer up to a month shorter than it is in the hottest deserts. Rainfall is both more abundant and more reliable in southern Arizona than in the hottest deserts. Annual rainfall averages 12 in. (300 mm) with up to 60 percent of the rainfall occurring during the summer thunderstorm season and the remainder between November and March.

The desert in and around Las Cruces and El Paso is still markedly arid but much colder than all the other deserts of the region. While the soils here have much of the same variability as do the deserts to the west, pockets of deep sand occur. Winter lows average around 25°F (−4°C) and almost half of the nights in December and January may be below freezing. Summer highs average 97° to 99°F (36° to 37°C) and are rarely up to or exceeding 105°F (41°C). Rainfall is a scant 9 in. (230 mm) per year. Summer and winter rainy seasons are split by long periods without rain.

Penstemon parryi with a blue wall, Schumacher garden

MILDER AREAS

On the extreme edges of the region we find areas that are distinctly different from the deserts. Elevation plays less of a role in defining these areas. The western edge is just as arid but has vastly milder temperatures. The eastern edge has significantly more rainfall, but its thin, rocky soils and high heat earn it a place in the region. From a plant's perspective, these are both extremely congenial locations in which to grow. In fact, most of the perennials in this book and many of the best arid- and heat-adapted perennials for the region come from these areas.

The western end lies over the mountains that surround the Coachella Valley of California and includes the huge sprawl of Southern California cities around Los Angeles, as well as most of Orange, San Diego, and Ventura Counties, especially the parts that are not directly adjacent to the Pacific Ocean. Winters are mild, with daytime highs similar to those of the hottest deserts. Freezing nights are uncommon in most of this area, but when they occur, they are of short duration, rarely lasting more than a few hours. Summer temperatures are the mildest within the region; only the most inland areas experience temperatures at or near 100°F (38°C) for more than a day or two at a time. Rainfall averages 8 to 10 in. (200 to 250 mm) annually and almost all of it falls during the winter.

The eastern edge of this milder region embraces those parts of central and southwestern Texas known as the Hill Country, the South Texas Plains, and the Rio Grande Valley. It includes the cities of Austin, San Antonio, Kerrville, Laredo, and Uvalde, among many others. Here soils are alkaline and, while many are thin and rocky, deep clays and loamy soils are scattered throughout. Rainfall is much more abundant here than in the rest of the region, up to 35 in. (890 mm) a year; however, it is far from even both from year to year and within a year. Long dry periods lasting months can be followed by torrential rains, and extremely dry years may be followed by incredibly wet ones. Winters are similar to those around El Paso, with freezing nights common in December and January. But again, sudden and unexpected extremes are the rule. A balmy week can be followed by spectacular cold within a day. Summers are hot and frequently more humid than in all the rest of the region, but temperatures rarely exceed 100°F (38°C) and then only for a day or two.

Taxonomic Note

The naming of species has baffled and bewildered gardeners and horticulturists since the entire effort began, but it is wise to remember that botanists and systematists are well-meaning and well-informed people. They are not out to make gardeners' lives a misery. They hope they are clarifying matters. Occasionally this is so; we have only to look at the salutary effort of breaking up the huge and unwieldy mess of *Opuntia* into some 17 other genera to see that breaking up, while hard to do, is often advisable. In addition, many plant scientists want to arrange and order species according to their perceived or known relationships and that can make for some shifting of names. Of course, names are meant to make it easier to talk to each other. Keeping all this in mind makes it easier to be kind to those who rearrange some long-known, favorite names.

For this book I relied on a number of sources. If the species was included in the Biota of North America Program (BONAP), I relied on that project's currently accepted name. This resource covers all species native to the United States and those that are naturalized. Mexican, Central American, or South American species are only included if they also occur in the United States.

For species that are native only south of the United States border, it was much more difficult to be current or sure. These areas have few up-to-date floras, but I relied particularly on the published floras of Texas, New Mexico, Arizona, California, and the Sonoran Desert, all of which are referenced in the bibliography. The unpublished flora of the Chihuahuan Desert was also used for species found in that region.

Sphaeralcea ambigua and *Encelia farinosa*

If the species had made it into the international database on accepted plant names called Species 2000, I used the name given there. A generous network of colleagues also was invaluable.

Cultivars and selections present another version of chaos. In most cases I relied on the most widely accepted and commonly used names in the region. I made only a minimal attempt to sort out whether all the similar forms of a certain species really merited a unique cultivar name. Readers need to be aware that distinct names can be assigned to the same taxon. This is true especially for species long in horticulture or grown on both sides of the ocean, where forms, selections, and cultivars may be reinvented or found by scientists on one side without those on the other side being aware of the "new" plant.

When it came to common names, I relied on my own common sense and what I have heard bandied about in local publications and gardening sources, and among other friends throughout the region. Most species have far too many common names, and many are just ridiculous (I strongly object to the too-common convention of names like Parry's penstemon simply because the botanical name is *Penstemon parryi*). In most cases I did not use Mexican common names unless they were widely used. Some authors include a number of Indian-language names for species in Mexico, but I resisted. Although these names are fascinating, I don't think they pass the common usage test.

I urge all readers to learn and use the botanical names all the time; it saves a great deal of confusion. The plant has no idea who it is; you name it so that you can call it something when you pass it along to your neighbor.

CHAPTER 2

Designing with Perennials

ALTHOUGH PERENNIALS HAVE BEEN USED since the dawn of gardening, particularly as culinary herbs and medicines, it was not until the 19th century that they began to take on the ornamental role with which we are so familiar. As that century matured, gardeners began to resist the increasing reliance on vast, formalized displays of annuals. These required not only colossal amounts of time and effort but also a bank account to match.

Gradually in England a minor rebellion ensued, spurred by the writing of William Robinson and later Gertrude Jekyll, to soften the look of gardens by relaxing the rigidity of planting and magnifying a garden's resemblance to natural areas. Flowering plants were essential in this view. While a lot of effort went into trying to have them look natural and unplanned, gardens based on this hugely popular position have become the norm for the last 100 years.

Gardens that employ a wide array of species, often in dense plantings with riotous color displays, are more accessible. Such a style can be done anywhere, on any budget, and with any amount of space. It was an idea that flourished, and thus the perennial garden was born. In its humblest and often most charming expression, this type of garden came to be known as a cottage garden. It throws all of its plants together and lets them more or less find their own design way. My great aunts in central Texas had cheerful plantings in the front of their farmhouses that were exactly like this. Plants were put in chiefly from seed, and each year a certain number continued to thrive, growing in a jumble with any newcomers that year.

Cottage gardens are seen throughout the American Southwest and, while they are often thought of and called natural or naturalistic plantings, I think they have much more in common with the wild array that my aunts as well as farm wives worldwide enjoyed. These gardens added just a bit of color to a drab front yard.

Odontonema tubiforme mixed with *Cycas revoluta* and *Coleus*

In England, cottage gardens took on features that defined them. They relied on a thick planting of perennials—the more bloom, the better—and roses, although they are shrubs, figured prominently. Like their humbler counterparts, these are colorful, exuberant gardens that when well done look as if they arose without effort.

Cottage gardens were the godmother of the naturalistic movement. Naturalistic gardening has become the style of choice in much of the country, but it dominates the Southwest. It began as a reaction to the strictures of an English-gardening style that did not seem to fit in well in the United States. It also had its roots in an increasing awareness that North America has splendid native species that were too often neglected in favor of species well known in European gardens.

Like the cottage garden, the naturalistic garden employs a casual aspect, as if the plants arose on their own. This style attempts to mimic the surrounding landscape, wherever it is used. In the Southwest, and particularly in the desert cities of Arizona, it has come to mean not only using desert and arid-adapted

Roadside planting of *Baileya multiradiata*

species but also spacing them widely and employing a generous mix of succulents, agaves, cacti, and other distinctive desert species.

Once perennials with their reliable and repeated bloom took hold in American gardens, designers began to play with the idea. Long ago and at the beginning of the popularity of perennials, some designers felt that color just begged to be organized, and so the perennial border emerged from the gardening muck. In this scheme, species are arranged to frame a lawn; they line it as you pass along and are often backed up by large hedges or large woods. Later, adventurous designers began to plant freestanding perennial beds where you could see the planting from all sides as you moved around it. These schemes or planting styles are still extremely popular and are widely employed in many parts of the world, but are uncommon in the Southwest. I think of this as a lack of gardening imagination and believe that a well-done border with desert species could be splendid.

The most organized expression of the perennial border is one that begins at one end of the color spectrum and ends at the opposite end. So if it began with reds, it moved to oranges, yellows, limey greens, purples, blues, lighter blues, and finally white as it progressed down the line. Few of these borders are built anymore—they are tricky to design and require meticulous attention to color, form, and care. But done right, they are just glorious and true works of art.

It is hard to talk of the historic desert garden, so few exist in this country. But in other arid regions, such as North Africa, parts of the Mediterranean region, especially Spain, and in pockets of the Middle East, models of ancient desert gardens exist. Gardening, even in deserts, is an old practice, and evidence of gardens and sometimes the species used can be found in selected excavations in these regions.

Most of these gardens were centered on water, either as a thin ribbon through the garden or as a fountain or well in its midst. Gardens were enclosed by walls, walkways were paved with packed dirt or stone, and shade both artificial and from larger plants was abundant. Color was seasonal, often in containers, and walkways, staircases, and door frames spilled out an abundance of color. You can find relics of these styles in many parts of Mexico, brought by the Spanish and embraced by Mexican gardeners. It is a beautiful model that is sometimes employed, but it is rarely used in the United States with the restraint needed to make it spectacular.

I am convinced that the best perennial gardens in the arid parts of the country are yet to be built. Talented and committed designers all over the region are doing exciting things with these species. Some of their work finds its way into these pages. I hope that by encouraging the use of the perennials so suitable for the region, this book will further inspire not only their use but also the gorgeous gardens to contain them.

Design Principles

Most serious gardeners fall into one of two camps in the design of their gardens: those whose primary interest and effort is to grow a wide range of plants, or those whose chief joy is in uniting plants into a pleasing whole. Richard Hartlage (1999) put it this way: "Those who will sacrifice the garden to the plants and those who will sacrifice the plants to the garden."

Gardeners in the first category tend to collect many plants, sometimes within a certain style or group. Frequently the mere absence of a particular species from their garden makes it an object of immediate desire. Gardeners in the second group tend to have more discipline, seeking out species with the right color, shape, or blooming season to round out a composition. Gardeners in the first group tend to have many plants floating around in pots waiting for a spot to open up for them in the garden, while gardeners in the second group tend to recognize the spot for a new acquisition as soon as it arrives.

Most of us fall somewhere in the chaotic and unapologetic middle, finding great delight in acquiring a new species, but wishing we had more nerve or discipline to fit together all our plants into a lovely garden. Many great gardeners feel uncertain and ill equipped to dive into the seemingly intimidating world of design.

Garden design is a term and an activity that many see as fraught with the weight and implications of a guarded mystery known only to highly creative and undoubtedly clever people. It sounds as if it must demand a gift and certainly extensive training. While training, talent, and experience are

Dalea capitata mixed with verbena in a raised rock bed

invaluable in any endeavor, anyone can absorb the basics, learning the guiding principles of garden design and launching a creative attack on their garden. As in other creative endeavors, most of us will manage to be adequate and have lovely, satisfying gardens. A sad minority will be completely inept, and even fewer will be brilliant, making plants reside in space in ways that are truly inspired, original, and spectacular.

Cranky contrarians insist that they just plant what they like, and if the results are not too good, so be it, it is done only to please the gardener, after all. I certainly urge everyone to be pleased with their garden, but this perspective really ignores the underlying issue. If you want more than just a smattering of plants thrown haphazardly into the ground, then a nod to the basic principles of design will help get you there.

Designing gardens or beds with perennials is especially satisfying because you are working with plants that will remain where you put them for a long time. In the Southwest and other mild climates, this permanency is enhanced because well-adapted perennials are not cut down by freezing temperatures, leaving huge blanks during the winter season.

Datura wrightii along a staircase

The basic design and arrangement of perennials in a garden can take on a number of recognized and well-used forms. In this region, few true perennial borders exist where perennials are mingled with grasses in a carefully planned bed that wanders alongside a lawn. This well-known, and frankly well-used, perennial planting has never achieved the prominence in this region that it has in most of the rest of the gardening world.

Perennial plantings in the Southwest tend to be mixed, or what English garden designer and writer Graham Stuart Thomas calls an "everywhere style." They are a collection of herbaceous plants generously blended with agaves, yuccas, dasylirions, grasses, cacti, and smaller shrubs with dazzling success. This mixing of perennials with many other types of plants is the dominant use of perennials in the region and is a striking example of the naturalistic or natural garden style. While little about such gardens truly mimics how natural systems look, the natural garden style takes great advantage of the unamended form of the plants.

Gardens are never confused with nature nor even particularly natural. Plants in gardens are considerably more abundant and grow much closer together than would ever be the case in nature. This is especially true when comparing deserts and arid regions with their gardens. Plants from widely disparate regions and of widely differing origins are gathered together to create the garden. Gardens simply do not exist without the intervention and attention of the gardener, but wise gardeners listen to the gentle voice of the natural world around them and choose plants that maintain their best form under local conditions while reaping the rewards of their heat and drought tolerance. This means choosing species that accommodate to the area's soils, grow exuberantly with minimal additional watering, and settle comfortably into the overall character of the region.

Attempting to pull together the needs of the plants and the desires of the gardener is what design is truly all about. The needs of the individual species are detailed in chapters 4 and 5. You must decide what you desire for your garden, but some general principles may help you find the path that takes you there.

Opinions vary on what the bedrock or core design principles are. I have selected ones that I think are most beneficial to the home gardener, that are useful in planning either a new garden from the ground up or an extensive renovation. Taking the time to apply at least a few of these principles to your planning before you put plants in the ground is an excellent way to minimize the agony of bad choices and maximize your success.

INTENTION

The first and perhaps most important principle is intention. What do you want out of this planting? Is it supposed to be colorful year-round or only in certain seasons? Is it a perennial bed destined to be a showpiece on its own or a backdrop for a larger, more complex garden scheme? Is it to be native, tropical, or an eclectic blend? Does it carry a theme or do you care? Is it meant to attract wildlife and, if so, what kind?

Intention is deceptive. Voicing your desire for a nice garden bed or some lovely color in the garden may seem simplistic, but giving thought and time to your interests and chief desires for the garden will pay off splendidly in the end. When using plants like perennials, mulling over what you want saves both time and energy and always offers better results.

To be sure you understand your intentions, make an informal list of what you expect from the garden or new bed. Include vague ideas such as beauty and color along with practical concerns such as a seating area, cut flowers for the house, or hiding that hideous fence. Try to keep the list to no more than five things. If the area is more or less blank and you are forming ideas for its first real garden, don't forget to consider whether a patio or other seating areas are in your plans and if structures such as ramadas or sheds will be needed. It is not necessary that they be built all at the same time, but if you know that someday you are going to want that patio cooking area established, it is foolish to plant a large shade tree

Lantana montevidensis massed with *Agave vilmoriniana*, Schumacher garden

over there. Answering these questions and putting them down on paper begins to give shape to your ideas and will help you determine the force of the next step, the site.

SITE

The site of the garden, the actual physical space it occupies, is a crucial note in the symphony that will be the garden, and it is surprising how strenuously it is ignored. Aspects of the site that impinge on your intentions begin with the dimensions, which firmly dictate how much room there is and therefore just how many plants will be able to live comfortably in the space.

Exposures, particularly in severe climates, force you to deal with the effects of the sun on your garden. Be sure you know which way the garden faces and how much sun is on it during the day. In the hottest deserts, it is particularly crucial to honor the relentless heat of western sun. Unshaded seating areas are a disaster on the western side of the garden in these deserts, but abundant shade can mitigate that. Enclosed spaces that face north and have almost no direct light in the winter are cold and may not be the finest choice for your tropical plants. By noting the exposures and overlaying what you want to do out there, you can avoid some uncomfortable and unfortunate plantings.

Justicia spicigera massed along a walkway (Mary Irish)

How cold settles in the garden can be just as important as how heat affects it. Many cities in the Southwest are built in and around small hills and mountains, and therefore gardens are built on lots with a lot of elevational change in a small area. Even if your garden does not have elevational changes, the neighborhood might. In gardens with great variations in elevation, know where the highest part of the garden is. That part will be both the warmest, as cold air slides downhill, and the driest, because water also follows a gravitational tug to the bottom.

Gardeners in cities such as Las Vegas, Palm Springs, and El Paso have to consider the wind when determining where and how to plant. Wind in these areas can be virtually constant, or at least seasonally so, and knowing the direction and seasonal shift of the wind will be important.

Flat areas may have poor drainage and may need some help to keep them from becoming monotonous. Low spots also may have drainage issues, but then maybe they are the perfect places to make even lower for a pond or below-grade seating area. Slopes are lovely, but often hard to navigate and can be subject to erosion. They can be terraced formally or informally; stairs make a lovely way to get around and, if wide enough, are a suitable platform for attractive pots.

Salvia leucantha in a mixed bed planting

Berlandiera lyrata and *Gaillardia aristata* in a mixed planting

When considering the site, don't forget what is in or adjacent to the garden that you cannot change. Sometimes this is a wonderful thing—a splendid tree or a rocky outcrop. Consider neighbors integral to the garden and work with them rather than against them.

Views can also be an unchangeable part of the site in beautiful ways such as a rocky butte, a mountain scene, or an impeccable view of the sunset. In other cases the neighboring view can be disastrous—the blank wall of a larger building, power poles and their tangle of lines, or your neighbor's car collection. In either situation the view from your garden is an important component of your garden now and you need to consider how you will either frame it and use it, or hide it and make it disappear.

Plants can drive your eye to and from a location. If you put in your most spectacular and long-blooming perennials directly under the huge white roof of your neighbor's garage, your eye will skip over the perennials and glue to the roof. If you have a lovely view of someone else's flowering tree or a natural scene, use your plants to bring it into your own garden.

If the long view is unfortunate, masquerade it with tall, complex plantings, closing down the dimensions of the garden to keep your eyes on what is happen-

Wildflower planting with *Penstemon eatonii* and *Baileya multiradiata*

ing only in the garden. The trick of drawing your eye upward by using narrow but tall plantings will secure the view down to your lovely perennials instead of over their heads and into the neighboring building or school yard. Arbors or walls with vines achieve much the same thing. When the horizontal view is compromised, go tall.

Another important aspect of knowing the site is to understand how water moves in and around it. What really happens out there when it rains? Does part of the area become a pond? Does the rainfall leave so quickly you wonder if it rained at all? How does water fall off the roof and where? If you don't have a clear idea of water movement on the site, turn on a sprinkler for an hour or so and find out. This is the only way to know if you have spots that will need some drainage work before you plant.

Again, a piece of paper is handy. Even if you cannot draw a stick man, start with a crude drawing, as much to scale as you can manage, that includes the shape of the garden or bed. Draw in the outline of all parts of the garden that are not available to plants, such as a house, driveway, and patio. Be sure to mark fences, large existing trees or other significant plants, as well as walkways. Mark out the cardinal directions and, if it is important, the wind direction.

For anyone who finds a plan view on paper either a challenge or impossible to interpret, try using the box-of-sand approach. I have used variations of this approach to teach the movement of sediment in rivers as well as the way in which plants can be used to aid in the heating and cooling of houses. Joe Eck, the Vermont-based author and designer, uses it to lay out gardens for himself and his clients. It is lots of fun, it is simple, and it has the same bonus that a paper drawing has—everything can be moved and changed with a flick of the wrist.

To use this method, simply take a box and fill it with sand. The size and shape are irrelevant, but the closer it resembles your garden the easier it is to visualize the result. Use paper cutouts, cardboard pieces, playing cards, or anything else you have to mark the nonliving parts of the garden. Set plastic trees and shrubs in the sand to lay out and arrange plants in the garden. Small twigs, prunings, and leftovers from floral arrangements are a few examples of things lying around that work just as well. This method is imaginative, it is three-dimensional, and it shares with the paper plan the obvious advantage of manipulating things easily and often. Just lift up a plant in the wrong place or a patio that failed and move it.

Evaluation and Contemplation

After you have laid out your intentions and have drawn up the existing garden, it is time to put them together. Either directly on the drawing or using tracing paper, draw out the areas and beds that are on your list. Put them somewhere; put them where you really like them, or where you imagine them to be, ignoring what is already there. It is only paper at this point. Now take a hard look. Is there a huge tree or hedge right where you wanted the perennial bed? Is the house too close to the wall on the south side to accommodate your mixed succulent and perennial garden concept? Answering questions like these will force you to meld your desires and intentions with the limits and constraints of the site. Once you have finished with this rough site plan, it is time to sit and look around, allowing yourself to live with your ideas for a while.

Contemplation is undervalued as a planning tool. The simple act of placing yourself out in the garden, sitting still and letting what is there and what you imagine float around in your mind a while is the best way to get the garden or bed project marching down the right track. You can nudge contemplation along by placing plants still in containers where you intend to plant them and leaving them there for a while. This practice is so common in my own garden that some plants remain in this hapless state for weeks waiting for their time to be planted, but I find it an invaluable tool in deciding how a plant will fit into the neighborhood where I have placed it. This trial placement helps you decide if the colors blend the way you imagined or if the texture is a pleasing contrast or jarring interruption. The question of whether the new plant makes the older plants look better or worse is quickly answered by looking at them together.

If an entire bed is to be established where none existed before, try using a hose, colorful string, or rope to lay out the dimensions and shape of the bed. You can do the same with a proposed building or patio. This preservation of the space for a future use serves you in two ways. First, it gives you a splendid and clear indication if your idea fits in. If you think it is too big you can reduce it. If it is not large enough you can expand it. If the corners aren't right you can adjust them and so forth. Second, it allows you to get on with other planting and work that will complement or enhance the space without waiting for that particular project to be completed. This is especially true of large areas such as patios, seating areas, and ponds.

When we moved into our present home, a large tree occupied the space where our main patio now sits. We quickly removed the tree and laid out the borders of the patio with cut stone. We swept the dirt until it was fairly level and clear and it stayed like that for years until we had both the time and means to pave it with the stone we wanted. In the meantime, we planted the beds that surrounded it and used it exactly as if it were completed. By the time the patio was installed, it seemed to fall naturally into the garden with the maturing perennial beds already surrounding it and trees already providing some shade.

In the arid cities of the Southwest, conversions have become popular. Although any garden can, and undoubtedly should, undergo a conversion from time to time, what is meant by the term in these areas is the shift from a garden that uses moderate to high amounts of water to one that uses lower amounts of water. It usually means eliminating or severely reducing an existing lawn.

These are garden projects that will find the planning scheme described above so useful. Taking out lawn where it once existed or reducing it dramatically changes the entire tone of a garden. The garden you once had is gone and a new one must be thought up to fill its place. While this can be a daunting task at first, it is also an opportunity to consider your new options and get what you really want out of your space.

SCALE

Scale is where many urban gardeners lose their minds. Perhaps the hardest part in understanding the scale of a plant in relationship to a building—usually the house—is allowing yourself to believe that plants grow. A sweet little 5-ft. (1.5-m) Aleppo pine (*Pinus halepensis*) looks like a miniature forest in its youth

Engelmannia peristenia, Lantana sp., and *Callirhoe involucrata* in a mixed planting

but will tower over a two-story house at maturity. Perennials that mature to 4 ft. (1.2 m) wide will smother plants put only 2 ft. (0.6 m) from them. Although it is often hard to endure the spacing necessary in a new planting, patience is advised unless you relish yanking out half of your plants within a couple of years.

Scale is just as important within an individual planting as it is in the overall garden. Although it is not necessary to march plants in lines by their height, as we were marched into church during my grade-school days, large ones will hide smaller ones from view, unless that is what you intend. In perennial plantings, using a few taller plants helps relieve the inherent boredom of plants that are roughly the same height. These can be set in the middle to make a focal point or used along an edge to encourage movement around a corner or to separate a large complicated planting area into sections that may be viewed from various angles. Selecting plants of differing heights provides interest and complexity in a garden planting, and is important in creating a pleasing arrangement.

ACCESS

When considering your garden scheme from either the paper or the box, or as you walk about, watch carefully how you travel around the garden. In whatever plan you have in mind, you need to be able to get to the back gate. If you have an entertainment area, it should be easily available from the kitchen or at least the house. When you or your guests get out of the car, you ought to be able to find the door to the house without confusion. And from personal experience I will tell you that if you have a site with a slope and you put in stairs to assist in getting up and down the slope, a wheelbarrow will not be able to climb the stairs. It, too, must have access to your proposed garden.

Access does not necessarily mean a runway directly from one point to another. In fact, it is much nicer to wander around a bit to find what you want. Give yourself and your guests a chance to look around before arriving at the destination. Invite a slower pace by using turns to spotlight a particularly wonderful plant, a piece of art, or a seating area. Seeing everything at once is rarely successful. Make walking in your garden more of an adventure, trying to find out what is around.

A smooth but wandering way through the garden will help you stay in touch with what is happening daily in your garden. The director of a public garden where I once worked refused to park in the privileged spot in the back of the garden close to the office. He preferred to walk through the garden every day on his way in and on his way out. It was his method of staying connected with what the place was all about. He failed to convince many others of his

Salvia greggii in a mass planting

preference, especially in Phoenix's summers, but it was a wise thought and one that can be emulated in even the smallest of gardens by giving yourself a reason to walk around as you take out the trash, contribute to the compost pile, or go to and from work.

ROOMS

It is popular to consider gardens or portions of gardens as rooms. This makes abundant sense in most of the Southwest where temperatures are ideal for outdoor living for a large part of the year. The idea is that a garden can be broken up into discrete areas either based on uses, such as pool area, play area, vegetable garden, seating, and so on, or simply for drama and interest in displaying the plantings. Even the smallest garden can benefit from this principle.

Don't give up the entire view of the garden the moment you come out the door. Place plants of varying scale in such a way that the garden does not offer up all its treasures in one glance. Use larger plants to back up a perennial bed near the house. When a path leads to one edge of the larger plants, it will also serve as an irresistible invitation to find out where it leads.

Placing furniture in an area almost immediately makes it a garden room even without living walls. Select spots that offer views of surrounding features or that make an excellent place to appreciate sunrise or sunset or where you get the best vantage of a particularly handsome flowering plant. Set out a chair or two and you instantly have a small garden room.

Great gardens also maintain a place for repose. This is at least one place, many if the garden is large enough, where you can stop, sit, and stare at the entire garden or perhaps just a part of it and delight in what has been done. Even a tiny garden, only a patio really, can achieve this with a small screen that keeps out the hubbub of the main garden or a well-placed arbor beside a large pot filled with plants that attract hummingbirds. It is a grace note that many gardens fail to achieve but all are the better for it.

HARMONY AND CONTRAST

Harmony in a garden is elusive, coming and going with seasons and the changes that occur over time with living things. It is that distinct feeling you have when all the components fall naturally into place, when everything seems inevitable and uncontrived. It is a scene that is clear in its meaning, where everything is in balance, and where certain pieces may stand out but not overwhelm. When you enter a garden that is in harmony with itself and the space it occupies, you mentally, and often literally, sigh with satisfaction.

Harmony sometimes happens entirely by accident. Don't let that worry you; it can be the best way. Looking for harmony in a garden encourages you to move things about, play around with what you think you want, try out different ideas and combinations. Harmony is one of the hallmarks of a great garden, and no matter how small the space, we can strive for harmony in it.

Ironically, one of the surest ways to achieve harmony is by the judicious use of contrast. Contrast in shape, size, texture, and color sharpens a planting in the same way that a nip of cinnamon livens up a sauce. Perennial gardens often suffer from a dreary sameness, filled with billowy leafy plants that are roughly rounded and full of nice flowers. Throwing in a few hard edges and rigid lines snaps the entire picture into focus. Gardeners in the Southwest are fortunate because countless species of agaves, yuccas, and their relatives can help achieve such contrast. Succulent like aloes and ocotillos, and infinite forms of cacti serve the same purpose.

White and particularly silver perks up all colors. Such tones are found in the leaves of selected perennials, and they are irreplaceable components of a truly harmonious planting. The leaf hairs that create these beautiful silvery casts are a response to hot, dry conditions, allowing gardeners in the region a wide array of such perennials. Some combinations of gold- or yellow-leaved plants can provide the same appeal. And oddly enough, certain pinks do an exquisite job of showing off other colors.

STYLE

I get immensely frustrated with the notion in the Phoenix area that a garden that uses a healthy dose of native and/or desert-adapted species must be planted in a naturalistic style. It certainly does not, and although that is a fashionable and certainly pleasing style, it is only that—one style. Style is a personal statement in your garden with a nod to the peculiarities of the local area, the house or surrounding buildings, and occasionally even the neighborhood. Gorgeous gardens

Terraced rock beds with *Penstemon parryi* and annual wildflowers

can be created with desert and arid-adapted perennials in a wide range of styles, perhaps in styles yet to be thought of.

Without a doubt, the most widely used style of planting perennials is in a bed that borders a lawn. Usually it is conceived with species that bloom over a long season and not all at once, but occasionally it is put together to form a living prism of plants on either end of the spectrum, with hot shades of red, orange, peach, and yellow giving way to cooler pinks, mauve, blue, lavender, and purple.

Nothing prevents the planning of a great perennial border using the type of plants in this book—it's just that such a border has never been done to my knowledge. And why must it border a lawn? Why not a graveled path or a beautifully laid stone walkway? A long sweep of perennials can look wonderful against a long wall or as an invitation along a walkway, but is probably disastrous when the background is a native preserve or unaltered natural area. Formal, even austere, houses may be most congenial to gardens that glean their interest and excitement from minimalist plantings, using texture and form more than color. Vivid color can light up a monochrome landscape where a judicious use of a few colors creates drama. With a cozy cottage of a house, a riot might look sensational, providing a rumpled, frumpy mass of varying perennials that is comforting in its randomness.

TIME

Finally, as you are ready to plunge in and begin selecting plants, making deci-
sions, and setting your choices in the ground, don't forget about time. You must
give your perennials and the garden that they inhabit time to grow and develop.
Particularly in the deserts, perennials do not spring forth in a giddy burst of
growth to make a perfect garden in one season. It routinely takes two or even
three seasons before perennials native to deserts and other arid regions are at their
peak. Accept the fact that time is required and savor the time it will take to have
your perennials fill in and become the garden in your mind.

Never forget that you are tending living things that will grow, change, and
die. Static gardens are hideous and boring, dull and pitiful in their sameness and
small expectations. Gardens that mutate, shift, and adjust are glorious creations,
changing with the seasons, enticing us always to come back and find out what is
going on.

Planning for Year-round Color

I hear the plea all the time—"I just want a nice-looking garden with color year-
round." It sounds so simple—and certainly a generous dose of perennials is a
great way to meet such a demand—but it takes some planning. In most of the
Southwest, the climate is mild enough and the sunshine sufficiently abundant
that gardeners, particularly those from more temperate areas, are moved to crave
consistent flowering in their gardens.

While year-round color poses no special challenge in most of Southern
California, especially outside the Coachella Valley, it requires much more careful planning elsewhere, particularly in the deserts. In whatever part of the region
you garden, it will mean devoting your perennial selection to as wide and as
diverse a suite of plants from congenial regions of the world as you can to satisfy
the hunger for year-round color displays.

In temperate zones, winter is a time of climatic rigor and gardening bond-
age; flowering is stymied and color in the garden comes from sturdy evergreens.
Summer is the glorious release from all of that, providing an abundant blitz of
color. But that is far from the case in most of the American Southwest. Summer
is not the joyous return of the carefree time of our childhoods and the release
of the garden into extravagant growth and glory. Summers in the low elevations of the Southwest are hot, in many areas astoundingly so, dry, and long
lasting. Along the eastern margin of the region, summers are less severe and

Dichondra argentea planted as a bench

summer-flowering species are much more abundant.

Look carefully at the bloom times for the perennials in this book when making selections; however, a few general guidelines may help. In the Sonoran Desert, an area of mild winters, winter and summer rainfall, and intensely hot summers, most perennials flower in winter or spring and nearly all are finished flowering by June. If your garden is dominated by Sonoran Desert natives, your chances of summer flowering from your perennials is drastically reduced; in fact, it is sunk, with desert senna (*Senna covesii*) the glorious exception. A few species repeat bloom in the fall, and a few others will continue through the summer if given extra water. Some of the species typical of this flora include desert marigold (*Baileya multiradiata*), globemallow (*Sphaeralcea ambigua*), brittlebush (*Encelia farinosa*), and some penstemons (*Penstemon parryi, P. eatonii*).

If your garden consists of chiefly Chihuahuan or West Texas natives, then your winter and early spring garden will be particularly lean in color from perennials. Species from the Chihuahuan deserts, and especially those that range into the Edwards Plateau region of Texas, offer the most choices for summer- and fall-flowering plants. This is a large region, but it has a more consistent rainfall pattern through the year, with assurance of at least some summer rainfall, cool winters with a moderate number of freezing nights but none with truly severe temperatures, and moderately hot summers that do not have the duration or extremes of the other areas. Here salvias (*Salvia* spp.), damianita (*Chysactinia mexicana*), pavonia (*Pavonia lasiopetala*), some penstemons (*Penstemon baccharifolius, P. triflorus*), and mistflower (*Conoclinium greggii*) offer reliable summer and fall flowering.

Species native to the Mojave Desert and most of the Southern California deserts grow in areas with colder, but still relatively mild, winters, receive almost all their rain in the winter, and endure intensely hot summers. These species also tend to be winter and spring flowering. At home here are chuparosa (*Justicia californica*), bladder pod (*Salazaria mexicana*), and most of the cool season annuals that we think of as wildflowers. Only a few of these species will bloom longer or out of season in this region.

Species that range into the California chaparral—the dry hills that block the Pacific Ocean from the deserts—tend to be extremely sensitive both to cold and to regular summer watering. Among these are white sage (*Salvia apiana*) and green brittlebush (*Encelia frutescens*).

In the warmest parts of the region, gardeners can reach into the tropics for summer-flowering choices. Yellowbells (*Tecoma stans*), cigar plant (*Cuphea ignea*), trailing lantana (*Lantana montevidensis*), and moss verbena (*Glandularia pulchella*) anchor summer-flowering gardens in these zones.

In seeking year-round color for a perennial garden, remember that not all color is derived from the bloom. Leaf colors, whether variegated in shades of cream, white, or yellow, or simply the myriad shades of green, gray, and white, can carry a bed through a season as well. The striking deep green of rosemary (*Rosmarinus officinalis*), turpentine bush (*Ericameria laricifolia*), or desert plumbago (*Plumbago scandens*), or the soft billowing gray of mugwort (*Artemisia ludoviciana*) or wormwood (*Artemisia arborescens*) can be just as pleasing as a huge splash of color.

Blending Perennials and Succulents

Throughout much of the Southwest various succulents grow naturally in and among the native perennials, shrubs, and trees. Cacti find their homes next to brittlebush or deer vetch (*Lotus rigidus*), agaves and yuccas are intermingled with showy mirabilis (*Mirabilis multiflora*) or globemallow. This blending of such disparate forms and textures also can be copied in gardens in the region. The rigid forms, crisp textures, colorful leaves and stems, and often generous flowering of most succulents, not to mention their endurance of dry soils and heat, can provide a burst of interest in any perennial garden.

The first step in blending succulents with perennials is to understand the cultural requirements of the particular species you want to use. While all succulents by their nature are adapted to dry soils in arid climates, they vary greatly in their acceptance of garden conditions.

Most agaves, yuccas, dasylirions, and nolinas grow naturally in areas with more rainfall than the deserts of Phoenix or Southern California. Therefore, they have no difficulty adapting to the seemingly generous watering schedule for

Ruellia brittoniana 'Katie' under Agave vilmoriniana

perennials in these regions. In areas with steadier summer rainfall, most of these desert species thrive on natural rainfall with only intermittent supplemental watering.

Cacti from the tropics and most prickly pears are tolerant of much more water than their relatives from the harsh deserts of southern Arizona and Baja California. South American cacti are even more tolerant, particularly the handsome, summer-flowering members of the genus *Echinopsis*.

Aloes are enjoyed throughout the warmer parts of the region for their winter flowering and attractive variety of leaf color and shape. The textural variety of sansevierias, dudleyas, and shrubby succulent euphorbias offers countless opportunities in gardens with warm winters.

All of these species want spectacular drainage, but then so do most of the perennials that thrive in this region. And as a rule, succulents are indifferent to the type of soil as long as such drainage is provided.

Shade may seem an odd specification for succulents, but in the hottest deserts of the Southwest, the sun's intensity is formidable and almost all succulents do best with at least a light or high, filtered shade. Many of these types of plants, particularly aloes and sansevieria, are unrivaled for their beauty in dry shady gardens.

Do not be afraid to experiment. Unless a species is rare and difficult to find or you value it above all plants in your garden, try it and see how it works. Great successes often come from the most unlikely pairings.

Undoubtedly the most difficult plants to put into mixed perennial plantings are those that have a strong and obligatory dormancy like boojum (*Fouquieria columnaris*) or the winter-dormant adeniums. They require special conditions that can make it arduous to find a workable combination.

Succulents in general do not appreciate consistently wet roots, and mixing them with perennials means noting not only their general watering requirements,

Mixed perennial planting with succulents

but also the style with which you are watering. Few succulents tolerate the rain-shower effect of a sprinkler or other overhead watering system. It is usually too much water, too frequently applied. Even when using soaker hoses or point emitter drip systems, it is best to place succulents a small distance from the water source. Roots will find what they need near these kinds of watering systems.

Using Perennials to Attract Birds and Butterflies

Rich is the garden that provides a home to a wide array of life beyond our own. The singing and merry antics of birds, the delicate attentions of butterflies, the rapid-fire hunting of lizards, and the endless parade of nearly invisible insects that make your garden their home add to our own enjoyment and succor the health of the garden. These are the pollinators and the pest control all working hard to eat and raise their young. Watching a hunting lizard is more than just a lesson in lizard tactics; it is witness to the fragile balance that moves a garden from being a static, pretty picture to a bustling center of life.

Melampodium leucanthum with succulents

BIRDS

What brings birds into the garden and keeps them there is an abundance of shelter including nesting sites, food, and water. Birds are always alert to the presence of potential predators and feel most comfortable when they have a suitable place to bathe, forage, or raise their young that allows them to hide when necessary. Birds are not just ornaments in the garden; they pollinate countless species while foraging around for food and consume an abundance of insects, some of which the garden is best off without.

Perennials rarely provide much shelter for birds, but the shrubs and trees that will also be part of a diverse and active garden do. Trees and shrubs of different heights and densities will allow almost any species to find a spot that suits. Doves like to roost overnight high up in the arms of trees, while quails prefer to nest below a dense shrub that falls all the way to the ground. Songbirds such as cardinals and mockingbirds prefer to nest about head high in a thick, tangled shrub, while cactus wrens seek out a place where they see all the action. Diversity of species is the key to a wide range of bird life in the garden.

Perennials, however, are abundant sources of food for numerous bird species. Because different birds have different food requirements, diversity again is the key to success. Goldfinches, sparrows, and house finches are seed eaters. They perch to feed and flit around the garden looking for whatever ripe seed is available on conveniently tall flowering stalks. Seeds of scarlet sage (*Salvia coccinea*), brittlebush, Mexican sunflower (*Tithonia fruticosa*), Mojave aster (*Xylorhiza tortifolia*), and mugwort, for example, bring these birds into the garden in droves.

Other birds such as towhees, thrashers, wrens, doves, and quail also eat seed but prefer to feed on the ground. They eat the seed that falls down where they can walk along and peck it out of the dirt. When planning perennials for these species, leave some room between the plants as the birds prefer to feed in the open, where they can keep a sharp eye out for trouble.

Thrashers and wrens, as well as mockingbirds and cardinals, also eat much fruit. They hunt down and devour even tiny fruit like that on lantana or the berries from Turk's cap (*Malvaviscus arboreus* var. *drummondii*).

For many of us, having birds in the garden means attracting hummingbirds. These astounding birds are nectar feeders, but so are orioles and to some extent house finches and verdins. Such species need an ample supply of nectar-producing plants to keep them coming to the garden. Provide a generous dose of salvias, penstemons, justicias, and Mexican oregano (*Poliomintha maderensis*) among others to satisfy their voracious appetites.

Hummingbirds, too, like to feed with some room. While the plants can be spaced close together, the birds will feed only on the outer edges of the plant, where there is ample room for a quick exit. Plants meant to attract hummingbirds can also be located on the edge of a large planting, where the birds will feed comfortably knowing there is an immediate escape route.

I am not a fan of the artificial feeding of birds. Most of the food is miserable, full of weedy species that don't do much for the birds and that do even less for your garden. Sugar water feeders are useful to bring hummingbirds into a newly planted garden, but if you are serious about inviting birds into your garden, plant a rich array of what they need.

Both birds and butterflies are attracted by color, but the precise hue is less important than you might think. Hummingbirds will feed on blue, white, pink, or red flowers. A bed planted for hummingbirds should have an abundance of red-flowering plants, but once the birds are settled in your garden they will feed on anything with good nectar.

While water attracts birds, it can be a mixed blessing. Birds are most attracted to quiet water where it is easy for them to stop and drink. A bowl or other

Queen butterfly on lantana

shallow container works best, but it must be changed often, sometimes daily, and birds can become deeply dependent on such water as well as bring in hordes of their relatives in unnatural and unwieldy numbers.

BUTTERFLIES

Butterflies use a wide range of perennials for food either as larvae or adults. Larvae or caterpillars certainly may be destructive if there are too many on a small plant, but the rule is, "No larvae, no adults." Most butterfly species are rigid in their requirements for larval food. Members of the carrot family (Cruciferae) and milkweed family (Asclepiadaceae), as well as many members of the sunflower family (Asteraceae), are strongly attractive to larvae of many butterfly species.

Adult butterflies prefer to feed on nectar and find it most readily from species in the sunflower, verbena, and milkweed families (Asteraceae, Verbenaceae, and Asclepiadaceae), just to name a few. Butterflies feed during the day, so day-flowering species most often in shades of red, orange, and yellow mean the most to them. Like some birds, butterflies prefer to feed out in the open where there is plenty of room. Plants have accommodated to this need by putting their flowers on the top of the plant or on long stalks high above the foliage. For butterflies, make sure that the plants are not overhung by trees or shrubs.

Providing water for butterflies is a bit different than for birds, as well. What butterflies really like is wet mud, or tiny ponds in the mud. Usually the act of watering around the garden is sufficient to provide what they need, but if you don't think so, select a place where you can keep a moist, muddy spot for them.

It is easy to forget the wildlife of the night, especially hawk moths and sphinx moths, when planting to attract wildlife. These large moths feed continuously through the summer on the large nectar-filled flowers of sacred datura (*Datura wrightii*) and four o'clock (*Mirabilis jalapa*). They are nearly as large as hummingbirds and make a fascinating addition to the life of your garden.

GUIDELINES FOR ATTRACTING BIRDS AND BUTTERFLIES
Keep the following guidelines in mind if you want perennials that will provide food and shelter for birds and butterflies.

Offer plenty of shelter near the perennials where small creatures can hide.

Leave behind tall stems and selected blooming stalks to serve as landing spots near the perennial bed.

Resist the urge to deadhead immediately after bloom, thereby allowing the delectable seeds to mature.

Plant a variety of species—the more different kinds of plants, the more different kinds of wildlife will be attracted to your garden.

Site plants where they get a lot of sun and in such a way that they provide exposed outer edges. Most birds and all butterflies feed on plants in sun, as well as on the outer edges of plants. Only ground feeders will burrow in and go into a covered area to feed.

Find out the food preference of the larvae that become the butterflies you love, and give some plants over to them.

Perennial Gardens Near a Natural Area

If you are fortunate enough to have a natural area, whether it is a park, a preserve, or the endless wildness of public lands, adjacent to your garden, it is important to consider both the garden and the wild area in your design and plant selection.

Ecologically practical and esthetic concerns must both be considered when living with the natural world as your next-door neighbor.

Perhaps the first and most important consideration is to forego planting any species known or suspected to escape and grow on its own without the intervention or attention of people. This does not mean that all species must be native, but it does mean that you need to do some research about species that might be in danger of taking over the truly native species outside your fence.

What is considered a pest is a local situation, and rare indeed is the species that is a pest no matter where it grows. Check with the local county extension gardening program or native plant society for lists of known or suspected plant pests in your area. Weedy species that escape and become ecological thugs are the exception rather than the rule in ornamental plants. In addition, problem plants are not threats in all areas, and a tame responsible perennial in one region might be a draconian monster in another. Problem species are specific to an area or a region. Knowing which are and which aren't problems or pests will save you a lot of grief and will spare your neighboring natural area even more.

Striking a balance between the esthetic or style of your garden and the surrounding scenery is a matter of both design and plant selection. When the view and the natural area itself are literally part of the visual space of the garden, they will all come together best if you attempt to blend them together.

In many cases, the easiest way to achieve balance between a planted space and a natural space is to incorporate many of the species growing naturally into the garden boundary so it becomes a blurry line between the two areas rather than a sharp edge. Use a mix of species on the edge, letting some of the toughest native trees, perennials, or shrubs fade into the natural landscape. Reserve the most exotic and least visually compatible species for parts of the garden nearest the house or areas inside courtyards and enclosed places. In this way your garden and the wildness beyond it blend gracefully from one to another, preserving the visual grandeur of the setting and incorporating it into the overall scheme of your garden.

To achieve a good blend between your garden and an adjacent natural area, incorporate views that are particularly exciting and take special note of areas in the garden that allow for the spectacle of a sunset or approaching storms. Invite these views to be an integral part of your garden. Set up seating areas intended only to view the natural areas for those times when you feel the need to gaze at the garden that is never tended.

CHAPTER 3

Care of Perennials

GARDENS ARE DIFFERENT FROM NATURE in many significant ways, and one of the most important of them is our own expectations. We want our plants to look good all or most of the time, and we want them to bloom longer, grow bigger, stay healthier, and live longer. To do all of that, plants need a bit of help from us. The great benefit of well-adapted plants is that they are forgiving when we forget or aren't as vigilant as we should be. A little slip-up does not make for failure; one missed watering rarely ensures decline.

Learning to maintain healthy, viable soil that offers appropriate nutrients to plants over the long term and mastering the timing of both planting and pruning will go a long way toward making your garden a raging success. Tips and comments in this chapter come from my own experience as well as those of other desert gardeners and have worked for me for years. But I suggest that you experiment and pay close attention to the particulars of your own garden when trying to determine what works best for you and your plants.

Soil

Soil is the heart and soul of a garden. It is there that all the success of the garden begins, and it is there that most failures originate. The more you understand your soil and learn to take good care of it, the more satisfying your garden becomes.

In the simplest terms, the duty of soil is to provide a place for plants to grow. The root system threads through the soil, holding the plant upright and in place, supporting it throughout its life. Roots are also the conduit through which the plant absorbs from the soil the water, air, minerals, and nutrients vital for photosynthesis. This absorption is greatly enhanced, in some cases solely performed, by a range of fungi we know as mycorrhizal fungi.

Soil is not one uniform material—a kind of inert lump into which we place plants. It is a cacophony of living and nonliving elements, blending and melding together to create a living organism. Soil has two basic materials—one mineral, the other organic—and is colonized by a wide range of insects, invertebrates, worms, bacteria, and fungi. The mineral composition of any soil is derived from the rocks of the region. Over thousands of years, wind and water wear them down into smaller pieces. As bits of rock, which may have been previously formed from volcanoes, sedimentation, or the metamorphosing action of pressure and movement, are worn down into ever smaller fragments—from boulder to cobbles, from gravel to sand—eventually they become small enough to aggregate with organic materials. This aggregation transforms an inert pebble into the mineral partner in soil.

Soils are frequently categorized by their texture, which is a reflection of the size of the mineral components. Clay soils have the smallest particles and sand has the largest. Silt is considered a midpoint in size. Rocky or gravelly soils have particles that are large enough to be easily visible without close inspection or magnification, much larger than sand.

The organic component of soil is a stew of fallen leaves, spent flowers, dead branches, seeds and their husks, rotting fruit, and ultimately the entire plant when it dies. This vegetable melee combines with the residue from the decay of the animals tiny and huge that have lived among the rocks and plants. All of this organic matter shows up in various states of decay, a situation that in turn provides a food-filled haven for the hordes of fungi, bacteria, worms and other invertebrates, and insects and their larvae that depend on decaying matter for food. These creatures eat up the residue and, by working it through their minute digestive systems, transform nutrients into solutions and chemical formats that are easily taken up by plants.

It all functions like a complex metropolitan area with spectacular internal order where everything is interconnected and interdependent, and the soil's health and vigor are dependent on a careful balance and its steady replenishment. Without a doubt, it is one of the most breathtaking natural systems and, unlike oceans, forests, or deserts, it all happens virtually outside of our view.

The complicated soil factory deconstructs the organic bundle of dead plants and animals, unlocking nutrients and offering them back to the next round of living plants. Soils that have an abundance of the nutrients and minerals required for good plant growth are usually called "rich" but this is misleading. Because plants and soils work together to create congenial and lasting relationships that allow them both to thrive, any soil can be a treasure trove if you match its inherent properties with the requirements of the plants placed in its care.

Most of the current Southwest was once part of a huge ocean that spread from modern-day Texas to the eastern half of California. Over time the ocean receded, leaving a complicated array of abandoned shorelines, sand dunes, coves, estuaries, and isolated lakes. These relics became the foundation of the areas with deep sandy soils. While these soils offer wonderful drainage, they contribute little else and are so poorly consolidated that they shift and move like the dunes they are. The water and its creatures have disappeared, but immense layers of the shells of tiny, unimaginably numerous sea creatures piled up. Gradually the calcium in the shells coalesced and was transformed into an undercoating of the limestone and other so-called chalky rock that lies beneath the region today. A few locales, particularly in Southern California and New Mexico, have vast sand deposits overlaying the limestone, another remnant of long-lost lakes.

Although the bodies of the sea creatures are long gone, their shells occasionally show up as imprints in the limestone itself—delicate reminders of the long, steady process of life being nurtured by the death and transformation of what came before. Over time these huge beds of shells became rock, were covered with other rock formations, and were bent and uplifted in the upheavals that resulted as the mountains of the Southwest were formed and undone. As these limestone beds were tilted and uplifted to face the elements, they were transformed and worn down by wind and water into cliffs and exposed ranges.

In many parts of the region these exposed limestone beds are near the surface and soils atop them are just a thin patina. Here soil finds its way between rocks and outcrops. In some parts of central Texas and in scattered locales around the region, the limestone base has been covered, often to great depth, by the floating debris of the mountains as they wore down. The rocks that formed these soils have been worn down for so long that only tiny mineral particles are left. We know them as tight clay soils, and they are probably the most difficult soils to work with because they combine clay's tendency to hold too much moisture, stay cold, and resist easy cultivation with high alkalinity.

In some parts of the region, water percolated through these chalky soils, especially those that were flatter and with poor run-off, and left a precipitate of calcium carbonate as it dried up. Over time this precipitate consolidated and formed an impenetrable rock known as caliche. Caliche may be a thick layer of rock unable to be moved by either pick or roots, or it may be fractured and fragmented into a rocky, rough-looking soil but one through which roots can penetrate with more ease. Both the underlying limestone in much of the region and the formation of these vast caliche layers have given almost the entire Southwest, especially the hot, arid parts, alkaline soils.

As the western United States has dried out over the time since the last Ice Age, the process by which dead animals and plants decompose in a given area also slowed down. Without sufficient moisture, the organic debris that falls on the ground will leave only minimal residual nitrogen in the soil. The increasing aridity of the region over time also reduced the total number of plants growing on a given plot, thereby reducing the total amount of organic matter available to the soil. Together these forces left many parts of the region—particularly the deserts—with beautifully drained soils rich in all nutrients and minerals save nitrogen.

What this means to Southwest gardeners is that to grow more than just locally native species they (the gardeners) must familiarize themselves with the soil that they inherit and find species which accommodate to it. All the species in this book were selected for their ability to thrive in this region but not all species, even those from similar areas, grow perfectly outside their native range without minor accommodation to their needs. Three strategies for success suggest themselves.

It is routine to hear newcomers to the desert regions of the Southwest bemoan the "poor soils," gardeners of the Coachella Valley sigh as they fight the fine sands, and South Texas gardeners wail over the wretched clay. But all these soils grow a vibrant mix of species. It is when we start trying to accommodate new-comers—our garden plants—to these soils that the fundamental nature of the soil and our gardening desires come into conflict. Making a match between an idealized garden soil and the one you are given requires an understanding of the soil, careful selection of species that thrive within its boundaries, and a gentle modification of its limitations.

First, grow an abundance of local or regional natives. These species are already perfectly suited to the soils of your garden and will have no need of arduous soil building to be grown well.

Second, to expand your choices beyond local or regional natives, choose species from analogous areas of the world. Deserts around the world share many traits and their plants have similar adaptations. The most critical similarity when choosing species from other regions is tolerance of soil alkalinity. Species that grow in extreme soil conditions such as high alkalinity or high acidity do not grow well in the reverse condition. Similarly, species that come from odd or rare soil types such as gypsum fields or serpentine hills may present huge challenges when grown outside those soils. Most species, even those from desert or arid regions, are less demanding, thriving in soils with a pH from 6 to 8.

Third, gently modify the soil of your garden, whatever its native state, creating a more congenial, less-demanding soil condition for all the species you grow. Modification of garden soils does not have to mean wholesale removal and arduous, time-consuming replacement of the soil. Not only is such practice expensive and difficult, it is jarring to think that you take a perfectly fine soil full of potential and discard it in favor of an idealized notion of good gardening soil. I find it ridiculous and entirely at odds with my first precept of gardening—it takes place where you live. If you live in the Southwest, you will garden in the Southwest, so you need to learn to live with the soils of the Southwest. Naturally, there is room for modest improvement, and in this region that means the introduction of more organic matter. Nothing is more successful at helping your soil, and therefore your plants, continue to thrive than the consistent addition of the holy grail of gardening—compost.

COMPOST

Compost results from the decomposition of dead plants. This partially decomposed material is black and crumbly, and holds a powerful blend of nutrients within its particles ready to be released to plants.

The chemistry that binds the organic matter to the mineral matter is complex, but the better the bond the more organic matter that can be attached. Compost, in ways that are poorly understood, helps make a surer bond. If a soil is too loose (sandy) or too tight (clay), then the available space for water and air between the soil particles is either too large and water rushes through the soil, or is too small and water sheers off the surface barely percolating downward. By holding more organic matter to the soil particles, compost has the seemingly contradictory property of both opening up tight soils and closing down loose soils, in both cases making a more perfect spacing. When spacing is optimal, water with its soluble nutrients and minerals and air becomes more readily available to plant roots.

A myriad collection of microscopic soil organisms—fungi, bacteria, other invertebrates, and insects—feeds on the decaying plants or animals and, through this digestion, releases nutrients back to the soil ready to be dissolved in water for uptake by plants. Many of these organisms travel with compost as it is turned onto the soil of the garden flourishing there as well. As the soil microflora grows and the entire soil system becomes more diverse and complex, the overall fertility and health of the soil increase dramatically.

Nutrients are held in the soil in a wide array of chemical formulations, but to be useful to a plant two things must happen: the nutrient must be soluble in water, and it must be in a chemical formulation that the plant can use. Here the pH of the soil plays a crucial role. Some compounds refuse to become soluble in high pH (alkaline) soils, and unless the entire compound is broken down and reformulated, the vital nutrient might as well be missing. The classic example of this action is chlorosis, a condition in plants where one or occasionally several minerals are lacking and leaves typically turn yellow or pale. While any deficiency can be called a chlorosis, iron chlorosis is well known to gardeners in areas with arid, alkaline soils. But the problem is not a lack of iron; it is the presence of iron in a formulation that cannot be taken up by the plant roots.

In a rough way there are two ways to approach the problem—provide another form of the same nutrient or change the conditions, making the nutrients more available to the plants. Soils rich with organic matter have somewhat lower pH, and a pH closer to neutral or lower often is all that is needed to release the nutrients so vital to a plant's well being. Of course, native plants are well adapted to their soils, and these chemical considerations are rarely of concern unless the soil in which you garden has been deeply disturbed.

In countless new housing developments, it is a routine practice to scrap all vegetation including the top layer of soil from the site, grade it, and then build a structure. Building alone causes some disruption; soil becomes compacted easily with heavy equipment rolling over it repeatedly. But the loss of the top layers of soil is the loss of most of the life of the soil, and homeowners in new subdivisions often have considerable difficulty getting new plantings to grow well.

The other common great disturbance of soil, and one that is equally destructive to the active life of the soil, is repeated tilling or digging. In most instances tilling, especially frequent or annual heavy tilling, just turns over the top living layer and buries it where water and air find it harder to penetrate. Soils in most of the Southwest are quite shallow, and turning them upside down can be lethal to all the life in them. In a new bed or garden it may be advisable to turn the soil or to disturb the surface slightly before planting. But if you add or permit to fall plenty of organic matter over the years, the soil will not need to be completely turned over again.

When soil has been deeply disturbed, it can be brought back to life in one of two ways: add copious amounts of organic matter in the form of compost, manures, clippings, or mulch, or grow things in it. All of it sounds like magic and it darn near is. Nothing substitutes for compost for long and nothing works nearly as well.

Making Compost

Making compost is quite simple. Find a place in the garden that is out of sight but handy to the kitchen and the garden. In the Southwest, compost piles need to be watered, so look for a place with a nearby water source. Pick a spot that is shaded for all or a great part of the day. If you want to keep the pile contained and can't snug it into the corner, use wooden pallets set on end, hay or straw bales, wire frames (although the compost can dry out quickly), or almost anything that is at hand. Each pile should be no more than 3 to 4 ft. (0.9 to 1.2 m) on a side and about that high. Piles that are too large, and especially too tall, become deficient in oxygen in the middle and don't decompose properly.

Add all the organic waste from your garden and your kitchen to the pile. This includes leftover vegetables and grains that are not full of oil, vegetable trimmings, coffee or tea grounds, clippings from pruning in the garden, debris from cleaning the sidewalk or the paths, old soils from repotting, and so forth. Forgo adding meat products or oils, as these additives attract vermin and can smell and decompose poorly.

As a rule of thumb, the hotter the pile the faster it breaks down, making compost ready to use quickly. But compost forms in almost any condition.

Oleander, eucalyptus, and palms are common ornamentals in most of the Southwest, but the leaves of these species are difficult to compost properly in home compost piles. Oleander is toxic in all forms and needs to be composted at hot temperatures to be safe; it is best to avoid adding it to home compost piles. Eucalyptus and palms take years to break down and need to be finely shredded before they are added to a compost pile; however, shredded eucalyptus leaves make a fine groundcover for a dusty pathway.

As the pile grows, keep it evenly moist, watering it if rainfall is scarce, covering it if rainfall is too abundant. Compost forms most reliably and abundantly when it is evenly moist and doesn't either dry out completely or become saturated and waterlogged.

Turn the pile, if you want, once a month or so. Many successful compost piles are never turned, and others are regularly turned. Turning aerates the pile, which increases microbial action and does help prevent waterlogging where that is a problem.

Even incompletely composted matter is excellent for your soil. Compost is a lot like spaghetti sauce: it is particular to each gardener, and developing your own formula and technique will be the one that works best for you.

Compost is done when it is dark—black is best—and crumbly in your hand, and has a sweet, earthy smell. It is widely known that there is never enough compost; you just keep the pile going continuously and use it where it will do the most good. If you want to use some of your compost as part of a container mix, put the finished compost through a screen or sieve so it is fine enough for the delicate roots of seedlings or newly potted plants.

Buying Compost

In many parts of the region you can buy a version of compost variously known as composted mulch, composted forest mulch, or composted soil conditioner. Most of these products work fine, especially as an additive to a new bed or as topdressing after planting. I think of them as feeding mulch. While most of these products provide plenty of benefit to soils, they are somehow never as potent as real compost. I find their best use is as a way to stretch the tiny amount of real compost that most of us are able to make.

SOIL PREPARATION

Various schools of thought on soil preparation have developed. In my garden in the low desert of Arizona, most of the ground is undisturbed, native soil, interlaced generously with broken caliche and various other rocky materials. It is highly alkaline, well drained, slim on organic matter, but otherwise healthy. It grows certain perennials better than any other soil—particularly local natives such as globemallow, brittlebush, and desert marigold—but it must be amended with organic matter for best results with species that are from semiarid regions or that are used to canyon or riparian habitats. Species such as salvias, justicias, and plumbago thrive with minor alternations to the native soil.

If an area has never been cultivated or has deeply disturbed soil, begin a new bed by gently turning the soil to a depth of a couple of inches (about 5 cm). Arid soils that do not have many plants on them, soils that have become badly compacted or have been dry for a long time, as well as soils that have been turned upside down during building can form a crust on the surface. It is important to break that hardened crust to allow subsequent amendments, water, and air to penetrate below the surface.

Add a 4- to 6-in. (10- to 15-cm) layer of any combination of compost, composted mulch, or forest mulch to a small proportion of composted steer or poultry manure and rake the mixture over the top of the soil rather than turn it in. It is impossible to put too much of this organic blend on the soil, and the worse the condition of the soil, the more amendment that will be needed.

In almost all parts of the Southwest avoid using peat moss as a soil additive or conditioner. It holds too much moisture when it is fully hydrated, and it dries out too fast, becoming a version of adobe that is slow to hydrate again. Peat moss is too acidic for most desert perennials and creates more problems for a garden than it solves.

Where clay soils dominate or drainage is poor, add sharp sand or gravel to the blend of amendments. With clay soils that have not been previously cultivated or are in bad condition, it is advisable to blend the mixture into the soil by turn-ing it in 4 to 6 in. (10 to 15 cm).

Water the area enough to penetrate at least 6 in. (15 cm) below the surface. Let the soil drain for a few days and repeat watering until the soil is well hydrated to a depth of at least 2 ft. (60 cm). Keeping the new bed moist helps establish the soil microflora that will bring your soil to life. If a bed cannot be planted right away, continue to keep the area lightly watered so it doesn't turn to dust while you wait to put in the plants. Watering will permit the organic matter to settle and keep it in place until you begin planting.

Besides low soil fertility, the other great challenge to growing desert and arid-adapted species is providing outstanding drainage. Almost all species in this book, and nearly all species from the type of environments covered in this book, grow in fast-draining soils either in gravelly washes or along rocky hillsides. In a garden setting, sharp drainage can be created in tight or poorly drained soils by using some combination of the following methods.

The easiest way to improve the drainage in a small or local area is to incorpo-rate a generous amount of gravel or rocky material. If you have the means and the energy, do this to the entire bed; otherwise, amend just the immediate area around the plant. A version of this idea is to build a slight mound of a planting hole where the area below the surface is almost entirely filled with gravel and the plant is placed on top of it.

Contouring is another technique for improving drainage. Again, it can be subtle involving only a small planting hole or part of a bed or it can involve large areas of the garden. By building small mounds or areas that are raised well above the ground level and then planting on the highest parts, drainage is much improved. This technique is excellent in areas with poorly or slowly drained soils and helps in areas that receive much more water naturally than a plant may be able to handle.

The most dramatic method for improving drainage is to build a raised bed. Raised beds can be built out of any material and can be designed to fit into any garden design. They are an excellent way to add interest and drama to a garden whether or not it has drainage issues.

SOIL MAINTENANCE

So much attention is given to soil preparation that it is easy to forget that soil needs to be maintained and tended over the long life of your garden. While soil preparation is a one-time activity to get an area ready for plants, soil mainte-nance is the continuous nurture and renewal of the soil to ensure that your plants thrive throughout their life cycle. It is a long-term arrangement between you and your garden's soil.

My scheme for maintaining the soil in the garden is simple and has yielded excellent results over the life of my garden. Every year, ideally twice a year, I add a generous layer, up to 4 in. (10 cm), of a combination of homemade compost and composted forest mulch or similar products, often with a small amount of composted manure, to the surface of the beds. These components are in roughly equal parts except for the manure which is added much less generously. I add this feeding mulch in April and in September, but you can adjust its application to anytime that is convenient for your garden.

In between these feeding mulches I apply "ordinary" mulch to all the garden beds. Depending on what is available, this might be chipped bark, straw, tree leaves, or any other type of loose organic matter at hand. The exceptions are beds or areas dedicated to local natives or species from extreme desert locales or those solely devoted to succulents. While these areas get the annual feeding mulch, they don't get the loose mulch because the plants in them do not thrive in excessively organic soils.

When applying mulch, do not use anything that is too green, particularly grass clippings, around your plants. If you have an abundance of green clippings, dry them thoroughly before adding them to the soil surface. Fresh grass will wrest too much available nitrogen from the soil for a short time while it is decomposing. Letting the grass dry and slightly decompose in a pile will prevent this nitrogen robbing from occurring in the garden. In addition, well-dried grass clippings do not resprout and regrow as they are spread around the garden.

Mulch has numerous advantages, but the main one is that it covers the soil, thereby slowing down the rate of evaporation from the soil. This reduction in evaporation results in more available water for the plants, which in turn means that you do not have to water as much or as often. Mulch also decays while in place, creating a miniature compost pile right where it is placed.

To prevent problems with rot or decay, spread mulch around plants without letting it run up the stems. Because mulch decays in place, it needs to be renewed from time to time. The frequency depends on what type of product you are using—barks are long lasting, but straw and clippings run out in a season.

The feeding mulch combination I have just described has been the lifeblood of my garden for years. Desert and arid-adapted perennials thrive with this diet of a gentle increase in the soil's organic content. The line is delicate between providing enough nutrients and care to desert and arid-adapted perennials so that they can prosper and thrive and simultaneously not providing too much so that the plants overgrow and become weak and short lived. Over time, the plant litter, leaves, fruit, and flowers of the garden plants themselves start to fill the beds, providing their own mulch.

Throughout much of the Southwest, but particularly in the hottest deserts, inorganic mulch is used widely. Most of it is crushed rock in an array of sizes. Rock mulch can be highly effective in holding down soil evaporation. Many annuals and some perennials thrive when grown with some kind of inorganic mulch around them, but inorganic mulch does not provide any nutrients to the soil; it is essentially neutral. In addition, it builds up enormous heat on the upper surface. Some species find this perfectly acceptable; others find it much too hot and they fail. It is wise to know the species you are growing and their resistance to reflected heat before putting rock mulch beneath them.

Timing of Planting

Although timing is important in planting all perennials, it is critical in the hottest deserts. In these areas gardeners need to promote vigorous and healthy plants that can withstand the long, brutal summers. One of the best ways to accomplish this is to plant perennials in the fall, allowing the plants to establish mature root systems before the summer heat sets in. For the Southwest that means planting from September through early November.

Fall planting offers two big advantages for perennials in the hottest deserts. First, fall is a long, benign growing season with some of the best temperatures available for these species. With luck, rainfall may occur in fall. During this season plants establish quickly and have up to two months of good growth before cooler temperatures slow them down. This means that they can grow larger, more vigorous root systems that allow the plants to resume growth quickly in the short, warm spring. By that time the plant will be well prepared for the rigors of the summer. No matter where a species originates, the summer of the deserts is what defines success or failure in perennials, and the better established the plants are before summer, the better they will be able to withstand it.

For perennials that flower in the spring and are semidormant in the summer, it is especially important to plant them in the fall. These species, particularly those that are native to the American deserts, begin to grow in the fall and maintain steady growth through the winter. By the time they have bloomed in the spring, the plants are shifting into a slower growth cycle that will ultimately result in a semidormant state for the summer. Because of this natural cycle, planting these species in the spring can result in high losses without careful attention to their care. If you must plant in the spring, be prepared to shade the plant more the first year than you will in future years and to water it often. Although it is tempting to buy spring-blooming perennials while in flower, they are best planted in the fall when they are small, homely little plants. You can trust that they will become the glorious delights we all want in the first spring after they are planted.

In milder areas or areas with regular freezes, fall planting must be carefully considered. Species need to be winter hardy and able to withstand intermittent or late frosts. The window for fall planting is shorter; late August and September are recommended. In these areas spring planting is more widely recommended for most perennial species.

Many summer-flowering perennials can be successfully planted in the spring in the deserts, as early as February and continuing through April. In milder areas, including central Texas and along the coast of California, spring planting times move forward one or two months from these dates, and summer-flowering perennials can be planted with ease into midsummer.

Exposure

Whether a species will thrive in full sun, partial or filtered shade, or full shade is addressed in the species profiles in chapters 4 and 5. A few general guidelines may help in making proper selection of a place for your plant to grow.

If you live in the desert regions be especially wary of the phrase "grows in full sun" when buying plants grown outside the region. Full sun in Phoenix, Tucson, or Palm Springs, particularly in the summer, is nothing like full sun in Indianapolis or Philadelphia on their best days. Because the air is so dry and the desert regions are closer to the equator than most of the rest of the country, sunlight is extremely intense. All that water vapor that makes uncomfortable humidity levels fills the air with minute sprays that diffuse the sunlight. Plants can tell the difference.

Unless the species is a local native or you have other reasons to believe it will tolerate full sun, all perennials grown in the desert regions do better with high, filtered shade or protection from the afternoon sun. In these regions filtered shade means the broken shade that comes from trees such as mesquite, palo verde, and others in the bean family or the kind of shade you get from a grove of date palms. It doesn't matter what species create the shade as much as the character of the shade: high enough over the plants to admit sunlight, yet lightly filtered enough to permit adequate plant growth. Dense shade such as from conifers and other evergreens or walls is substantially different from a plant's perspective. Perennials that do well in such heavy shade, particularly if it is dry shade, are prized and are noted in the species descriptions.

Even species that are native to the region may not tolerate full sun if their origins are in canyons or riverside areas. Keep this in mind as you evaluate which plants will or will not thrive in full sun. These species particularly resent growing in too much sun with rock mulch. Some species do unexpectedly well in full sun if their roots are heavily mulched to keep them cool and they have adequate water.

No matter where you live, full sun in the winter is entirely different from full sun in the summer. Almost anything can be grown in full winter sun, but whether that translates to full sun in the summer is a matter of experience and trial and error. In Southern California, where the moderating effect of the Pacific Ocean noticeably lowers the intensity of sunlight, full sun is desirable for almost all perennials in this book. This part of California can be very dry, often going without rain from March to October, but air temperatures do not soar above 90°F (32°C) for long. Under these conditions perennials from desert or arid-adapted regions are growing in ideal circumstances and will thrive in full sun year-round.

Water

I doubt that anything puzzles gardeners using desert or arid-adapted species more than when, how, and how much to water. Watering schedules and recommendations are as numerous as gardeners. Here are mine.

Perennials as a rule have shallow root systems. They rarely extend more than 2 ft. (0.6 m) below the ground. Therefore, in evaluating when and how much to water, bear in mind that you want to soak the root zone to that depth with each watering. Watering intervals or the period between waterings is the time it takes for the soil to dry out to within the last 6 to 8 in. (15 to 20 cm) from the surface. This interval may be as often as every three days in the summer in the hottest deserts or as infrequently as every other week in milder, wetter ones. The variations in weather and soil type are numerous, and it requires some experimentation to find the right blend for your garden.

Although it sounds obvious, one of the best ways to find out when and how much to water is to watch your plants. Plants that wilt dramatically have used up all the available water and are near the point of breaking down. Try to time watering to avoid this condition; it is enormously stressful for plants. For example, if you are watering every four days and your plants begin to wilt on the evening of the third day after watering, you may need to increase the frequency of watering to every three days, increase the amount of water with each watering so that the plants "last" for four days, and/or apply a generous layer of organic mulch to help prevent rapid soil evaporation which robs plants of the water you are providing.

Applying water slowly so that it soaks in deeply is always preferable to a quick and shallow watering. Spray heads or oscillators are inefficient watering devices, allowing a lot of water simply to evaporate in the air, but they cover a lot of area quickly and when carefully managed can work well. They are also handy in a pinch. Use spray heads and oscillators when evaporation is lowest, usually after dark, and avoid windy days.

A modification of flood irrigation by soaking an area with a hose that runs slowly over a long time works well for densely planted or well-contained areas. Water needs to run slowly enough to soak in thoroughly but not run off the bed. Slight mounds or depressions within or around the bed are helpful to keep water confined to the bed so that it slowly percolates into the soil.

Drip irrigation is king in much of the region but especially in the hottest deserts. It is an excellent watering technique for perennials because they rarely have large or deep root systems. A wide array of drip irrigation emitters is available in a bewildering number of styles, but they boil down to two general types: fixed and variable. In fixed emitters, which may look like buttons, flags, or little spaceships, the amount of water that will be delivered is set by the size of the opening on the emitter. Such devices typically deliver 1 or 2 gallons (4 to 8 liters) of water per hour.

In variable emitters the top rotates to open up tiny ports around the cap. These devices are rated to go from 1 to 10 gallons (4 to 40 liters) per hour. How well calibrated they are is a subject of much controversy. I don't care; I find them useful and flexible. I find that variable emitters allow you to place plants closely and use only one emitter for a group by opening it up widely to increase the amount of water. You can also increase the amount of water a plant receives as it grows, or adjust the amount by season. Both fixed and variable emitters are able to be shut off completely. This feature is handy as the plants mature, when they need less frequent watering or when one of them inexplicably dies.

The spacing of emitters is something of an art form. In densely planted beds, it is rarely necessary for each plant to have an emitter. Putting one emitter in the middle of a trio or between two plants is often plenty. The point is to deliver enough water to soak the entire root zone of the plants to about 2 ft. (0.6 m), and if that can be accomplished with fewer emitters, all the better. In addition, many species find a dedicated emitter delivers too much water, but being in the vicinity of one is perfect.

A soaker hose is another version of drip irrigation that is easy to use for watering perennial beds. Water oozes out the entire wall of the hose, spreading gently and evenly over a large area. This type of hose can be joined to a conventional drip system or run on its own. It is especially successful in densely planted beds where individual emitters are intrusive or difficult. In addition, unlike standard emitters, soaker hoses can be shallowly buried or covered with mulch to disappear entirely from sight. A covering not only looks better but also prevents the hose's premature disintegration from sun exposure.

No matter which type of emitter or watering system you use, watch your plants. Drip systems work well, but they are not maintenance free. Check the various components of the system often for leaks, blown-out emitters, wet spots with no plants, spontaneous ponds, and plants that are dry or wilting much sooner than all the others on the system.

In areas with salty or mineral-laden water, and that includes most of the deserts in the United States, water may become increasingly salty over the course of the summer. It is common to find a drip system that was functioning perfectly in May is clogged and failing by August. As salts build up, chiefly from the water, they plug the minute holes quickly. Once a month, particularly in the summer when the system is running most frequently, take off the end cap and run the system briefly to flush out any salts or debris that may build up in the line. Do the same with individual emitters on a regular basis.

Automating a watering system with a timer will give you back your life. Not only are such systems very convenient, but when properly set and maintained they also provide plants with the correct amount of water—no more, no less. The most common type of timer is electronic, and it seems that every one of them is a bit different. It is worth the time and trouble to learn how to use the timer and how to program it to suit the needs of your garden. A few pitfalls with timers can be avoided if you are forewarned.

First, not all species are compatible in their watering needs. It is important that species with similar watering requirements be run on a single station (valve) rather than all plants run on one station throughout the garden. If you get more stations than your timer can handle, add another timer.

Second, timers are touchy about power interruptions and lightning. Power outages, even the most minor blip in the power supply, will shut off the timer, sending it into its default mode, which is typically a daily watering for 10 minutes. A strong lighting strike near your property, even if it doesn't touch your house or yard, can blow out an electronic timer.

Reliable battery-operated timers are available. I find these especially useful for areas that do not require a continuous irrigation system such as wildflower or annual beds, for plantings that are unusually distant from the main timer, or for areas with special watering needs like vegetable gardens. These timers attach directly to a faucet and then to a hose or irrigation system. Good ones are highly reliable, inexpensive, and easy to use.

Fertilizer

I am not a strong advocate of regular or steady fertilization for most perennials. Inorganic or artificial fertilizers are applied too generously and much too often. Although results can be dramatic in the short run, fertilizers are not nearly as effective as compost and mulch and other organic additives in building and maintaining a healthy soil.

Most fast-acting fertilizers are applied as a supplement to existing soil nutrients that may be either missing or in short supply. All inorganic fertilizers work very fast, but they do not stay around long. To achieve those deep green leaves, huge blooms, or longer blooming times, you must use such fertilizers often. But using them abundantly involves paying a price, not only in money but also in soil health. Alkalinity and aridity cause many fertilizer formulations to build up toxic loads of mineral salts if you aren't religious about leaching the ground regularly. It just isn't worth it to me, so I take a slower approach.

Maintaining and building a healthy soil is the best fertilizer you can provide for your plants. As described previously, putting down a thick covering of mulch throughout the year and supplementing it with compost or similar products once or twice a year is more than sufficient to meet the needs of almost all perennials and especially those from arid or desert regions. Most fertilizers add nitrogen, often in extravagant doses, and most perennials from arid or desert regions have an innate ability to thrive in soils that are low in nitrogen. While plants will live on nitrogen boosts, it is neither necessary for their health and performance nor desirable.

Composted steer or chicken manure is widely available in many areas and is used as a fertilizer by many gardeners. Other gardeners are hesitant to use these products because they can be salty if they are not composted properly, increasing an already salty soil and water condition.

Several ways of handling manure products will both minimize the salt problems and get the most effect from the product. First, know your products and buy those that work best in your soils.

Second, do not overuse these products. It is not necessary to add them often; once or twice during the growing season is more than enough. Using such products too often can indeed build up unhealthy amounts of salts, releasing excessive amounts of nitrogen and causing plants to grow leaves at the expense of flowers.

Third, water both before and after applying manure products. This helps leach out any residual salts and settles the product into the upper reaches of the soil so that it won't wash away in the next rain.

Fourth, whether you start with fresh manure or are buying a dried manure product, be sure that it is well composted before you apply it to the ground around your plants. Composted manure that you puchase in bags should be slightly dry, not powdery, and have no smell. If it is otherwise, throw it on your compost pile for a few weeks or months before using it. If you are fortunate enough to have a ready supply of fresh manure, pile it along with other vegetable leavings and let it sit for a season before applying the mixture to the ground.

If you are uncertain about the condition of any manure or believe that you have an inferior product, pour it on the ground, mix it with any other type of organic matter, and let it sit for a few months. Keep it moist but not wet. This shorthand compost pile will help relieve the product of any unwanted salts.

Perennials in Containers

Plants growing in containers require soil, water, and fertilizer regimens that are significantly different from those given plants in the ground. The restricted space of a container can increase the heat load of the soil dramatically, and plants in containers must be placed carefully to avoid too much heat during the summer.

The limited soil and frequent watering that leaches out nutrients very quickly are conditions inherent in container growing. To maintain vigorous plants, provide a rich soil loaded with organic matter right from the start. In created soils it is important that each of the big three nutrients—nitrogen, phosphorus, and potassium—are present in sufficient amounts, and that a healthy dose of micronutrients is available as well. Adding these minerals to the soil blend will help assure that your container-grown perennials remain healthy throughout the year.

Lantana montevidensis mixed planting in a container

Tithonia fruticosa in a container

If you want to use an inorganic fertilizer, add a slow-release, pelletized form to the mix either when you plant or at the beginning of the growing season. Replenish it every three or four months. If you do not use inorganic fertilizers, apply a layer of compost, mulch, or a blend of the two to the top of the pot every three or four months. Once a year renew all the mineral components you added originally to the container. When growing perennials that have a slow or dormant period, add nutrients to replenish the soil or fertilizer only during active growth.

Water-soluble fertilizers have nutrients already in solution and therefore these formulas act even more quickly than dried formulations. Just like the dry formulations, the water-soluble fertilizers whether inorganic or organic do not last long and need to be reapplied frequently, often every two weeks, to be consistently effective. I find this an impossibly difficult, expensive, and time-consuming process for long-lived perennials and look for methods that last longer, build up good soil nutrition, and save my time for more interesting projects.

Recommendations for watering perennials in containers are hard to generalize because conditions through the region are so different. As a rule, containers will need to be watered about twice as often as plants in the ground. In the hottest deserts even large containers may need to be watered daily during the hottest part of the summer. Clay pots lose moisture faster than plastic and need to be watered more often than their plastic counterparts. However often the plants are watered, always water thoroughly until water comes out the drain holes at the base of the pot. The soils in pots can build up salts quickly if they are not leached out often, and watering thoroughly will help prevent this problem.

Pruning

I love to prune. It is satisfying to see a wild array of unruly stems, stalks, and flowers end up as a neat bundle of tidy splendor. Pruning, however, is not a task to be taken up lightly, and it never is performed on a calendar date or because you have nothing better to do in the garden. Pruning is a technique for enhancing the appearance or flowering of a plant, or for correcting damage or poor growth. Each species account in chapters 4 and 5 offers specific timing and pruning style recommendations. Here, however, let us consider why it may be desirable to prune as well as how best to prune.

The reasons to prune are numerous and the ways to perform successful pruning are even more numerous, but fundamentally the pruning of perennials falls into two categories: removing flowers or removing foliage.

REMOVING FLOWERS

Pruning out pitiful flowers that are long past their prime before they fall off naturally is a cosmetic flourish that greatly enhances the look of any perennial planting. When done properly, pruning out older flowers often encourages another bloom and can make for a longer, more exciting flowering cycle in the garden. The oddly morbid term for this kind of pruning is *deadheading*. While you can casually walk around the garden and literally pinch the spent flowers off the plant as they fade, more careful deadheading will have better overall results.

Unless you have the kind of fingernails that I only dream of, removing spent flowers with your hands usually does not result in a good cut. Use scissors, floral shears, or razor-sharp pruners for the best cut and the least damage to the stem.

If the plant has solitary flowers on thin stalks, remove spent flowers by cutting the stalk back to the first lateral bud whether it is a flower bud or a leaf node. Blanket flower (*Gaillardia aristata*), desert marigold (*Baileya multiradiata*), and Angelita daisy (*Tetraneuris scaposa*) are examples of plants whose flowers are removed this way.

In species with more complicated flowering, where flowers are held on branched stalks, deadheading is different and can be done in two ways depending on the style of flowering. When a tall main stalk is branched into three to five small or minor stems, as is common in salvias, one of the minor branches will flower and fade, then another will begin and finish, and so on until the entire stalk has bloomed out. Depending on your preferences and just how it all looks, each minor branch that finishes blooming can be pruned to its junction with the main stem as it fades. Many gardeners prefer to wait until the entire branched stalk has bloomed at which time they prune back to its junction with the leaves growing at the base of the plant. In most salvias and other species with this style of flowering, because the leaves are held in a low basal set, pruning out the old flowering stalk means cutting it nearly to the ground.

In other species, such as brittlebush (*Encelia farinosa*), Mexican hat (*Ratibida columnifera*), and ageratum (*Ageratum corymbosum*), the flowers are also held on a tall, branched inflorescence but there is no low, basal growth of leaves; rather, the leaves are held on tall stems which may branch repeatedly. In this case, pruning the spent flowering stalk means cutting it back to the first lateral bud.

Perennials such as penstemons and Rodney's aster (*Symphotrichum praealtum*) have a tall inflorescence without clearly defined branching that holds congested clusters of flowers. For species like these, wait to cut out the flowering stalk until all the flowers have opened and faded. Then cut back the stalk to either the basal growth or the first lateral bud.

Leaving flowering stalks to complete the entire reproductive cycle by setting and maturing seeds can inhibit another flowering cycle. Taking away the flowers before seed is set frequently results in the formation of another blooming cycle. Members of the sunflower family are especially sensitive to this cycle and can be nudged into numerous blooming cycles by regular deadheading.

Occasionally, it is desirable to time blooming. If the garden is going to be the location of an important event or activity you might want a particular perennial or set of perennials in bloom at that time. Pruning out flowers that are too early can delay blooming until the desired time. But here is a caution about this technique with many desert-adapted perennials: species from the most arid regions are often reluctant to return to bloom when conditions become too hot, the days are too long, or the ground is too dry. They are programmed to bloom when conditions are best for seed set, and trying to trick them out of these cycles can be difficult and result in no flowers at all.

Of course, if you want to keep seed, you have to leave the entire flowering stalk on the plant until the seeds are ripe. While this can be unsightly for a time, it is rarely necessary to keep every flower to have an adequate amount of seed, and the rest can be cleaned away. Keeping the flowering stalks until there is seed is also a fine way to encourage birds in the garden. Again, you can leave a little for the birds and clean out the rest to make things tidier.

PRUNING FOLIAGE

Pruning foliage from perennials goes by many names—cutting back, pinching, pinching back, or thinning—all of which sound more like a dietary desire than a gardening practice. Foliage in perennials is pruned for a wide array of reasons, including to encourage the plant to rapidly increase growth, making it look lush and dense; to thin out congested or closely growing stems, resulting in a plant with an open, sparse appearance; to secure a more upright or rounded shape; to reduce its overall height; to correct errant or unruly growth; to remove pest or disease damage; or to mitigate the ravages of animals, storms, or severe cold or heat.

In addition to pruning for all these reasons, sometimes the reason for pruning is merely preferential based on the individual whim of the gardener. Because pruning can change the shape and height of a plant, gardeners with a tidy or formal garden can use selective and judicious pruning to maintain a plant's final height more or less permanently and therefore maintain a particular effect. Some gardeners don't like plants to touch or fall into one another. Regular pruning keeps a perennial with runaway tendencies tidy and in its own space.

Although I love the practice of pruning, I believe that most perennials are pruned much too often and far too aggressively. Every time you get the urge to prune ask yourself, "Will the plant be healthier after I prune it? Will the plant look better after I prune it?" and most importantly of all, "Does the plant really need to be pruned or am I just looking for something to do outside?" It sounds trivial but not to your plants.

I like my plants to grow into their natural form, so if they become too large or too unruly, or look out of place, it often means they are in the wrong place. No amount of pruning and cajoling is going to make this better. Far better to yank out a plant and put in something better suited than to continually and relentlessly cut the plant back. Pruning is like giving blood—it is a wonderful and beneficial act full of promise and healthy opportunity, but if done too frequently it can be the death of you or your plant.

Regardless of why a plant is pruned, pruning must be done with care and attention. Proper pruning is a fine art that improves with practice. Nothing is mysterious about it, but these general guidelines may help.

Always prune to a leaf node or junction in the stem. This will prevent the grue-some sight of a lovely perennial smothered with bare, slashed stems. Pruning out tip foliage unleashes a wash of hormones and other signals from the plant to mitigate the damage. When you want the plant to be fuller or have more stems, this response is just what you want.

Prune with an eye to the natural form of the plant unless you are practicing the specialized art of bonsai or topiary. Reducing height by taking out the one or two problem stems results in a much more balanced plant than just whacking it back from the top.

Use the right tool for the job. Most perennials have stems that are small enough to be pruned with either handheld bypass pruners or floral shears. Anvil pruners are not sharp enough and usually mash the stem rather than make a clean cut. In selected situations sharp hedge pruners can be useful. Scissors are adequate for perennials with exceptionally thin stems.

Prune at the appropriate time of year for the species and the type of pruning. Pruning at inappropriate times can vastly increase the time it takes the plant to recover, leaving you with a pathetic version of the plant for months instead of weeks. Poorly timed pruning also opens opportunities for pests, diseases, sunburn, or cold damage that did not exist before you pruned. It can also so shock a plant that it dies from the stress of pruning. The same response that encourages a flush of new growth when you prune at the beginning or in the midst of a growth cycle will be dulled by pruning when the plant is not actively growing.

Follow any hard pruning with a deep watering. Pruning is stressful and removes many leaves that provide photosynthetic activity for the plant. Your perennial will do better if you shower it with extra attention after pruning rather than walk away satisfied with its new look.

Avoid applying any fertilizer for at least two weeks after pruning. This is especially critical after a hard prune or if you have been forced to prune out of season because of damage. Fertilizer can be too strong for the young growth, and plants may burn or react by slowing growth.

How you prune is roughly dictated by what you want to achieve. When the goal is to reduce the overall size of the plant, two ways present themselves.

Pinching or pinching back is the practice of cutting off a plant's terminal buds. When this is done while the plant is actively growing, the plant will respond by regrowing more than one tip where previously there was one. To pinch back a stem, remove only an inch (2.5 cm) or less of the tip. Repeat this cut two or three times over a season if desired, but stop four to six weeks before blooming begins. Most perennials have a strong growing season in advance of blooming, and that tendency is helpful in determining when to prune. In addition, any perennial that has terminal blooms (arising from the tip of the stem) will require that the tip be undisturbed to set flowers.

The other way to reduce the size of a perennial is to prune selected stems that are growing too long. Here the cut is made deep in the plant, ideally at the base of the stem to be cut. When plants are cut this way the actual wound is invisible. This type of cut is quick and easy, and frequently all that is needed to bring the plant down to size is to remove two or three stems. Although best done when the plant is actively growing, this type of pruning isn't as time sensitive as pinching back and can be done anytime it won't seriously affect flowering or vigor.

Thinning is the removal of selected stems to create a plant that has a lighter, open, less dense look. Take out stems that are crossing onto each other, growing too close together, or branching abundantly. Cut the stems as far back into the plant as possible. Thinning is often done in humid climates to increase air flow through a plant to help prevent mildews or other fungal infections.

Perennials sometimes need a hard prune. This is a drastic pruning technique that removes a large volume of the plant, often taking out almost all its height. It results in a dramatic change in the looks of the plant for a brief time. Because this type of cut can kill a plant, it is critical to perform hard prunes at the proper time.

In a hard prune, the plant, regardless of the number of stems, is cut to within 6 or 8 in. (15 to 20 cm) of the ground. This cutting will induce a flurry of growth, particularly of new stems, and within a span of a few weeks the plant will return to its regular, fully leafed form. Generally a hard prune is done shortly before the plant's most active growing season or directly after flowering. Although it is brutal, this type of pruning can be a splendid way to bring a languishing perennial back to life and to correct damage from a bad cold spell, a devastating hot spell, or the catastrophic attention of a rambunctious dog.

When damage to a plant is less dramatic, a modified version of a hard prune can be done. Instead of cutting the entire plant back, severely prune out only the dead or damaged portion of the plant, ideally to a junction with another stem. If the plant is lopsided or out of balance after pruning, remove one or more other stems to restore symmetry. Quick regrowth will also correct this temporary imbalance.

When freezing temperatures have damaged a perennial, always wait to prune until all danger of frost is past. Pruning earlier exposes the stem to the possibility of more cold damage, and any new foliage that sprouts is easily ruined by a subsequent freeze. Patience pays off even if the plant looks dreadful.

When damage is caused by severe heat, the timing of pruning is also important and it pays to know your plants. Summer-growing, tropical species can be pruned in the summer and, because they grow in the heat, they recover quickly. Species that actively grow in spring or fall can be severely damaged by pruning in the heat of the summer since pruning opens up new stems to sunburn and resulting damage. It is especially critical in the extreme heat of the deserts to wait until temperatures have moderated in the fall before pruning out damaged stems to restore shape or adjust.

Insects, Pests, and Diseases

When I first moved to the desert environs of Phoenix I thought that the area had no insect pests or plant diseases worth noting. I had come from the Louisiana Gulf Coast and nothing in arid Arizona matches the intimacy with which I had learned to live and cope with insects and plant diseases in those reclaimed swamps. I soon learned that while these garden marauders were dramatically reduced, a few remained. My experience in Phoenix is common throughout the Southwest, although central and southern Texas can lay claim to a more abundant insect and disease fauna.

I have to admit that I take a live-and-let-live approach to almost all insects that are labeled as pests. Most species are a fleeting presence in the garden and tend to erupt into Stygian hordes of destruction only when plants are deeply stressed or genetically susceptible to their predations or when a collusion of environmental conditions creates unnatural numbers of the insect. Learning about the preferences and life cycles of these insects helps keep it all in perspective and make for clear determinations of when to proceed with some kind of control. It is also important to recognize that most of the insects you see in the garden are not the ones causing destruction, but are more likely to be your partner in creating the balance and harmony that is the best safeguard against pestilential insects.

The few strategies I adhere to when dealing with insects and their possible damage to my plants are as follows: look often and carefully at your plants, be clear that the insect you see is the one that is causing the problem you notice, and deal only with the exact insect that is causing the problem.

These same strategies apply when dealing with disease—it is critical to know what is going on so you can treat it appropriately. Nothing is as destructive and as wasteful as the conditioned response to launch an assault over the entire spread of the garden with a wide-ranging poison when you see a notched leaf, a wilted stem, or a blackened twig. It is never a good idea to douse plants with pesticides on a regular schedule with the imaginary idea of preventing damage; you are only making your plants and the garden in which they live a sterile, hostile place where ironically a lethal infestation is then much more likely to get a foothold and cause extensive damage.

In the garden, a wide array of insects that eat each other and healthy plants that resist and ward off disease is a more certain prevention to the ups and downs of insect and disease predation. Watching plants carefully is simple and so rewarding. We grow them to enjoy them, so getting out and doing that up close is our reward for all the care we have lavished on them, as well as the quickest way to spot any trouble early. Early detection means noticing subtle symptoms such as yellowing leaves, chewed segments, browning tips, or a general fading that marks the first stages of decline.

Noticing a problem in its early stages does not necessarily reveal the cause. Yellowing leaves may result from heat stress or a mineral deficiency, or they may only be old leaves that are ready to fall. They may indicate overwatering or be common at that particular time of year. Chewed leaves might indicate the feeding of a caterpillar, the innocuous cutouts of leaf cutter bees, or the scars left by a bird pecking at a delectable nymph. Then again they might be the nibble marks of a small rodent.

Browning tips can signal salt build up in the soil, but they can also result from drying winds or a mineral deficiency. Old leaves that are going to fall off anyway regularly turn brown.

Plants can look puny because they are water stressed, in which case a good soak will fix them up. They might be showing incipient signs of root rot that is preventing water and nutrients from rising through the roots to the stems, or they might just be too hot or too cold. Plants that are preparing for dormancy often look peaked and begin to lose a leaf or two shortly before they drop all their leaves for the long rest. Newly established plants can be alarming and display all kinds of dreadful symptoms before they finally set and take off in their new location.

With these few examples, you can see that noticing a problem in the plant is only the first step, and figuring out what is causing it is the next and most necessary step. Knowing what is wrong or what is responsible allows you to choose what to do about it or whether the situation is worth dealing with at all. Ask yourself if this problem will severely cripple the plant or cause all the fruit or flowers to vanish, or if is it only a slight blip in the life of the plant. Find out if it is a short-term problem or something that will only get worse if left alone. Many insects and some diseases are extremely sensitive to changes in their environment, and their activity in your garden is linked to a particular part of their life cycle. It pays to know if you can wait out the problem with gentle control or if an all-out assault is necessary.

In addition, I urge you to take a hard look at the cultural practices you have exacted on your plant. Cultural failings on our part are much too often the actual source of plant problems and we are loathe to acknowledge it—taking the much easier road of blaming that dang whitefly and or that dratted powdery mildew for the damage. For most diseases the surest control is to plant species that are either resistant or chiefly so. Maintaining healthy, lively soil and keeping plants from undue stress go a long way toward keeping plants disease free.

When you are assessing the damage, watch for signs of underwatering or overwatering, too much or too little sun, and bad timing when planting or pruning. Many diseases and insect infestations are secondary symptoms when the root cause can be laid at our own hearth.

Sun stress and associated heat stress are a common occurrence in the deserts and show up as yellowing, occasionally browning, of leaves or stems. This type of stress usually comes on suddenly, within a day or two of a plant being transplanted or moved into a hotter or sunnier location, or when a sheltering limb is pruned away. Sunburn and heat stress can also occur after ill-considered pruning in the summer or anytime too much foliage is removed from the plant.

Overwatering and underwatering are difficult to diagnose; the symptoms can sometimes be the same—pale yellowing leaves. Stems and leaves that become soft or blackened indicate overwatering or extremely poor drainage. Wilting, of course, makes underwatering a snap to diagnose.

Keeping a sense of perspective about pests and diseases is essential for both your peace of mind and for your garden's health. If you recognize that a healthy and diverse garden with living soil is your goal, then a few yellow leaves or nibbled stems are a small price to pay for the range of life that lives in your small area.

DAMAGING INSECTS

Not many insects plague perennials in the Southwest. A few of the most common that might occur are listed here.

Aphids

These tiny sucking insects can be found anytime of year, but they seem to be most prevalent in the spring and the fall. Aphids are drawn to parts of the plant that are rich in nitrogen and therefore they relish tender, new growing tips, flowers, and flower buds. Their eggs are virtually invisible, but the immature stages (nymphs) show up as small yellow or whitish circular eruptions on the leaf underside. The adults look similar but they have legs and move around. Modest numbers rarely harm a healthy plant.

Vigilance is key in dealing with aphids. Running your hand over the leaf or tip to kill off the daily invasion, using a strong jet of water on the leaf or tip daily, or smothering the aphids with insecticidal soap helps keep the numbers down. Maintaining healthy plants without overfertilizing them also helps keep the balance of aphids in the garden at manageable levels. If a plant has become so infested that it is declining, your best option may be to cut it back severely if that is possible or remove it and start again. Even if you kill all the aphids at this point the plant's chance of a decent recovery may be minimal.

Cutter or Leaf-cutter Bees

These are not really pests, but their telltale circular or semicircular cutouts on leaves tend to put them in the category for many gardeners. The bee takes the leaf segment back to its den and uses it to line a nest for her eggs. The damage occurs only in late spring or early summer, and it is entirely cosmetic. The plant will fully recover, and secondary problems from the holes in the leaves are not likely. You can hardly see the bees, so any spraying is merely a wild guess, and they are better pollinators than we are. Wise gardeners leave them alone.

Spider Mites

Like aphids, these nearly microscopic creatures suck out nutrition from a plant leaf. The leaf of a heavily infected plant is stippled with yellow. Spider mites are frequently red, and you can tell if you have them by placing a white piece of paper under the leaf as you shake it. The crawling bits of dust are the spider mites.

Spider mites thrive in dusty, dry conditions. One of the best ways to prevent them is to keep plants clean; spraying them with water every few days will ensure that spider mites do not reach astronomical proportions. Dust is a way of life in areas that do not receive regular rain, so gently cleaning your plants with a spray is your best defense. Leaves that are heavily infected become mottled and discolored and fall off. Clean up any fallen leaves that are infected to help keep down the population of these minute creatures.

Whiteflies

The adult whitefly is small and extremely mobile. You find whiteflies on plants by flicking a leaf and watching as a cloud of white particles erupts. Many researchers believe that the adults cause little harm, using plants only as a resting place, but all agree that the nymphs are sucking devils. Nymphs are tiny, rounded creatures that may be almost clear whitish or yellow. They are commonly found on the undersides of the leaf.

Huge infestations can decimate a plant in hours. Whiteflies prefer leaves that are thin and soft, such as those of lantana, hibiscus, tecoma, and most vegetables. Symptoms of large infestations include discolored and distorted foliage and copious honeydew on the leaves, which encourages a bloom of sooty mold and premature defoliation.

In some parts of the Southwest, especially near agricultural fields, these insects can arrive in clouds in the late summer. Major eruptions have decimated miles of melons and other crops. One year these insects were so numerous that they formed a haze in the sky in the Phoenix area. That year we not only saw them, but we also breathed them and we ate a great number of them. After that, a surge of research emerged on various ways to control these agricultural pests, including hormonal lures, targeted sprays, and cultural practices, and gardeners have been the beneficiary. Numbers have never again approached anything like those infestations in the years since.

No control is effective in removing all whiteflies from a garden—you can only hope to keep them down to manageable numbers. The adults are on the move, and the ones you may be lucky enough to remove today will be replaced by new ones tomorrow. Spraying them off daily with strong water and covering precious crops or plants with row covers or other shelters aids in keeping the numbers down. While insecticidal soaps and a few other insecticides do kill adults, the whiteflies are usually so numerous that those controls are only reasonable within closed systems like greenhouses. Many predatory insects eat whiteflies or their larvae, and encouraging a bountiful fauna of good bugs is perhaps your best defense.

Psillids
These tiny sucking insects strongly resemble whiteflies, and it can be difficult to tell them apart. They tend to occur quickly in the late spring or early summer, often in great numbers, and then disappear. Psillids are usually a greater problem on woody plants, and a significant infestation can defoliate a tree quickly. Control measures used for whiteflies are generally the only measures available to help with psillids.

Grasshoppers
As with whiteflies, you may find one or two grasshoppers in your garden in some years, while in other years you have to fight them off with a broom. With their long legs and great mobility, grasshoppers in large numbers can become a huge problem. They eat voraciously while they are around.

If you find only one or two, as I always do in the late summer around my potted plants, simply remove them individually and dispatch them with a rock, tool, or scissors. *Nosema locustae* is a protozoan disease of grasshoppers sold under the trade names NoLo Bait, Grasshopper Spore, and Semaspore. Young grasshoppers are the most susceptible to this disease, and some species of grasshopper are not affected at all. The effectiveness of this product hinges on proper timing and use of quality strains and is only worth it for huge infestations.

Caterpillars

This is a catchall phrase for the larvae of moths and butterflies. All caterpillars are eating machines; they only live to grow up large enough to pupate and ultimately to harness enough energy to transform into their adult stage. The variety of size, shape, coloring, and other markings is profound.

Again, the numbers are the critical factor in determining whether control measures are needed or not. A few caterpillars are easy to either tolerate or deal with by directly killing them manually. Larger infestations may need more dramatic measures.

When I was a girl my sisters and I had various duties in the garden. One was monitoring the immense, deep green tomato hornworm that can strip a tomato plant overnight. When we found one, we cut off the branch where it was found and stomped it dead with our feet or a shovel. This sure-and-direct method is still the best method for dealing with marauding caterpillars.

The less vigilant or more squeamish gardener can rejoice in the harnessing of a bacteria, *Bacillus thurengensis* (Bt), that has gone a long way to helping gardeners control excessive numbers of caterpillars. Bt is available in numerous formulations; many target only one species, so be sure you know which one is useful for your situation before applying it.

I urge caution in dealing with caterpillars. These bloated creatures last only a short time in the garden and become the exquisite butterflies that we all go to so much trouble to attract. Many also become the humble moths that pollinate vast numbers of our annuals, perennials, and vegetables throughout the year. Go easy on the caterpillars, dealing only with the ones that are truly causing a problem.

Ants

While ants in the garden are not a pest in the true sense of the word, large numbers of ants or ants in the wrong place can be a problem. Not only are they annoying when they build their nests right where you need to kneel, walk, or sit, but they also can in some cases encourage aphid populations. The excess sugars and sap emitted from aphids is known as honeydew. This substance attracts the fungus that grows as black mold or sooty mold. Ants like sooty mold and, although they can harvest it directly, some ants colonize and "farm" aphids for it, pulling in aphid eggs to overwinter in their chambers. Keeping ants under control can help control aphids and associated diseases in some instances.

BENEFICIAL INSECTS

In what might be termed a revolution, pest and disease control methods have an increasingly large number of advocates for what is known as Integrated Pest Management (IPM), or ecologically based pest control. This is a version of the quaintly termed methods known as organic gardening. These terms are not synonymous—pure organic gardeners never use an inorganic product formulation for any type of control. Each method, however, hinges on the concept that pest control is best done in a targeted fashion with prevention and accurate identification as the keys to success.

One of the chief resources of all these methods is the use of so-called beneficial insects, those little warriors of the insect world that are parasites or predators on the insects that we deem pests. It has become a flourishing industry. When properly encouraged, a mighty army of beneficials can be your best assurance of healthy plants; however, there are a couple of caveats. Many of the insects sold as beneficials will not be native or comfortable in your area. Countless numbers of them last only a few weeks and never set up the colonies that you wish they did; this is particularly true of lady bugs. Take great care in buying beneficials. Purchase only those that attack what you need them to and that can live well where you do. It is also vital that their life span coincide with your insect problems.

The more beneficial plan in my view is to encourage these helpful predators to flourish in your garden by the twin methods of creating a diverse and healthy garden from the soil up and of eschewing pesticide sprays that kill broadly and without discrimination. Believe me, they will come. Although countless species of insects feed on one another, some of the most well recognized and those that turn on the garden pests are mentioned here.

Trichogramma *Wasps*

These wasps are tiny insects that eat the eggs of many moth and butterfly species but are never effective against caterpillars. Therefore, any release of one of the countless species of *Trichogramma* wasps must be when moths or butterflies are laying eggs. Unfortunately, moth and butterfly eggs are laid long before the destruction of the caterpillars becomes noticeable and abundant. Although the wasps are fierce predators, their life cycle must coincide with that of their prey. These wasps are a good example of the importance of knowing what your beneficials eat and when.

Praying Mantids

Praying mantids are a large group of predatory insects with a truly astounding ability to feed on other insects. Watching these silent, still hunters reminds me of watching herons—they freeze and hold for an endless amount of time waiting for an unlucky passing victim. When praying mantids strike, they are so fast and accurate that their insect prey seem to vanish rather than be caught. Praying mantids are indiscriminate, however, and trying to increase their numbers in your garden might jeopardize beneficial insects and bees as well as the ones you want them to eat. In addition, praying mantids are fiercely territorial and won't permit other mantids in the vicinity; in the end, only one mantid will be left. Therefore, trying to increase pest control by buying more praying mantids and releasing them has limited success, but finding them around the garden is a great joy and is to be celebrated.

Aphid Lions

Despite the picturesque name, aphid lions are actually the larvae of both green and brown lacewings. They feed on a wide array of insects including aphids, leafhoppers, mealybugs, whiteflies, psillids, and insect eggs. The adults are tremendous predators of aphids and other insects.

Beetles

Lady beetles or as they are more commonly known, ladybugs, are the darlings of the beneficial insects business and the species most likely to fail when you buy them. They are territorial, prefer habitats that they pick over the ones you pick for them, and are driven by migratory necessities that may or may not coincide favorably with your release. When they are around, however, they are voracious feeders on a wide array of insects and mites.

Ground beetles with their gaudy black or dark metallic backs and rove beetles are both small hard-shelled insects. The former favor ground-dwelling insects while the latter feed on fly larvae.

Miscellaneous Insects

Syrphid or hover fly larvae are described by one author as the "connoisseur of aphids," and these abundant insects help control even large infestations of aphids. Other useful and highly visible insects around the garden include stink bugs with their shieldlike body and revolting odor, assassin bugs, big-eyed bugs, and damsel flies. The minute pirate bugs are tiny black-and-white insects that burrow into the folds and bases of leaves and stems to feast on hidden thrips, spider mites, and insect eggs. Even those insects that require us to be cautious around them, such as paper wasps and yellow jackets, feed on caterpillars. Their benign cousins, the hunting wasps, also feast on leafhoppers, caterpillars, and beetles.

The remarkable creatures known as spiders can provide abundant control for an array of leaf-eating and leaf-sucking insects including beetles, caterpillars, leafhoppers, and aphids. This is particularly true of the more cryptic species rather than the flashy web weavers.

Because the adult forms of many beneficial insects feed on nectar or pollen, while their larvae feast on your pests, providing a garden with a wide diversity of flowering plants makes them feel at home. In the end, a lively healthy garden with vigorous plants in a wide array of species that are well adapted to the area's conditions encourages the vast intertwined insect population that will feed and sustain itself within your garden, offering unexpected protection to your precious ornamentals.

DAMAGING ANIMALS

Gardeners in certain locations such as on the outskirts of town or near a park or preserve can have their gardens inhabited by any number of animals that are destructive to their plants. Rabbits, gophers, deer, numerous small rodents, and in some places javelina—all are unwelcome visitors that can chew their way through a garden in a matter of hours.

Gardeners plead for a sure and certain fix for the invasion of these animals, believing that lures, repellants, and other fantastical formulations will ward them off. I am often reminded of medieval charms and exhortations, and I am certain they work just as surely as most of the lures and repellants on the market. The only thing that works permanently for all these creatures is a fence.

Fences come in many forms and, depending on your budget and your garden, you can use any or all of these suggestions. If you can fence the entire perimeter of the garden, it will be a serious deterrent to most animals. Animals like javelina are unable to move through a block fence or other sturdy wall, but rabbits are geniuses at finding the minutest slit beneath a gate to secure entry. Deer can be fenced out, but the fence has to be extremely tall, well over their leaping height. Ground-dwelling rodents, such as gophers and the other smaller chewing rodents, are not deterred by a fence at all; they simply burrow under it.

Fences can also be temporary. Rabbits are common throughout much of the Southwest and represent a significant pest in the garden. They are especially fond of the plants you put in yesterday and devastate new plantings without protection. A small temporary fence of chicken wire, hardware cloth, or similar material is the only deterrent I know that works. Although the fence is hideous, it does not have to be permanent. Once the plant is large enough to both survive a minor chewing attack and have some semiwoody growth at the base, the corral can be removed. Rabbits will eat absolutely anything if they are hungry enough, including cacti, agaves, and other plants that are not touched in normal times, so some sort of protection for new or tender plants is unavoidable.

Ground-dwelling rodents are the most trying animal invaders in my opinion. Every part of the region has its own species, but in my garden, ground squirrels and some small mice tunnel throughout areas of the garden that have well-turned soil. I cannot bring myself to use the baits and poisons on the market, but they may be effective. These products are not selective and, if you choose to use them, be sure they are not accessible to your pets.

Even when using such products, no guarantees are made. Rodents are prolific, and the loss of one clan is the opening another clan was waiting for. The move to recolonize your garden will happen quickly. I have fought these creatures with a host of removal techniques in a nursery yard I once ran and only a cat kept them at bay and even then only when she was right there.

PLANT DISEASES

Disease is the invasion of a plant by bacteria, fungus, or virus. Although the incidence of some of the most devastating plant diseases is low in the Southwest, a few diseases can plague perennials in the region.

Bacteria

Bacterial diseases are often the direct result of injury to a plant. Poor pruning practice, such as bad timing or too much damage to the root during planting, is a common reason for a bacterial infection to invade a plant. Good hygiene and good cultural practices will reduce the probability of bacterial infections dramatically. The black goo oozing out of leaves or stems that is a symptom of overwatering is the work of bacteria that attack weakened plant tissues.

Fungus

Fungal diseases are more common in perennials than bacterial ones. The wide number of infections by the fungi *Rhizoctinium* and *Phytophora*, known as root rots, can erupt quickly in warm, moist soils. Fungal diseases are dependent on environmental conditions that become congenial for their increase. *Penstemon* species, particularly the desert ones, are highly susceptible to root rots in late summer when summer rains create the moist, warm conditions that the fungus favor. Again, prevention and cultural practices are key to keeping loses from fungal infections at minimal levels. Good drainage, proper watering, and plenty of sun are a few strategies to keep summer root rots at bay.

Keep plants healthy and be sure that drainage is excellent. Water only when your plants need it; do not be tempted to overwater your perennials just because you are hot. Standing water or overly wet soils is a breeding ground for a wide range of fungal infections. When a plant becomes diseased, either remove it or remove the infected portion to minimize the spread of the fungus.

Powdery Mildew

One of the most common diseases of perennials is powdery mildew. This fungal disease first appears on the underside of the leaf as a whitish or mottled spot. The next phase of infection is the part with which we are most familiar—the white webby surface that holds the spores. If left to spread, powdery mildew can debilitate a plant, and therefore prevention is vital.

Powdery mildew is encouraged by high humidity and lack of air circulation as well as by temperature fluctuations. Warm, dry days followed by cool nights are ideal circumstances for the fungus. Growing plants so close together that air circulation is significantly reduced is also encouraging. For many perennial species the best prevention is to choose resistant forms, but keeping plants healthy and well spaced will keep this fungal infection under control. Clean up regularly around plants and do not leave infected leaf litter around the base of the plant especially over the winter. Such litter is full of spores. Clean mulch helps control the disease by preventing splashing which can fling spores from the ground up to the plant.

Virus

Viruses are just as insidious in plants as they are in people. While few viral diseases affect perennials, when they occur the symptoms are clear. Leaves will have oddly patterned yellow or white areas, or show deformed or irregular growth on lower stems or tip (although this symptom alone can also be the work of thrips) or an unexplained and sudden wilting or death of all or part of a plant. No treatments are available for virus attacks. Remove the plant as soon as you are certain of the presence of a virus and destroy the plant without putting it in the alley or the compost pile.

Propagation

Propagating plants is so much fun, it is a wonder we don't do it more. I believe too many people think of it as mysterious or especially difficult. It can be both, but it is successful and relatively easy once you master a few principles. It is delightful fun to make plants that you can give away to gardening friends. Basic propagation skills also allow you to grow species or varieties that are not widely available in your area. Three types of propagation are presented here—by seed, by cuttings, and by layering.

PROPAGATION BY SEED

Timing can be important in germinating seeds successfully and is often the reason for poor or erratic germination. In addition, many if not most desert and arid-adapted species have strong protections on the seed to hold off germination until conditions are just right. These can include chemical inhibitors, hard or impermeable seed coats, or a need for seed to age (known as after ripening) once it has fallen from the plant. Some species need cool soils to germinate, others need hot soils. Find out as much as you can about the particular species you are growing before you set out. In the hottest parts of the Southwest, if you are unsure, plant seed from September to February. Extremely hot weather can be hard on seedlings. Unless you know they love it, try to get plants up and growing well before the hottest weather sets in. In less intensely hot climates, plant seed you are not sure of from late winter to early summer.

I plant all seed in a mix of equal parts vermiculite and perlite. I do this to prevent problems with fungal disease like damping off. Make up the mixture, wet it thoroughly, and then fill clean containers with it. If you prefer to add some good quality, sterile potting soil, do so, but watch for signs of fungal infections.

Sow seed over the top of the mixture and then cover with a light coating of the same mixture. Water again. Seedlings are fragile and using a powerful hose spray can shift them, move them around, drown or damage them. Misters or fine-spray nozzles help immensely.

Put the containers in a place that has bright but indirect light and cover them to prevent moisture loss. A greenhouse or a cold frame is ideal. If you do not have such a structure, cover the entire container with a loose shroud of plastic. The plastic storage bags made for food storage rather than those for the freezer are excellent. Plastic that is not even slightly permeable can cause problems by allowing too much moisture to be held around the seedlings. You can also cover the pot or container with a milk jug or a quart-size (liter-size) plastic beverage container from which the bottom has been removed.

Secure the plastic around the container with a string or rubber band. As long as water droplets are visible on the inside of the plastic or other covering, it is not necessary to water the seeds.

Most seedlings do not need any supplemental nutrients until they are growing true leaves. They can, therefore, be left in a sterile mix until they germinate and have grown up to five true leaves. Once they have up to five true leaves, seedlings should be moved out of the sterile mix and into a good-quality, well-drained potting soil.

When transplanting seedlings, grab them by the leaves, never the stem. If you break or damage a leaf, the plant will regrow quickly, but if you break or damage the tiny stem, the plant will die. Move plants from the potting mix to the growing mix with the least amount of root disturbance you can manage. Lift seedlings with a spoon or small trowel so that the entire root system stays intact. When the mix is moist the roots usually hold together well.

Once transplanted to a growing mix, the seedlings should be watered thoroughly. For at least a week or two keep them in the same location where they were growing before being transplanted. This means replacing whatever covering you had to keep them moist. Too many changes at once in the growing environment of tiny seedlings can be lethal.

Newly transplanted seedlings must not be allowed to dry out, but they also must not be inundated. Spray nozzles or misters are excellent tools to get just the right amount of water to the seedlings. Just as when the seed is germinating, do not water the transplants if droplets of water appear on the inside of the plastic covering. After a week or two gradually allow the seedlings more and more light, moving them to a semishaded location where they are subject to normal air temperature. Soluble fertilizers, whether organic or inorganic, give young seedlings a boost as they begin to grow. Slow-release fertilizers used at low dosages are also helpful and you do not have to remember to apply them on a schedule.

Keep potting up the seedlings until they are large enough to plant in the ground. If you are keeping the plants over the summer, put them in a pot that is large enough not to dry out daily and keep them well watered throughout the summer. In the deserts it is vital to keep seedlings and other potted perennials in the shade during the summer.

PROPAGATION BY CUTTINGS

One of the most delightful ways to propagate a favored perennial is by taking off a piece, plunging it into a hormonal bath, planting it in a humid chamber, and hoping for the mysterious miracle of root growth. This way you can save and pass along a precious plant that may have been passed along to you from someone especially dear. It is also the way to maintain a spontaneous—or purposeful—hybrid that turned out to be exceptional or to continue a truly hardy, resilient, long-blooming, or early-flowering form that you were lucky enough to find. Mastering the making of cuttings is simple; all the hard parts are up to the plant.

The three kinds of cuttings are identified by the age of the stem. Hardwood is the oldest part of the stem and is at least two years old. This part of the stem is nearly impossible to bend without breaking and is usually a darker color than the rest of the stems.

Semihardwood is last year's growth and can be hard or nearly so but is more pliable than the oldest part of the stem. It, too, can break when bent, but with gentle pressure will curl and curve minimally. It can be darker, like hardwood, than the newest stems.

Softwood is the growth put on in the current year and can be as young as just a few weeks old. It includes the tip which is the newest extension of the stem. Softwood, as the name implies, is extremely pliable and in almost all perennials can be curled around your finger without breaking it. When the stem piece is new, just a few weeks old, it is often referred to as tip growth. When it is just a bit older, a few months, it is known more commonly as softwood. Either way it is young and delicate.

The greatest success in almost all perennials, particularly those of desert or arid-adapted origin, is from cuttings of semihardwood or softwood that is not new but has lived on the plant for some time.

Before considering making cuttings from a plant, look at it carefully. The plant must be healthy, vigorous, and robust. It must not be stressed by heat, cold, or lack of water. In addition, it is often best to take cuttings from a plant that is not in bloom, although you can work around this by simply removing all the flowers from the cutting you take. Most importantly, the plant must be actively growing when you take the cutting. The hormones that will induce rooting rage through the plant when it is growing well, and without them your cutting effort is a waste of time.

Begin by preparing a rooting mix that may be the same as the one described previously for seeds, or a good, sterile potting soil. Sterility is important at first because cuttings need to be kept moist to induce rooting, a condition that is ripe for the formation of soil-borne fungus and bacterial infections.   .

Next, have on hand some kind of rooting hormone. Many formulations, both liquid and powder, are available and all of them work well. Dip 'N Grow, Horminex, and Hormodin are some of the most common. Use the one that is easy for you to locate or has worked well for you in the past. All hormone formulations need to be used within the stated shelf life on the container and kept refrigerated when not in use.

Take cuttings that are about 4 in. (10 cm) long; longer stems can be cut into pieces. If you cannot get all of the cuttings in the mix right away, or the weather is hot and dry, plunge the cuttings immediately in a container of water while you work. For longer storage, keep them cool in a refrigerator or cooler. Putting cuttings in freezer bags with a moist paper towel keeps them fresh for a few days if you cannot get to them right away. But no cuttings will survive longer than a week without being put in the growing mix, and some will not last beyond two or three days.

Remove all the leaves or flowers from the part of the stem that will be beneath the soil. It is better to strip them with your fingers rather than to cut them off because the wounding action of stripping helps induce the nodes to begin the rooting process and exposes more of the bud to the rooting hormone. If there are flowers anywhere else on the cuttings, remove them. If there are large leaves on the stem remove them or cut them in half; they will only rot in the moist atmosphere necessary for rooting.

Any type of container that holds up the cuttings will do. It must have drain holes, however, because you don't want water standing around the stems. More than one cutting can be put in the container, but it is best if the cuttings do not touch each other. Water the mix well before putting in the cuttings and pat it down so that it is firm. Dip the end of the cutting and all visible nodes in the rooting hormone; then push the cutting into the container far enough so that it will stand up on its own.

Like seedlings, cuttings need to be kept in a place that has bright indirect light and is consistently moist. If you don't have a greenhouse, cold frame, or mist system, then cover the container with the cuttings as you would a seedling growing chamber. If there are droplets on the inside of the plastic, there is no need to water. About once a week take off the plastic, check for any signs of disease, water if needed, and gently prod the cuttings. The cuttings will have grown roots and are set when they will not pull out of the pot with gentle pressure and won't rock around the container in response to gentle pushing. The time it takes to establish roots is variable, depending both on the species and on the growing conditions; it can range from two to eight weeks.

Once roots are well set, remove the plants and transplant them to individual containers. Keep these young plants in the same gentle atmosphere for at least a week before letting them begin to grow in normal light, heat, and air. Once growth has resumed you can begin to feed them with a gentle soluble fertilizer or a minute amount of time-release fertilizer. Be careful not to overfertilize young cuttings too quickly; they are easily shocked and burned.

Propagation by Layering

Layering has gone out of favor for most gardeners, but it can be an easy way to increase certain plants in the garden. It is a modified version of making a cutting that takes place in the soil adjacent to the plant.

Species that can be layered most easily are those that grow long stems rapidly during their growing season. These stems are pliable enough to fall over, with or without your help, or grow close to the ground. Species that have brittle or upright stems do not work well with this technique.

Begin layering while the plant is actively growing, but keep in mind that it can take up to two months to get roots using this method so begin early in its growing season. Take a stem and gently lay the upper portion of it along the ground. With a metal hairpin stake or similar tool, press the stem down into the soil about an inch (2.5 cm). Cover the portion that touches the soil with more soil. This can be repeated along a long stem if there is enough room. Take care not to bury the tip. Some growers slightly scratch or wound the stem, then apply some rooting hormone to it before covering it with soil.

Keep the area moist, but not excessively wet, and after about three weeks gently tug on the stem where it meets the ground. If there is not strong resistance, leave it alone, checking it every week or so. Once the stem resists being tugged, an indication that it has rooted, cut the rooted portion away from the stem. You can leave on the tip of the plant or not. Pot up the new plant in a good-quality potting mix, put it in a shady place for a couple of weeks, and keep it evenly moist. Once the plant is beginning to grow on its own, increase the amount of light. It will be ready to replant by the next growing season.

CHAPTER 4

Plant Descriptions

Acalypha monostachya

Acalypha monostachya
Round copper leaf

FAMILY: Euphorbiaceae.
DISTRIBUTION: In the United States in central and southern Texas, as well in Mexico from southeastern Chihuahua and Coahuila south to Oaxaca and Puebla at elevations from 2500 to 4300 ft. (800 to 1290 m).
MATURE SIZE: 6 to 18 in. (15 to 46 cm) tall and spreading to 3 ft. (0.9 m) wide.
BLOOMING PERIOD: April to November.
EXPOSURE: Full sun in all areas but the deserts, where filtered shade or morning sun is needed. HARDINESS: Root hardy to 10°F (−12°C).

Round copper leaf is new to most gardeners in the region, but it has been grown as an ornamental for many years by native plant enthusiasts, particularly in Texas. Most gardeners are more familiar with its tropical relatives, chenille plant (*Acalypha hispida*) and copper leaf (*A. wilkesiana*).

This species grows from numerous stems with a semiwoody base. The stems elongate over time, rooting as they go, forming a mat or spreading ground-cover.

The leaves are round, and both they and the stems are covered with fine hairs. Leaves are deep green with a strong reddish cast that is exaggerated when the weather turns cold. Ultimately, plants are all or mainly deciduous in the winter.

Plants are dioecious (female flowers on one plant and male on the other) with the flowers held in long, terminal spikes. Occasionally, plants have female flowers on the lower part of the inflorescence and males above. Flowers lack a true corolla; the floral color is derived from the long, exserted pistils that are brilliant red. The selection 'Raspberry Fuzzies' found by Wade Roitsch in the western Texas Hill Country is a prolific bloomer with rosy-red flowering heads that look like erect bristles.

Grow round copper leaf in alkaline soils with superb drainage. I have grown it for a time in a large container with rich, well-drained, soil, and although it does well, it is important in these conditions to not overwater the plant.

The mounding habit, long and exuberant flowering, and the increasing red of the leaves in the fall make this species a great choice for blending into perennial plantings or to relieve the monotony of too many rosette-formed succulents. When planted in a large container or raised bed, it provides a soft maroon underlining to the planting.

Agastache cana
Mosquito plant, hummingbird mint

FAMILY: Lamiaceae.
DISTRIBUTION: In the United States from extreme western Texas to south central New Mexico at elevations of 4000 to 6000 ft. (1200 to 1800 m).
MATURE SIZE: 8 to 39 in. (20 to 98 cm) tall and as wide.
BLOOMING PERIOD: June to October.
EXPOSURE: Filtered shade or morning sun in all areas.
HARDINESS: Cold hardy to at least 20°F (−7°C), root hardy to much lower temperatures.

Mosquito plant is an erect perennial with 10 or more branched stems per plant. Although the stems are herbaceous, they turn woody at the base as they age.

The leaves are 0.5 to 1.5 in. (1.5 to 4.0 cm) long, more or less heart shaped, and covered with fine hairs that make them feel rough. Although the species has deep green leaves, the leaf color of the cultivars and selections varies. Mosquito plant derives its odd common name from the practice of rubbing the skin with the extremely aromatic leaves to deter mosquitoes.

Flowers are held on a loose raceme that rises high above the foliage, and the entire inflorescence is showy with abundant flowers. Individual flowers are tubular with flared lobes and range in color from pink to rosy lavender, including

Agastache cana (Wynn Anderson)

white. Flowers are lightly fragrant, and a large planting can provide a delicate aroma throughout the garden.

Mosquito plant needs to grow in moderately fertile, but exceptionally well-drained soils. It will rot easily in dense, clay soils. In gardens in higher elevation of the West it has good drought tolerance, but in the hotter summers of the lower elevations it should be watered regularly through the summer to maintain good form and good bloom. Cut back the entire blooming stalk when flowering is complete to keep the plant tidy and to encourage further blooming.

'Heather Queen', the selection with probably the longest ornamental history, is described as the most heat tolerant of the cultivars and it is also one of the tallest at over 30 in. (76 cm). It has rosy-red flowers that are profuse on its tall stems. Another selection, 'Purple Pygmy', grows to 16 in. (41 cm) and is a deep rose-lavender shade. The selection 'Sinning' (also sold under the trademark name Sonoran Sunset™) is a moderate-sized plant, up to 15 in. (38 cm) tall, with blue-green foliage and rose-lavender flowers. *Agastache* 'Desert Sunrise', a hybrid of *A. rupestris* and *A. cana*, blooms orange, pink, and lavender.

Although this species has been favored in temperate-zone gardens in the United States and England for a long time, it is barely known in the lower elevations of the Southwest. This is a shame, for it is lovely, durable, great species for a dry, shady location. In addition, a number of Southwestern native species of the genus are never used ornamentally but would be worth experimentation. Mosquito plant is untested in the hottest deserts and may be unsuitable for those areas.

Other commonly found related plants may also be suitable for the region. *Agastache* 'Firebird', a hybrid of *A. pallida* (synonym *A. barberi*) and *A. mexicana* 'Toronjil Morado', grows to only 1 ft. (30 cm) tall and has vivid red-orange flowers. *Agastache pallida* (synonym *A. barberi*) 'Tutti Frutti' has stiff, purple stems and fragrant, rose-lilac flowers. A yellow-variegated selection with blue flowers sold by some as *A. cana* 'Golden Jubilee' is actually a selection of *A. foeniculum*. It was named to commemorate the Golden Jubilee of Queen Elizabeth and was rated an All-America Selection in 2001.

Ageratum corymbosum
Butterfly mist, blue mist, flattop ageratum

FAMILY: Asteraceae.

DISTRIBUTION: In the United States in southern Arizona, Hidalgo County in New Mexico, and western Texas. In Mexico from Chihuahua to Jalisco and south to Guatemala at elevations from 1700 to 11,000 ft. (520 to 3300 m).

MATURE SIZE: 6 ft. (1.8 m) tall in nature, usually 2 to 3 ft. (0.6 to 0.9 m) tall and wide in cultivation.

BLOOMING PERIOD: September and October, but in some parts of the range from May to November.

Ageratum corymbosum (Mary Irish)

EXPOSURE: Filtered shade or morning sun in the deserts, full sun or filtered sun elsewhere.

HARDINESS: Cold hardy to at least 22°F (−6°C), root hardy to 12°F (−11°C).

Butterfly mist has numerous branching stems rising from a semiwoody base. The stems are green and upright.

The 1.5- to 4.0-in. (4- to 10-cm) lanceolate to linear leaves are arranged in opposite pairs up the stem. They are apple green with wavy margins and are dimpled on the upper surface and rough to the touch.

Flowers are held in congested heads that are 1 in. (2.5 cm) across. The rayless flowers range from a soft, sky blue to lavender or dark blue. The prolific flowering heads are held well above the foliage and seem to float over the plant as the mist for which it was named.

Butterfly mist grows best in somewhat fertile soils with excellent drainage. It is susceptible to chlorosis in soils that are poorly drained or depleted, or from overwatering. In the deserts, butterfly mist needs at least weekly watering in the summer, sometimes more if the temperatures are severe, to maintain good form and for continued flowering. Like most perennials that grow in the summer, this one benefits from a heavy mulch that helps maintain the balance between the need not to dry out and excessive watering.

Butterfly mist tends to have a lot of leaf loss over the winter. It is, therefore, good practice to prune it in the early spring to shape it up and relieve it of these dreary winter leftovers. It can be tip pruned lightly for shape through the summer, but don't take off too much.

I am a great fan of this species. It holds up to intense heat much better than the similar mistflower (*Conoclinium greggii*), and is a reliable and consistent bloomer in the late summer, which is a challenging time for good colorful plants in the hottest deserts. But I am not alone. Butterflies, particularly queen butterflies, are wild for butterfly mist and will smother it when they begin their migration. I understand it contains a chemical that assists in mating, always a strong inducement to visit.

Angelonia angustifolia
Summer snapdragon

FAMILY: Scrophulariaceae.

DISTRIBUTION: From southern and tropical Mexico through Central America to Ecuador and Colombia at elevations from sea level to 1000 ft. (300 m).

MATURE SIZE: 2 to 3 ft. (0.6 to 0.9 m) tall and 1 ft. (0.3 m) wide.

BLOOMING PERIOD: May to October.

EXPOSURE: Full sun to filtered shade in all areas but the hottest deserts, where filtered shade or morning sun is best.

HARDINESS: Root hardy to around 25°F (−4°C) but recovers slowly from cold damage.

Summer snapdragon is a multistemmed perennial with erect, smooth, green herbaceous stems. The 2- to 3-in. (5- to 8-cm) leaves are dark green, linear with a sharp tip, and gently toothed along the margin. The leaves are packed up the stem, and the plant looks full and lush.

Flowers are held in an upright spike that can range from 9 to 12 in. (23 to 30 cm) tall. They have the inflated tube and flared lobes typical of the family and occur in shades of pink, lilac, lavender, purple, or white. Flowers have prominent nectar guides that vary in color from dark purple to pale lavender.

Summer snapdragon grows best in fertile, well-drained soil that does not dry out significantly in the summer. Thick mulch in the summer, particularly in the deserts, helps keep it evenly moist. Waterlogged or tight soils cause significant yellowing and chlorosis, a condition that unless corrected quickly kills the plant. I tried summer snapdragon once in deep shade and it was not a great success. Plants were smaller with less flowering than those with at least half a day of sun.

Two main series or lines of cultivars of this species are available, AngelFace™ and AngelMist™, both with a full range of colors including bicolors. The AngelFace™ series was mainly developed in Europe but is found throughout the American Southwest. It was tested in various trials in this country with excellent results. Most of the colors in this series are dark and intense, and the plant is shorter with more numerous stems than the type.

The AngelMist™ series was developed in the United States chiefly in response to viral problems in older cultivars. When the older cultivars showed susceptibility to cucumber mosaic virus in some conditions, horticulturists chiefly in Florida developed this new series to mitigate that problem. This is now the series that is most commonly

Angelonia angustifolia

sold throughout the American West, but you can find many of the old cultivars for sale with or without their names.

Summer snapdragon is a wonderful perennial for gardens in hot summer areas with plenty of sun and good, well-amended soil. Because of its need for fertile soils and steady watering, it makes a delightful potted plant either mixed with other perennials or as the base for a potted shrub. I grew one at the base of a potted bougainvillea and found them a wonderful combination.

The flowers have a pleasant fragrance and make sturdy, long-lasting cut flowers. Many gardeners and one trial by Cornell University report that the plant is rarely browsed by deer.

I began growing summer snapdragon with an unnamed white selection, which thrived for the entire summer until the cold weather of November finally did it in. The next year I put in a number of the available color selections scattered all over the yard. The plants in full sun and those with purple flowers were infinitely superior to the others. Over the years I have tried several cultivars and locations and still hold that the purple and white are the sturdiest for hot summer areas and that plenty of sun is mandatory.

Anisacanthus quadrifidus

Anisacanthus quadrifidus
Flame anisacanthus, hummingbird bush

FAMILY: Acanthaceae.
DISTRIBUTION: From southern and western Texas in the United States into the states of Coahuila, Tamaulipas, and Nuevo León in Mexico at elevations from 1000 to 5000 ft. (300 to 1500 m).
MATURE SIZE: 2 to 4 ft. (0.6 to 1.2 m) tall and about as wide.
BLOOMING PERIOD: May to October.
EXPOSURE: Full sun even in the deserts.
HARDINESS: Cold hardy to 5°F (−15°C).

Flame anisacanthus has numerous branching stems from a stout woody base. Young branches are coated with fine hairs, making them whitish, but they lose these hairs and turn tan with age.

The 1.5- to 2.0-in. (4- to 5-cm) leaves are deep green, linear to lance shaped, and closely packed onto the stems. Plants are all or nearly deciduous in the winter.

The red-orange flowers are held on slender terminal racemes. Each flower is 1.0 to 1.5 in. (2.5 to 4.0 cm) long. The corolla is tubular with lobes that are pointed and flared at the tip.

Flame anisacanthus grows in a wide array of soils but does best in lightly amended, well-drained, even rocky soils. In the deserts it is necessary to water every two or three weeks in the summer to maintain bloom and keep plants vigorous. In other locations, it needs little more than natural rainfall.

Four varieties of this species have been described, but it is the widely distributed var. *wrightii* (synonym *Anisacanthus wrightii*) from which nearly all ornamental plants are derived. The form known in Texas as 'Selected Red' has much deeper color than the type, and 'Pumpkin' is a light, orange color. Some forms are more compact and shorter than the type, as well. Var. *brevilobus* is offered from time to time, especially in the Phoenix area. This variety has extremely thin leaves and is more compact than the type. Its flowers are more red than orange.

Flame anisacanthus is a tough but outstanding species that mixes well with large succulents such as agave, prickly pear cactus, or chollas, providing color and contrast to their sharp, hard edges. The late-year bloom makes an outstanding display just about the time the garden has given up on color. One individual in my garden was placed where the setting sun would shine through its flaming flowers. I recommend using it in such situations; it was a stunning display in the late summer. Even in the hottest deserts, flame anisacanthus can be grown well on minimal summer watering in native, unamended soils.

Flame anisacanthus can be severely pruned when it first shows leaves in the spring, but it usually looks best if it is lightly tip pruned intermittently through the early spring to encourage fuller growth.

Hummingbirds are attracted to the flowers, which because they bloom for such a long time keep providing food for these charming visitors throughout the summer.

Aquilegia chrysantha
Golden columbine

FAMILY: Ranunculaceae.
DISTRIBUTION: In the United States from the mountains of Colorado and Utah south into Arizona, southern New Mexico, and western Texas at elevations from 3500 to 9500 ft. (1100 to 2900 m). In Mexico in the mountains of Sonora and Chihuahua, barely into Coahuila.
MATURE SIZE: Basal growth 8 to 10 in. (20 to 25 cm) tall, flowering stalks up to 3 ft. (0.9 m) tall.
BLOOMING PERIOD: March to September.
EXPOSURE: Filtered sun or deep shade throughout the region, full sun in selected situations in the American West or in higher-elevation gardens.
HARDINESS: Cold hardy to below 0°F (−18°C).

Golden columbine grows numerous short, leafy stems from a somewhat swollen base during its first year. Large, leafy flowering stalks begin to form in the second year. Although often considered a biennial, golden columbine may live up to five years depending on conditions.

The parsley-shaped leaves are compound, in three parts, and held on a thin stem. The thin, light-green leaves are up to 2 in. (5 cm) long and vary from slightly pubescent to smooth.

The 3- to 4-in. (8- to 10-cm) flowers are held on tall, branched stalks in a loose panicle. The open-faced corolla tapers sharply to the junction with the petiole. A

Aquilegia chrysantha

spur, or attachment behind the petal, is one of the distinguishing features of the entire genus; spurs range from 1 to 6 in. (2.5 to 15.0 cm) or more in length. The flower is deep, golden yellow.

Golden columbine grows in fertile, well-drained soils, but I have had excellent results in native, unamended soils that are shady and cool. It is important that plants not dry out significantly while they are actively growing. Keeping the roots cool with either a thick application of mulch or a shady location is important for the vigor and flowering of this species. Amazingly, golden columbine can grow in almost full sun in even the hottest desert if the roots are kept cool and moist.

Pruning golden columbine can be difficult at first. Flowers open in sequence, and dead flowers and newly emerging buds can occur on the same flowering stalk. If this is a problem, the old flowers can be pruned out to the first lateral branch as they decline. Prune out the entire inflorescence once all flowers are finished. Columbines are vigorous reseeders in the right growing conditions, and pruning out finished flowers quickly helps hold down the amount of seed that is matured.

In the western United States, few named cultivars or selections of this species are sold, but in other parts of the country, as well as in England, a number of appealing selections would be interesting to try. 'Yellow Queen' is a tall selection, up to 3 ft. (0.9 m), with a heavy bloom of large, bright yellow flowers with long spurs.

Var. *hinkleyana* (synonym *Aquilegia hinkleyana*) is endemic to the Big Bend area of western Texas and adjacent Mexico and has been a favored choice for Texas gardens. This variety is similar in appearance to *A. chrysantha*, but often superior in performance in the hottest parts of the region. The Texas superstar selection 'Texas Gold' is from var. *hinkleyana* and grows up to 2 ft. (0.6 m) tall and as wide with deep yellow flowers.

'Blazing Star', a hybrid of *Aquilegia canadensis* and *A. chrysantha*, has excellent heat tolerance, good size, and flowers that are bicolored red and orange. Forms with double flowers in yellow and white are known as 'Flore Plena' and 'Alba

Plena', respectively, and an interesting form named 'Silver Queen' has white flowers with yellow stamens.

The well-known columbine, *Aquilegia canadensis*, with its rich assortment of red and yellow flowers is a good choice for gardens than have ponds or a shady stream where its need for cool, moist soils can be met.

Aquilegia longissima is another species from the canyons of the regions that could be used more than it is. It resembles golden columbine, but the spurs are enormous, up to 8 in. (20 cm).

Golden columbine blends well with other perennials and provides a stunning display in the spring. The graceful, nodding flowering stalks are irresistible and, in the hottest desert cities, bloom later than the main burst of spring flowers, extending the wildflower season by a few weeks. In cooler or milder areas, golden columbine blooms through the summer.

The plant's ability to grow and bloom well in shade makes it useful in odd corners and nooks in the garden that are too shady for most other colorful perennials. Let it seed freely around the garden, and bloom will be even more vigorous and plentiful as plants mature at different times.

Artemisia arborescens
Giant mugwort

FAMILY: Asteraceae.
DISTRIBUTION: Mediterranean Europe.
MATURE SIZE: 4 to 6 ft. (1.2 to 1.8 m) tall and as wide.
BLOOMING PERIOD: April to June.
EXPOSURE: Full sun or filtered shade.
HARDINESS: Leaves and stems are damaged at 18°F (−8°C), but the plant
  recovers quickly.

Giant mugwort stretches the line between perennial and shrub with its larger size. The stems are woody at the base, but the open form and delicate leaves make the plant more useful in the garden as a large perennial rather than a shrub.

The leaves are up to 4 in. (10 cm) long, more or less evenly cut into deep lobes. They are coated with fine hairs that provide the distinctive silver to white color. In some forms, the leaves are narrower but still much dissected, giving them a fernlike appearance.

Artemisia arborescens (Mary Irish)

The flowers are tiny and innocuous, held on terminal racemes. They are whitish yellow to white and, although the flowering stalk is held above the foliage, the flowers are not showy.

If there is significant summer damage or dead stems, or if the plant has become unruly, it can be pruned in the early fall just as it begins to grow. It will tolerate a severe pruning in which it is sheared to the ground but will recover better if pruning is of selected stems or at the tips.

Of the artemisias described here, giant mugwort is the most tolerant of rocky, unamended soils, extreme heat and sun, and minimal watering. In the summer in the hottest deserts, it is more or less dormant, losing many of its leaves and reducing to a white ghost for the duration of the summer heat. Growth resumes with the cooler temperatures of the fall and continues vigorously until the following summer. Even in less rigorous areas, giant mugwort needs to be grown in soils with low organic content and outstanding drainage.

Giant mugwort has a long and distinguished ornamental history. It has been used for medicine and insect control, as well as for ornament for centuries. The leaves are aromatic, and the stems make attractive wreaths or dried arrangements.

Use giant mugwort among other Mediterranean perennials such as lavender, rosemary, and germander, or among rugged natives such as creosote and globe-mallow because it will thrive on the benign neglect so useful with those species. Its clear, silvery foliage makes a stunning backdrop for greener plantings, and it mixes well with summer dormant bulbs.

A few selections have been made, chiefly in Europe. 'Faith Raven' is widely regarded as synonymous with 'Powis Castle', but the diminutive 'Little Mice' with its congested leaves on a plant rarely over 12 in. (30 cm) tall would be a worthy addition to desert gardens.

Artemisia ludoviciana
Western mugwort, silver wormwood

FAMILY: Asteraceae.

DISTRIBUTION: Virtually all of the United States except Florida, but particularly common in the western half of the country. In Mexico widespread from Baja California, Sonora, Chihuahua, and Coahuila at elevations from 500 to 8500 ft. (150 to 2600 m), occasionally higher. One variety ranges as far south as Guatemala.

MATURE SIZE: 1 to 3 ft. (0.3 to 0.9 m) tall and as wide.

BLOOMING PERIOD: May to November.

EXPOSURE: Full sun or filtered shade in the deserts, but full sun elsewhere.

HARDINESS: Cold hardy to below 0°F (−18°C).

Artemisia ludoviciana

Western mugwort has numerous stems that begin erect but may recline and spread as they mature. Plants are rhizomatous and quickly grow multiple stems from the base.

The leaves are highly variable and range from 2 to 4 in. (5 to 10 cm) long. They are gray-green but have variable amounts of minute hairs that make the leaves appear silver-white to gray. Most leaves are linear but may also be serrated, loosely toothed, or lobed.

The rayless flowers are almost invisible in loose racemes. The tiny heads are 0.25 in. (0.7 cm) in diameter and are white to yellowish white.

Western mugwort has been cultivated for so long and is native over such an immense range that it performs beautifully in almost any circumstance. In the deserts it prefers excellent drainage and appears to have no preference on soil type. Water Western mugwort carefully; it does best with supplemental irrigation in the summer as long as the drainage is sharp, but prefers to grow on the dry side through the winter when it is at least semidormant.

If pruning is needed to clean up the plant or reinvigorate it, cut it down to 6 in. (15 cm) in the late fall as it becomes dormant, or in the early spring just before it begins to regrow.

Because of its winter dormancy, it is best to plant mugwort in the spring so there is ample time for the plants to become established.

Many people are allergic to the pollen of this species, and cutting off flowering stalks as soon as they form can help relieve this problem.

The species has three principal cultivars. 'Silver King' is an old selection that is thought by some to be from var. *albula*, which is found in the western United States and eastern Mexico. It is upright with an open, loose form, growing 3 ft. (0.9 m) tall and as wide with 0.75-in. (2-cm) long leaves. 'Silver Queen' is much the same but somewhat more compact, with larger, more lobed leaves. 'Valerie Finnis' is a beautiful form with tight, compact growth to only 12 in. (30 cm) tall and wide. Its 4-in. (10-cm) leaves are gray-green with a silver cast below and nearly white above with broad lobes.

Plant Western mugwort generously among either desert perennials or succulents for a strong contrast of both color and form. Because it spreads quickly, it is useful as erosion control on steep, hot, dry slopes. This species is the most shade tolerant of all commonly grown artemisias, especially in the deserts.

Western mugwort is essentially dormant in the cold part of the winter and during that time can become reduced in size and will cease to grow. I once tried to move this species in the cool temperatures of November, a time when most perennials move effortlessly in my area, and it sulked so badly and for so long that I thought it was dead. I found out later that this was a common response to moves in cool seasons. Use my experience and relocate any of your plants that are in the ground in early spring just before they begin to regrow.

The long stems and fragrant leaves make this a splendid choice for either dried arrangements or wreaths in the fall. In many areas, artemisias are used to prevent insect infestations in furniture, linens, and other cloth.

Artemisia 'Powis Castle'
Mugwort, wormwood

FAMILY: Asteraceae.
DISTRIBUTION: A hybrid (*Artemisia arborescens* × *A. absinthium*) of garden origin. Used ornamentally throughout the world.
MATURE SIZE: 3 to 4 ft. (0.9 to 1.2 m) tall and spreading up to 5 ft. (1.5 m) wide.
BLOOMING PERIOD: Erratic bloom from November to March, but most individuals do not bloom.

Exposure: Full sun or filtered sun in all areas but the hottest deserts, where filtered sun or morning sun is preferred.

Hardiness: Cold hardy to at least 0°F (−18°C), reported tolerant of even lower temperatures by some authors.

Artemisia 'Powis Castle' is the most well-known and widely grown artemisia with the possible exception of Western mugwort (*A. ludoviciana*). A dense plant, this hybrid has numerous thick, semiwoody stems that form a tight mound.

The leaves are up to 3 in. (8 cm) long, finely cut, and white to silvery white from their coating of fine hairs. Clustered at the ends of the branches, the leaves form repeated rosettes that give the plant its fluffy appearance. The leaves are aromatic and make good additions to dried arrangement or wreaths.

Artemisia 'Powis Castle'

Although 'Powis Castle' occasionally blooms, flowering is sparse and erratic, so pollen problems are minimal.

'Powis Castle' is tolerant of a huge range of soils from dry and rocky to tight clays. It is the most tolerant of all artemisias to hot, humid conditions; however, it must have excellent drainage. In the deserts it tolerates weekly watering in the summer without rotting or falling over, but in cooler or moister areas watering should be minimal to prevent both of these problems. Plants can become leggy or lose all but their terminal leaves over time unless they are kept tidy and tight with occasional pruning either in the early fall or early spring. This mugwort should never be sheared or pruned to the ground. If you need to reduce its height, take out one or two of the oldest and largest stems only.

This hybrid was introduced by Jimmy Hancock, head gardener at Powis Castle, Wales, around 1972. Some confusion exists whether he found the seedling or it was given to him, but regardless, it was an instant success.

'Powis Castle' is one of those astounding plants that appears to be able to grow anywhere and is therefore endlessly useful in the garden. Use it to light up a perennial planting that suffers from too much green or to smooth the edges of a poolside planting or a patio boundary. It can be planted as a low, informal border or as a background for smaller perennials.

Asclepias curassavica

Asclepias curassavica
Blood flower, butterfly weed

FAMILY: Asclepiadaceae.
DISTRIBUTION: South America. Widely grown and frequently naturalized in warm regions of the world.
MATURE SIZE: 2 to 4 ft. (0.6 to 1.2 m) tall and 1 to 2 ft. (0.3 to 0.6 m) wide.
BLOOMING PERIOD: April to October.
EXPOSURE: Full sun or filtered shade in all areas but the deserts, where filtered shade or morning sun is preferred.
HARDINESS: Cold hardy to at least 20°F (−7°C). Leaves and stems may be lost at higher temperatures, but the plant recovers quickly.

Blood flower has 10 to 15 erect stems rising from a semiwoody base. Those stems often branch once or twice as they develop.

Leaves are much longer than they are wide, deep green, and up to 3 in. (8 cm) long. They frequently show prominent veins that may be reddish in color.

The flowers are clustered in dense heads at the ends of the branches and are red to red-orange, often with combinations of red, orange, and yellow on various parts of the flower. One of the most common combinations is an orange calyx and a yellow corolla, although nearly any combination of color is possible

The floral structure of all members of this genus is complicated. Each flower has five calyx lobes that typically reflex downward. Five corolla lobes are upright and end in points or acute tips that look like the points on a crown.

Blood flower grows well in any kind of soil from fertile garden soils to unamended desert soils. It gets largest and most prolific with increased soil fertility as well as with regular watering.

In the summer in the deserts, water every four to seven days to maintain bloom and vigor. This species is either dormant or deciduous in most areas in the winter, and watering should be minimal. In frost-free or mild areas where it remains evergreen, water every two to three weeks in the winter.

Butterflies are strongly attracted to blood flower and the Gulf fritillary, which serves as one of its principal pollinators, also favors it. Monarch and queen butterflies are known to use it as a depository for their eggs.

I first found this species growing in the sidewalk in Houston, Texas, and brought a few seeds home. It is a star in the summer garden here in Phoenix and isn't nearly as aggressive as it can be in other areas, although it will reseed where there is ample water. I find this trait useful because in the hottest desert gardens it is not especially long lived.

Use blood flower generously within a perennial planting or other garden area to provide a bright note of color in the summer. Put it where you can see it often so you can enjoy the butterflies that crowd the bright heads.

Asclepias linaria
Pine-leaf milkweed, needle-leaf milkweed

FAMILY: Asclepiadaceae.
DISTRIBUTION: In the United States in desert regions of Southern California, southern Arizona, and far southwestern New Mexico at elevations from 1500 to 6000 ft. (460 to 1800 m). In Mexico from Sonora and Chihuahua south to Oaxaca and Zacatecas.
MATURE SIZE: 2 to 3 ft. (0.6 to 0.9 m) tall and 1 to 2 ft. (0.3 to 0.6 m) wide.
BLOOMING PERIOD: March to October.
EXPOSURE: Full sun, filtered shade, or morning sun in the deserts, full sun elsewhere.
HARDINESS: Cold hardy to 25°F (−4°F).

Pine-leaf milkweed has grayish stems, typically 20 or more, that rise from a semiwoody base. The branching of the stems gives the plant more substance than the small number of stems might suggest.

The leaves are thin, 1.0 to 1.5 in. (2.5 to 4.0 cm) long, and spiral up the stem in pairs. The overall effect is of a soft, green brush.

The flowers are clustered at the ends of the branches into dense heads that are 1 to 3 in. (2.5 to 8.0 cm) across. Flowers are pure white, waxy, and with the distinct coronet of the genus.

Pine-leaf milkweed is tolerant of any well-drained soil, although it has a thicker, lusher appearance in a fertile soil. Drainage is important; plants quickly become yellowed and chlorotic in poorly drained soils. Moderate supplemental

Asclepias linaria (Mary Irish)

watering, once a week in the hottest desert areas, improves the appearance and prolongs the bloom. In more moderate climates, water much less often.

During the winter, pine-leaf milkweed often loses a large proportion of its leaves and quits growing. It quickly revives when the weather warms. Prune out old or failed stems as far back as possible in the late winter or early spring.

Like all milkweeds, pine-leaf milkweed is extremely attractive to butterflies both larvae and adults. Tiger moth larvae prefer it to feed, and countless moth and butterfly species imbibe its nectar. Its long blooming season makes it even more useful to these pollinating insects.

This is another of those arid-adapted perennials whose delicate appearance belies its toughness in dry, hot conditions. Mix pine-leaf milkweed generously in a perennial planting to help carry a bed through the summer. Use it as a background for succulents with hard edges such as cactus, agave, or yucca, where it provides textural contrast. Plant it liberally so the impact of the bright white blooms and the open form are exaggerated and enhanced.

Asclepias subulata
Desert milkweed

FAMILY: Asclepiadaceae.
DISTRIBUTION: In the United States in the deserts of Southern California, southern Nevada, and western Arizona from sea level to 2500 ft. (800 m). In Mexico in Baja California, Sonora, and Sinaloa.
MATURE SIZE: 3 to 4 ft. (0.9 to 1.2 m) tall and up to 3 ft. (0.9 m) wide.
BLOOMING PERIOD: April to December, but most prolific in May and June.
EXPOSURE: Full sun even in the deserts.
HARDINESS: Cold hardy to 25°F (−4°C).

Desert milkweed is a forest of thin, erect stems that rise from a semiwoody base. The stems are covered with a fine wax that gives them a gray-white cast.

The leaves are ephemeral and may be on the plant only in the earliest part of the year. They are threadlike, up to 2 in. (5 cm) long, and begin green but may fade to gold or golden brown.

The flowers are held in 1- to 2-in. (2.5- to 5.0-cm) congested heads, and the waxy corolla is white to yellowish white. The horn-shaped pods are more than 3 in. (8 cm) long and begin pale celadon-green but fade to brown as they mature. Like all

Asclepias subulata (Mary Irish)

milkweeds, this one has seeds that are each attached to a filmy plume; this plume serves as a parachute, allowing the delicate seed to float away on the wind as the pod opens.

Desert milkweed is an extremely xeric species and grows best in dry, alkaline, unamended soils with excellent drainage. Even in the deserts, plants achieve the best form when grown with only minimal and infrequent supplemental watering. Water it only when it has been a long time between rains or if it begins to dry out at the tip of the stems.

Desert milkweed rarely need pruning, but if there is an ungainly stem or two that needs removal, cut as far back to the base as possible in the summer. The milky sap can cause dermatitis in sensitive individuals so wear gloves and avoid contact with the sap.

Many gardeners are leery of the aphids that crowd this plant in the spring and fall, but these insects rarely cause much damage to the plant. In general, they are resting in between mating bouts or migratory pushes. Clean them off with strong jets of water or scrape them off with your hand. The red tarantula wasp and other harmless wasps often use this species as a resting place or for a romantic rendezvous; mating pairs are found in abundance all over the stems in the late spring. These insects cause no damage or other problems for the plants.

Desert milkweed is a tremendous choice for areas in the garden that do not receive regular irrigation or are very hot. The plant looks much more delicate than its performance would suggest and makes a pleasing contrast with the hard, firm edges of cacti, agaves, or other desert succulents. It is especially effective in mass plantings where the open, light form is overcome by sheer volume.

Butterflies are strongly attracted to all species in this genus, and this one is no exception. Some butterflies find the stems suitable for feeding their larvae, but most use it as a nectar source for adults.

Aster filifolius
Wild aster

FAMILY: Asteraceae.
DISTRIBUTION: South Africa including the Cape, KwaZulu-Natal, and
    Transkei up to 6000 ft. (1800 m).
MATURE SIZE: 3 ft. (0.9 m) tall and as wide.
BLOOMING PERIOD: February to April.
EXPOSURE: Filtered shade or morning sun in the deserts, full sun elsewhere.
HARDINESS: Cold hardy to at least 25°F (−4°C).

Wild aster is a loosely branched perennial from a woody base. It is a lanky plant, but the stems rise and fall in a picturesque fashion. Over time it forms a low, mounding plant.

The leaves are thin and needlelike, less than 1 in. (2.5 cm) long, and are tightly clustered, like a fascicle, on the stems. They look like small brushes poised at the end of the stems.

The 1-in. (2.5-cm) flowering heads are on the ends of the stems. Ray flowers are widely spaced and sparse and are light lavender to blue. The disk flowers are yellow.

Wild aster grows best in fertile, well-drained soil that can be allowed to dry out between waterings. Plants that are overwatered or grown in poorly drained soils quickly become pale and chlorotic. In the hottest deserts, plants need to be watered every week or two in the summer to prevent dieback, but watch the plant carefully for signs of overwatering.

Because of its tolerance for drier soils, wild aster blends well with succulents or Mediterranean species. Its open form provides a good contrast for denser, leafier species, and the surprise of the flowers is welcome in the late winter. Use wild aster where the flowers will be noticed in the early spring but where other summer-growing perennials might cover up the less attractive foliage in summer.

Aster filifolius

Baileya multiradiata
Desert marigold

FAMILY: Asteraceae.

DISTRIBUTION: In the United States in deserts of southern Nevada, southwestern Utah, Southern California, Arizona, central and southwestern New Mexico, and western Texas below 5000 ft. (1500 m) in elevation. In Mexico in Sonora, Chihuahua, Durango, and Coahuila.

MATURE SIZE: Basal growth 6 in. (15 cm) tall, flowering stalks up to 12 in. (30 cm) tall, spreading 6 to 12 in. (15 to 30 cm) wide.

BLOOMING PERIOD: November to April, with occasional flowers year-round.

EXPOSURE: Full sun even in the deserts.

HARDINESS: Cold hardy to at least 10°F (−12°C).

Desert marigold is a plant in two parts. The first plant is a foliage plant with deeply lobed, 2-in. (5-cm) gray-green leaves that are covered with a plush of white hairs. This plant is a tight, low-growing mound that looks like a firm cushion.

The second plant is a flowering plant with numerous fine stalks, each with a single brilliant yellow flower so prolific it appears to be another mound, this time a yellow one. Flowering heads are 2 in. (5 cm) across with countless ray flowers piled one over the other and thickly set, yellow disk flowers.

Desert marigold prefers to grow in rocky, alkaline soils but will survive in other types of soil as long as the drainage is outstanding. Water intermittently in the winter growing season, just enough to keep plants vigorous and blooming. Water carefully in the summer, enough to keep the plant healthy but not so much

Baileya multiradiata

that it will rot. One of the hardest lessons of using Sonoran and Baja natives is that it is possible to rot them out in the hot soils of summer with too much water.

Most plants are started from seed, but germination can be erratic. Seed is planted in the fall and may or may not result in the great displays so popular in the spring. Without doubt, the plants do best with a light gravel mulch. They may be started from small transplants, but transplanting is much more successful in the fall than the spring. Rarely is spring long enough for plantings to become well established.

Prune plants to a few inches above the ground in the fall to remove summer-damaged stems and rejuvenate the plants, but cut off spent flowering stalks anytime.

This is one of the bedrock species of most so-called wildflower gardens in the southwestern United States. It is a cheerful species that when grown in stupendous abundance can create a memorable image. It makes a generous display, covering the ground as grass and offering up a blizzard of its lovely blooms when conditions are to its liking. It is also effective as a solitary plant at the base of a rock or emerging from a tiny crevice. The plants are pretty, the flowers are delightful, and however they are used they should be given prominence. Because of its great drought tolerance, this species is easy to blend into natural plantings or with succulents.

Desert marigold can be fickle about where it thrives; in some gardens it is nearly a weed, in others it is barely able to find a foothold. This is particularly true when planted from seed, so try using the more reliable transplants if you have had trouble getting it established. Plants are short lived but reseed generously in most dry gardens, especially in rocky locations or yards with abundant rock mulch, coming up in surprising places.

Barleria cristata
Philippine violet

FAMILY: Acanthaceae.

DISTRIBUTION: India and Myanmar. Widely used in warm regions and naturalized in the warmest parts of Florida.

MATURE SIZE: 3 to 6 ft. (0.9 to 1.8 m) tall and 3 to 4 ft. (0.9 to 1.2 m) wide.

BLOOMING PERIOD: September to November.

EXPOSURE: Filtered sun or morning sun in most locations, full sun in milder climates or along the coast.

HARDINESS: Leaves and stems are damaged at or near 32°F (0°C), but the plant recovers quickly.

Barleria cristata

It is amazing to me how many excellent ornamentals from the Indian subcontinent take to dry, even desert, conditions. This is yet another example. Many members of this genus are well known in northeastern gardens as flowering house or patio plants, but this dense, full perennial does beautifully in the ground. I no longer remember why I started growing it, and kick myself roundly to this day for killing it accidentally when I tried to move it, but it was an outstanding choice for many years.

It grows into a multistemmed erect plant. The leaves are dark green, with dimples along the surface as if the veins were lightly collapsing, and with smooth margins.

The flowers are 1.5-in. (4-cm) trumpets of lavender, purple, or occasionally white, and forms with stippling or veining of purple on white are known. The flowers are held in axillary spikes and are profuse during the blooming season. The 1-in. (2.5-cm) tubular corolla ends with flared lobes.

Grow Philippine violet in fertile, well-drained soil. For best results in the hottest deserts, water it regularly in the summer. It is immune to any level of heat, although relief from afternoon sun helps keep it in better condition. Like many tropical species, it thrives in the difficult conditions of high heat and hot, humid soils that are common in much of the region. It is best used in areas with frost-free or mild winters.

Berlandiera lyrata

Berlandiera lyrata
Chocolate flower, greeneyes

FAMILY: Asteraceae.
DISTRIBUTION: Widespread in the middle of the United States from Kansas and Colorado through Oklahoma, western Texas, Arizona, and New Mexico. In Mexico from Chihuahua and Coahuila, though Durango, Aquascalientes, Nuevo León, and Tamaulipas, as well as northern San Luis Potosí and Zacatecas at elevations from 4000 to 6600 ft. (1200 to 2010 m).
MATURE SIZE: Basal growth with stems that extend from 8 to 18 in. (20 to 46 cm) above this base and spread as wide.
BLOOMING PERIOD: May to October.
EXPOSURE: Full sun or filtered shade throughout the region, protection from full sun or west-facing sites in the hottest deserts.
HARDINESS: Cold hardy to below 0°F (−18°C).

Chocolate flower is a variable perennial that may rise up with numerous stems or remain low, almost sprawling, on the ground. The leaves are oblate to spatulate, gray-green with deep, widely spaced lobes. Leaves range from 2 to 6 in. (5 to 15 cm) long.

Flowers are composed of a few bright yellow rays and dark brown disks. The heads are held on thin stalks above the foliage and smell precisely like chocolate. The fragrance is powerful and evocative, and on a warm late spring morning the entire garden is filled with the seductive aroma of that heavenly confection. After the bloom the light green receptacle framed by rows of green bracts stays on the plant for weeks. It appears to be a new type of flower and helps make the plant attractive for an even longer time. The receptacle also dries well.

Chocolate flower does best in fertile, well-drained soils that are not allowed to completely dry out during the summer. In the hottest deserts, water once or twice a week in the summer and provide heavy mulch to retain moisture. In other areas, water every 7 to 10 days. In the winter, plants often do fine on natural rainfall.

Prune spent flowering heads often to encourage repeat blooming.

The deep yellow flowers and burnt toast brown centers are an irresistible combination when mixed with other perennials. Their long blooming season helps carry a bed through the summer.

Butterflies are strongly attracted to the flowers for their nectar. The Texas native greeneyes (*Berlandiera texana*) is similar but seldom seen in the trade. Two hybrids, *B.* ×*betoniciolia* and *B.* ×*humilis*, may also be available from time to time.

Buddleja marrubiifolia
Woolly butterfly bush

FAMILY: Buddlejaceae.
DISTRIBUTION: In the United States in far western Texas. In Mexico from eastern Chihuahua, northwestern Durango, Coahuila, western Nuevo León and Zacatecas, and northeastern Nuevo León at elevations from 2300 to 7900 ft. (690 to 2400 m).
MATURE SIZE: 3 to 4 ft. (0.9 to 1.2 m) tall and as wide.
BLOOMING PERIOD: March to August, occasionally into the fall.
EXPOSURE: Full sun even in the deserts.
HARDINESS: Cold hardy to 15°F (−9°C).

Woolly butterfly bush is so densely branched that a well-grown plant resembles white balls in the garden. This outstanding natural form is just the beginning of its charm, however.

The leaves are ovate to oblong, 0.5 to 1.0 in. (1.5 to 2.5 cm) long, and although gray-green are so smothered with velvety, white hairs that they look white. The margins are crimped along the edge.

Flowers are held in small stalks above the foliage and are crowded into rounded heads. Each flower begins yellow or yellowish white and fades to orange. The entire head is 0.5 in. (1.5 cm) or less around, so the overall effect is of orange marbles.

Woolly butterfly bush requires an alkaline soil with extremely sharp drainage. It is quickly killed with too much watering or soils that do not drain sufficiently. In the summer, even in the hottest deserts, watering once a week or less often is sufficient for established plants. In the winter in all areas, natural rainfall is sufficient unless there is an extended dry spell (over a month without rain).

Buddleja marrubiifolia

This species has an excellent natural form, but should it need pruning or shaping it is best to prune in the early spring before flower buds begin to set.

As its name suggests, woolly butterfly bush is highly attractive to butterflies. Its summer flowering habit makes it a particularly good choice in a mixed butterfly garden to help keep these tiny visitors fed throughout the summer.

Woolly butterfly bush blends well with native desert shrubs or perennials for a colorful, year-round planting. Mix it with natives such as globemallow (*Sphaeralcea ambigua*) and brittlebush (*Encelia farinosa*), whose cultural needs are similar but whose blooming period is different. Because of its requirements for good drainage and minimal water, it blends well with cactus and other succulents. The white foliage is arresting and can be a cooling note in a hot location. Use around pools or patios because of its tendency to attract butterflies and its tidy appearance.

Calliandra eriophylla
Fairyduster, false mesquite

FAMILY: Fabaceae.

DISTRIBUTION: In the United States from southernmost California west through the deserts of Arizona, New Mexico, and western Texas at elevations from 400 to 5000 ft. (120 to 1500 m). In Mexico in Baja California, Sonora, Chihuahua, Coahuila, Durango, Zacatecas, and Nuevo León south to Puebla.

MATURE SIZE: 1 to 3 ft. (0.3 to 0.9 m) tall and as wide.

BLOOMING PERIOD: February to May.

EXPOSURE: Full sun even in the deserts.

HARDINESS: Cold hardy to at least 15°F (−9°C).

Calliandra eriophylla

Fairyduster looks more like a miniature shrub than an herbaceous garden perennial, but it is so small and, under cultivation, is so tidy that it must be included. The smooth, gray branches are flexible and prominent, particularly when the plant is deciduous.

The 1-in. (2.5-cm) leaves are composed of two or three pairs of pinnae with 14 to 16 leaflets; all this within the space of an inch (2.5 cm) makes for an incredibly small, delicate leaf. Leaves are widely spaced, sparse even, along the stem during the dry season or as the summer approaches, but become both darker green and more abundant during wetter and cooler times. Leaves are coated with sparse hairs, giving them a slight silver cast.

The flowering head is 1.5 to 2.5 in. (4.0 to 6.4 cm) across. The corolla lobes are minute, and four to six flowers are clustered so tightly they form a ball. The stamens are highly exserted, up to four times longer than the corolla, and provide the familiar puff ball look of the flowers. The color begins white but fades from pale pastel to deep rose-pink. The mature pods are flat and, when they split open, the two halves form a coil on the plant that persists for months.

Fairyduster grows best in a well-drained, even rocky soil. Otherwise, it is not fussy about the fertility or composition of the soil. It should be watered regularly, every two weeks in the winter in the hottest deserts but much less often elsewhere. Continued regular watering through the spring prolongs the life of the leaves and the flowering, but ultimately plants become at least semideciduous as the summer heats up. Intermittent watering in the warm weather keeps the plant in good condition through the summer, but overwatering or too frequent watering may result in rotting problems.

Deer find fairyduster a delicious food in the wild, and many people who are familiar with the plant's short, tight stature in nature are astounded by its rounded, full form when garden grown. This means that it is an easy plant to prune hard if you desire, but any pruning should be done in the fall.

Fairyduster blends beautifully with native plants in dry gardens, out on the edges of a planting where watering is minimal, or incorporated into a seasonal wildflower display. It is attractive to both butterflies and hummingbirds.

Unnamed hybrids of this species and its close relative, Baja fairy duster (*Calliandra californica*), hold their leaves all year and flower in an array of watermelon tones. One such hybrid, 'Sierra Starr', was developed by Greg Starr of Tucson, Arizona, and has been introduced by Mountain States Wholesale Nursery. It is a deep, watermelon red on plants with lush, deep green foliage. 'Maricopa Red' is a selection from Desert Tree Farm of Phoenix that is much redder than typical. White-flowering forms are also found from time to time.

In Texas, this fairyduster can be easily confused with the much more widely distributed *Calliandra conferta*. *Calliandra eriophylla* has three or four pinnae, each with 4 to 12 leaflets, while *C. conferta* has only one pair of pinnae on the leaf with 7 to 10 leaflets.

Callirhoe involucrata
Wine cups, poppy mallow

FAMILY: Malvaceae.

DISTRIBUTION: In the United States from Wyoming and North Dakota to Missouri, south to northeastern New Mexico, Oklahoma, central and eastern Texas. In Mexico in Coahuila and Nuevo León.

MATURE SIZE: 12 in. (30 cm) tall and spreading 2 to 4 ft. (0.6 to 1.2 m) wide.

BLOOMING PERIOD: April and May in the deserts, continuing through September in more moderate regions.

EXPOSURE: Light, filtered shade or an east-facing site in the hottest desert areas, full sun or filtered shade elsewhere.

HARDINESS: Cold hardy to at least 0°F (−18°C).

Wine cups grows from a basal set of leaves with extended runners that spread far from the base. The plant produces a deep taproot that increases over the years.

Callirhoe involucrata

The leaves are wide, nearly round, and palmately lobed. The depth of the lobes varies greatly; some plants have deeply incised lobes, others merely suggestive of wavy margins. Leaves are widely spaced on the stems.

Flowers are up to 3 in. (8 cm) across with open, cuplike form so typical of the family. Color ranges from pink to lavender, purple, and white, but the dominant color form is reddish purple.

Wine cups grows best in fertile, well-drained soils that do not dry out entirely. This species is more or less dormant during the winter with either a few basal leaves evident, or deciduous, depending on temperatures. Growth begins as a low, mounding plant in the early spring with the runners extending later in the season. After flowering, leaves begin to fade, and by early summer plants need to be cut back to the basal growth.

I am deeply fond of this species and wonder why it isn't grown more in the region. It is a bedrock of central Texas wildflower displays and, in regions where it is native, requires minimal care. In the deserts, it blooms later than most wildflowers and before the summer tropicals begin, filling in a flowering gap for perennials during the late spring.

Two varieties are somewhat different from the type. Var. *tenuissima* is a fine-leaved form from Coahuila, Mexico, with light lavender flowers. Var. *linearifolia* has leaves that are so lobed they look like the halberd of the French *fleur de lis* and white flowers with varying amounts of streaking in rose or pink.

Many authorities report that this species is attractive to lacewings, which are widely valued beneficial insects. Lacewings are ferocious predators of aphids.

Because of the spreading habit, wine cups is a good choice to fill up a shady corner or put it in the front of a border or bed where it can spread onto a patio or path while blooming. Plants can be used with summer-flowering bulbs such as rain lilies (*Zephyranthes* spp.) that will not begin to grow until wine cups has faded.

Calylophus berlandieri

Calylophus berlandieri subsp. *pinifolius*
Square-bud primrose

Synonym: *Calylophus drummondianus*.
FAMILY: Onagraceae.
DISTRIBUTION: In the United States from southeastern Colorado and southwestern Kansas to eastern New Mexico, Oklahoma, Texas, and Louisiana. In Mexico from northern Coahuila to northwestern Nuevo León and Tamaulipas.
MATURE SIZE: 4 to 16 in. (10 to 41 cm) tall and 10 to 16 in. (25 to 41 cm) wide.
BLOOMING PERIOD: March to October.
EXPOSURE: Full sun, filtered sun, or morning sun in all areas.
HARDINESS: Cold hardy to 0°F (−18°C).

Square-bud primrose is a low-growing, spreading perennial, but in some forms may have erect stems and form a mounding plant. The leaves are 1 to 3 in. (2.5 to 8.0 cm) long, dusky or dark green, and narrow. Leaves are smooth with slightly toothed margins.

The 1- to 3-in. (2.5- to 8-cm) flowers are bright yellow, thin petaled, and solitary. Flowers open during the day and last one day, but are prolific through the blooming season. They have variable amounts of dark purple to brown at the base of the petals, a feature that is much sought after in selections offered for sale.

Square-bud primrose is distinguished from its near relative, sundrops (*Calylophus hartwegii*), by its more bushy habit and flower buds that have prominent ribs on four sides, making them look square.

Square-bud primrose is not particular about the type of soil as long as it has excellent drainage. Although it thrives with supplemental watering in the hottest deserts in the summer, care must be taken to avoid wet or waterlogged soils. This is not a long-lived species, but runners root readily and in some areas plants will reseed easily.

I think both square-bud primrose and sundrops are outstanding groundcovers or space fillers for dry gardens throughout the region. Use this primrose mixed with flowering perennials or shrubs, planted within the well of a tree, or in a crowded planting to line a walk or driveway.

Calylophus hartwegii

Calylophus hartwegii
Sundrops

Family: Onagraceae.
Distribution: Widespread in the United States from Colorado to Kansas and Oklahoma, south to Texas, central and southern New Mexico, and southern Arizona at elevations from 4500 to 7500 ft. (1370 to 2290 m).
Mature size: 6 to 12 in. (15 to 30 cm) tall and spreading 2 to 3 ft. (0.6 to 0.9 m) wide.
Blooming period: March to October.
Exposure: Full sun, filtered shade, or morning sun, but not deep shade.
Hardiness: Cold hardy to below 0°F (−18°C).

Sundrops is a sprawling plant with weak, spreading stems. The leaves are linear and 0.5 to 1.5 in. (1.5 to 4.0 cm) long usually with entire margins but occasionally with tiny teeth. The leaves are deep green and densely covered in fine hairs which give them a velvety texture. The leaves, however, vary greatly over the range of the species.

Flowers are axillary, bright yellow, and 0.5 to 1.0 in. (1.5 to 2.5 cm) long. Flowers in bud are more or less round without the sharp angles that quickly separate this species from square-bud primrose (*Calylophus berlandieri*).

Sundrops grows in virtually any well-drained soil. I have grown it in native, unamended soils and found it an excellent perennial. Water carefully in the summer in the deserts; it does best with intermittent deep watering rather than continuous moisture. In the hottest areas, it is semidormant during the summer and it can be rotted out without careful attention to its watering.

Flea beetles may cause superficial damage in early spring, but are a short-lived problem. Prune any winter or insect damage in the early spring.

Sundrops resembles its close relatives in the genus *Oenothera*, but you can tell the difference by looking at the stigma. In *Calylophus* the stigma is shaped like a club or a knot, in *Oenothera* it is shaped like a cross.

Few groundcovers do so well in the rocky, arid soils and intense heat of the deserts as sundrops. This one is superb, and its glorious, bright yellow flowers offer even more interest to the planting.

I like to allow some plants to grow mingled with each other, and once I let sundrops find its way through a black dalea (*Dalea frutescens*). The large, brilliant yellow flowers of the sundrops combined and contrasted perfectly with the fine-textured, deep indigo of the black dalea. Sundrops can also be used to hang over a wall or raised planter or to provide the understory for a dry perennial garden.

Chrysactinia mexicana
Damianita

Family: Asteraceae.
Distribution: In the United States on limestone soils in the Edwards Plateau and Trans-Pecos areas of Texas and in southern New Mexico. In Mexico in Chihuahua, Coahuila, Nuevo León, and Tamaulipas west to Durango and Aquascalientes and south to Puebla and Veracruz at elevations from 1000 to 10,000 ft. (300 to 3000 m).
Mature size: 12 to 24 in. (30 to 60 cm) tall and as wide.
Blooming period: April to September.
Exposure: Full sun in all areas, although filtered sun or morning sun is tolerated in the hottest deserts.
Hardiness: Cold hardy to 0°F (−18°C).

Damianita is a low-growing, crowded plant with numerous branching stems held closely together. The aromatic, resinous leaves are 0.25 in. (0.7 cm) or less in length. They are needlelike and deep green.

The terminal flowers are showy and virtually smother the plant when in full bloom. Individual flowering heads are 1 in. (2.5 cm) across and consist of 10 to 13 bright golden yellow ray flowers and golden yellow disk flowers.

Damianita grows best in well-drained soils that are not overly enriched. In the deserts, this species should be watered regularly through the summer to maintain vigor and for increased bloom. Although damianita will subsist on extremely modest watering regimens, it becomes reduced and nearly dormant on this type of summer watering. In more moderate areas, including its natural range, damianita performs well on natural rainfall except during a protracted dry spell. It is

Chrysactinia mexicana

best to avoid overhead watering, which makes plants floppy and promotes a fungal infestation that can collapse the plants.

Damianita will tolerate a hard prune to reinvigorate the plant, but this should be done only in cool weather. Pruning in hot weather can be destructive to the plant.

Damianita is low growing enough to be used as a groundcover if planted closely together. It also makes a pleasant border or boundary for a larger bed or along a walkway or path. Putting it where the sharp fragrance can be brought out by frequent brushing of the foliage makes it delightful not only to look at but also to smell. It looks so much like a smaller version of turpentine bush (*Ericameria laricifolia*) that many gardeners use them both because of their different blooming times.

Conoclinium greggii

Conoclinium greggii
Boneset, mistflower

Synonym: *Eupatorium greggii*.
FAMILY: Asteraceae.
DISTRIBUTION: In the United States from south-eastern Arizona and New Mexico to western Texas and south along the Rio Grande Plains. In Mexico from central and eastern Coahuila to northern Zacatecas, Nuevo León, and San Luis Potosí.
MATURE SIZE: 18 in. (46 cm) tall and 24 in. (60 cm) wide.
BLOOMING PERIOD: April to October.
EXPOSURE: Filtered sun or partial shade in the deserts, full sun or filtered sun in milder or coastal climates.
HARDINESS: Root hardy to 0°F (−18°C).

Boneset has numerous, weak stems that are more or less upright and rise from a semiwoody base. The leaves are ovate but deeply dissected, recalling the fronds of ferns.

The terminal flowering heads have numerous rayless flowers in a 1- to 2-in. (2.5- to 5.0-cm) head. Flowers are pale lavender to blue and may be so dense they cover the plant.

Boneset prefers to grow in fertile, enriched soils that are well drained. Water regularly throughout the summer; in fact this species is especially tolerant of hot, humid summers and does well under those conditions. Perhaps for that reason, it is a bit more reluctant in the low deserts, often suffering in the hot, dry summer and failing to achieve its most beautiful form for the fall flowering. Gardeners in less rigorous, but still warm climates, find it outstanding. In the hottest deserts its close relative, blue mist (*Ageratum corymbosum*), is much tougher in the intense heat of these areas.

Butterflies find this species irresistible, and it makes a good foundation for a butterfly garden. Its delicate pastel flowers float over the top as spun frosting, allowing it to soften and provide a light textural contrast to a perennial garden. Use it generously to get the full effect of the filigreed leaves and gossamer flowers.

Convolvulus cneorum
Bush morning glory, silverbush

FAMILY: Convolvulaceae.
DISTRIBUTION: Spain, Italy, Croatia, Albania,
   and adjacent islands.
MATURE SIZE: 2 to 4 ft. (0.6 to 1.2 m) tall and as
   wide.
BLOOMING PERIOD: March to October, often
   ceasing by June in the hottest deserts.
EXPOSURE: Full sun even in the deserts.
HARDINESS: Cold hardy to 15°F (−9°C).

Convolvulus cneorum

Bush morning glory is entirely different in form
from the vining morning glories so familiar in
our gardens. This species grows numerous sturdy
branches forming a low mound.

The leaves are lanceolate, 1.0 to 2.5 in. (2.5 to
6.4 cm) long. They are a dusky grayish green and
the coating of fine hairs, especially on the underside of the leaf, makes them
silver in some lights.

The flowers are held in a loose panicle at the ends of the stems and are so
prolific the species appears to change color when it blooms. One to six flowers
grow on each panicle. The 1.0- to 1.5-in. (2.5- to 4.0-cm) flowers are pure white
with a yellow throat.

Bush morning glory must have an alkaline soil with superb drainage to look its
best. In clay or other tight soils, it can develop severe root rot problems and fail
quickly. In areas with abundant summer rainfall or humid conditions, it should
be grown on gravel or in raised beds.

Water generously in the winter, but be sure the ground is nearly dry between
waterings. Like most Mediterranean natives, this one must be watered carefully
in summer; too much water encourages rotting, while too little water risks losing
the plant.

I once recommended this species for a roadside planting, thinking it would
look so luxurious in the somewhat stark surroundings. But it was voted down
by one of the committee, because she thought it looked like dirty tissues on the
roadside. I am still astonished that anyone could take that position; I find this

species charming and know of few others that can match its ability to be so lovely in such dire circumstances. Even in Phoenix it thrives on roadside plantings or in narrow roadside medians—and there can be no hotter or more difficult situation—but so much for personal taste.

It is important when choosing bush morning glory that you recognize its need for stunning drainage and modest summer irrigation. It blends well with other Mediterranean species such as rosemary and lavender, and with those from the California chaparral such as Cleveland's sage (*Salvia clevelandii*) or bush snapdragon (*Galvezia juncea*), which also appreciate a modest summer water regimen.

Cuphea ignea
Cigar plant

FAMILY: Lythraceae.

DISTRIBUTION: Southern Mexico to Guatemala and the West Indies, particularly Jamaica.

MATURE SIZE: 1 to 3 ft. (0.3 to 0.9 m) tall and as wide.

BLOOMING PERIOD: May to October.

EXPOSURE: Filtered shade or morning sun in all areas but the California coast, where full sun is best. In the hottest deserts, it will also grow well and bloom in full shade.

HARDINESS: Leaves and stems are damaged below 32°F (0°C), but the plant is root hardy to 20°F (−7°C) and recovers quickly.

Cigar plant has a tidy habit with numerous erect stems arising from a semiwoody base. The narrow lanceolate leaves are 1.0 to 1.5 in. (2.5 to 4.0 cm) long and deep green with bronze or red overtones.

Flowers are tubular, less than 1 in. (2.5 cm) long, and bright red-orange, although pure red, pink, white, and yellow forms are known. The flowers are composed only of the calyx; there is no true corolla. The lobes can be tipped with black, purple, or white, features which are the source of many of the named selections.

Cigar plant prefers to grow in fertile, well-drained soils with consistent watering throughout the summer. It quickly becomes chlorotic in infertile or poorly drained soils. Providing a layer of compost or mulch during the summer helps prevent drying out and chlorotic leaves.

Several cultivars are known but only 'David Verity' is common in the region. This selection is a compact, bushy plant with deep orange flowers that have a small whitish tip. It is vigorous growing with abundant and consistent flowering. 'Starfire' is rose pink as is 'Flamingo Pink'. 'Lutea' is yellow and somewhat smaller, only 12 in. (30 cm) tall and wide. 'Black Ash' is an odd combination of a white flower that is rimmed in either red or black. It, too, is only 12 in. (30 cm) tall and as wide. Solid red forms also exist.

Cigar plant, like all members of the genus, is strongly attractive to hummingbirds and is a worthwhile addition to any garden that hopes to invite these remarkable birds. The great benefits of this plant to gardeners in warm deserts are its excellent flowering in significant shade and its tolerance of any amount of heat. It is sometimes difficult to find good flowering plants for such areas, and considering how useful shade is, any species that will lighten up dark areas is to be enjoyed. Use it in large containers, raised shady beds, or in the wells of trees.

Cuphea ignea

Cuphea llavea
Bat-faced cuphea, red cuphea

FAMILY: Lythraceae.
DISTRIBUTION: From southern Mexico to Guatemala.
MATURE SIZE: 8 to 12 in. (20 to 30 cm) tall and spreading up to 3 ft. (0.9 m) wide.
BLOOMING PERIOD: March to October.
EXPOSURE: Filtered shade or full shade in the deserts, full sun or filtered shade in milder or coastal areas.
HARDINESS: Cold hardy to 30°F (−1°C).

Bat-faced cuphea is one of those species that you can hardly believe is true. It is a low-growing, sprawling plant with many stems that arise from a central point.

Cuphea llavea

The ovate to lanceolate leaves are deep green with slightly wavy margins and occur in pairs up the entire stem. It is the flowers, however, that are so distinctive and the source of the common name "bat-faced cuphea."

The calyx is large, covering much of the corolla, and is deep green often with dark purple or black tips. The corolla is made up of four abortive lobes below and two hugely inflated or flared ones above and is usually scarlet red. The entire effect is of the mouth of a bat, with red Mickey Mouse ears repeated on the plant. In some individuals the tips of the calyx are black, in others they are white; but the plants grown commonly in this area usually have purple tips.

Bat-faced cuphea prefers to grow in rich, well-drained soils that are consistently watered through the summer. Heavy applications of mulch or compost during the summer are also helpful. When grown in these conditions it will thrive and bloom prolifically through the summer, but insufficient water, poor drainage, or impoverished soils will cause severe chlorosis and quick decline.

This is a fine choice for a shady garden; it offers a quick respite from the deep green gloom that often defines such spaces. Hummingbirds are strongly attracted to it as well. Use it in a large container close to a seating area where the oddity of the flowers can be appreciated, or in the wells of large trees.

Although known for some time in other parts of the world, this is a recent arrival in the desert parts of the Southwest. In Europe and Australia this species is referred to as 'Tiny Mice', a name that may also apply to a dwarfed selection. 'Firefly', a hybrid between this taxon and creeping waxweed (*Cuphea procumbens*), has six flared rose-pink corolla lobes, two of which are larger than the rest. This hybrid is often known as *C. llavea* var. *miniata*, a name which has no botanical standing. 'Georgia Scarlet' is a popular selection in the Southeast and has intensely red flowers. Some authors also suggest that the *C. llavea* of gardens is actually *C.* ×*purpurea*, a hybrid between this species and *C. procumbens*.

Dalea capitata
Lemon dalea

Dalea capitata

FAMILY: Fabaceae.

DISTRIBUTION: In Mexico from Coahuila, Durango, Zacatecas, San Luis Potosí, and Nuevo León at elevations from 5500 to 7700 ft. (1670 to 2350 m).

MATURE SIZE: 12 to 15 in. (30 to 38 cm) tall and spreading up to 3 ft. (0.9 m) wide.

BLOOMING PERIOD: April to June and again from September to November.

EXPOSURE: Filtered sun or morning sun in the hottest deserts, full sun to filtered sun elsewhere.

HARDINESS: Cold hardy to 0°F (−18°C), but the plant is deciduous at about 25°F (−4°C).

Lemon dalea is a delicate, spreading perennial with thin stems that may be erect or crawling. The leaves are less than 1 in. (2.5 cm) long but pinnately compound with three to five pinnae per leaf.

The pealike flowers are equally tiny and held in short, terminal spikes. The bracts may be green or dark reddish brown and often showy, while the flowers are light custard yellow to deep butter yellow.

Lemon dalea grows best in mildly fertile but sharply drained soils. Soils that are too tight or too consistently wet may cause rotting problems. Water at least weekly in the summer in the hottest deserts; elsewhere it can survive on much less water. I have found this a short-lived species in the Phoenix area, but even the modest reduction in summer heat offered by Tucson and other locations with slightly higher elevation provides more congenial conditions for this species.

The trailing habit makes lemon dalea a splendid choice for large containers or in a raised bed where it can hang over the wall. It can also be used as a groundcover or to fill in a small enclosed part of a bed or patio planting. When mixed with other perennials it should be kept to the front as it is easily overtaken by larger species.

Lemon dalea is strongly attractive to butterflies, and its fall blooming habit makes it a favorite to help attract migrating butterflies in the Southwest.

Dalea frutescens

Dalea frutescens
Black dalea

FAMILY: Fabaceae.

DISTRIBUTION: In the United States from southern Oklahoma and southern New Mexico into northern and western Texas. In Mexico in Coahuila, Chihuahua, Nuevo León, and northern Zacatecas at elevations from 2000 to 7500 ft. (600 to 2290 m).

MATURE SIZE: 3 to 4 ft. (0.9 to 1.2 m) tall and as wide.

BLOOMING PERIOD: August to November.

EXPOSURE: Full sun throughout the region including the deserts.

HARDINESS: Cold hardy to 15°F (−9°C), root hardy to 0°F (−18°C).

Black dalea is a rounded perennial that resembles a small shrub with its semiwoody base and sturdy whitish stems. The leaves are pinnately compound with 10 to 20 tiny leaflets per pinna. The entire leaf is up to 1 in. (2.5 cm) long and deep green.

The tiny flowers are held in 1-in. (2.5-cm) congested clusters at the tips of the stems. Individual flowers range from a rosy purple to dark purple. Although they are bicolored on close examination, this feature is not evident from a distance.

Black dalea in the colder parts of the region is deciduous but in the warmer areas it simply loses a small number of its leaves over the winter. It requires extremely good drainage for best performance and is excellent in rocky soils. Plants grown in wet or poorly drained soils fail quickly.

Even in the hottest deserts, black dalea requires only minimal summer watering to maintain good form and growth. In my own yard, it grows with watering every other week in the summer, although somewhat more frequent watering would be acceptable.

The light, airy look of this perennial makes it a wonderful contrast in dry, hot gardens where its delicacy offers strong contrast to the hard, firm edges of succulents or other desert perennials. The fall-flowering habit is widely appreciated in the hottest deserts where it blends well with other fall-flowering species such as California fuchsia (*Epilobium canum*) and many justicias. I long enjoyed a pairing of this species with sundrops (*Calylophus hartwegii*) where the large yellow flowers were set off by the dark purple of the dalea. It is also useful for planting against a hot wall or near a pool where reflected heat is intense.

Dalea greggii
Trailing smokebush, trailing indigo bush

FAMILY: Fabaceae.

DISTRIBUTION: In the United States in western Texas and southern New Mexico. In eastern Mexico from Chihuahua to Tamaulipas, south to Zacatecas, San Luis Potosí, Puebla, and Oaxaca at elevations from 1700 to 6000 ft. (520 to 1800 m).

MATURE SIZE: 6 to 24 in. (15 to 60 cm) tall and spreading 3 to 4 ft. (0.9 to 1.2 m) wide, occasionally to 6 ft. (1.8 m).

BLOOMING PERIOD: April to November, with heaviest bloom in spring and fall.

EXPOSURE: Full sun or filtered shade.

HARDINESS: Cold hardy to 15°F (−9°C).

Trailing smokebush is an intricately branched perennial that forms a gentle mound from a semiwoody base. The fine, herbaceous stems elongate and sprawl along the ground, rooting as they go. The leaves are tiny, less than 1 in. (2.5 cm) overall, and are pinnately compound with two to four pairs of leaflets per pinna. Leaflets are blue-gray with fine silvery hairs.

Flowers are pealike and held in 0.25- to 0.5-in. (0.7- to 1.5 cm) congested heads at the ends of the stems. They are surrounded by large bracts and are further crowded by a hairy pappus. Although the flowers are typically blue to indigo, they are commonly bicolored with yellowish upper lobes and rosy-pink lower lobes; the entire head is so small it is hard to distinguish such fine differences.

Trailing smokebush grows best in sharply drained, even rocky soils, with minimal watering. In the hottest deserts, water two or three times a month in the summer, much less frequently in the winter. This species resents overhead watering, which can cause rotting problems. Plants that are overwatered tend to grow exceptionally tall from the base before spreading out and look like relic volcanic mounds isolated from each other. With more modest watering, plants spread gracefully and more uniformly over the ground.

Dalea greggii

Pruning is rarely required, but if it becomes necessary, cut the plant back in the early spring to reduce the size or reinvigorate it. In areas with colder winters like Las Vegas, the plant can be deciduous or partially so.

This species is an excellent choice for slope stabilization or erosion control. The silvery cast of the foliage provides a pleasant contrast when interplanted with colorful perennials or as textural relief in succulent gardens. Plants root along the stems freely and fill space quickly. They also reseed freely to further expand the planting.

Like most of its kin, trailing smokebush is highly attractive to butterflies, both adults and larvae.

Datura wrightii
Sacred datura, angel's trumpet, toloache

Synonyms: *Datura inoxia* subsp. *quinquecuspida*, *D. metel* var. *quinquecuspida*, *D. metelioides*.

FAMILY: Solanaceae.

DISTRIBUTION: In most of the United States from California to Virginia, most of the Midwest, and the upper Atlantic states. It is especially common in Southern California, Arizona, New Mexico, and western Texas. Some authors suggest it ranges south into South America as well.

MATURE SIZE: 3 ft. (0.9 m) tall and spreading 6 to 10 ft. (1.8 to 3.0 m) wide.

BLOOMING PERIOD: March to November, usually in response to deep watering or rainfall.

EXPOSURE: Full sun, filtered shade, or full shade in all areas.

HARDINESS: Root hardy to at least 10°F (−12°C), although leaves and stems are deciduous in all areas.

Sacred datura is a large, gangly perennial with big, hollow stems arising from a swollen tuberous root. Plants are winter deciduous but increase annually in size as the tuber grows.

The leaves are 5 to 8 in. (13 to 20 cm) long. They are gray-green, heart shaped, and either velvety or sticky with resinous hairs.

The flowers are stunning with 6- to 8-in. (15- to 20-cm) long flaring tubes. While in bud, the corolla lobes wrap at the tip like a fist that has closed but open suddenly and dramatically at night. Flowers are fragrant, often so much so that they can be smelled dozens of feet from the plant. Their delicious, sweet perfume reminds me of jasmine. Like the flowers of many night bloomers, these flowers are pure white, but there are forms with lavender flowers, as well.

The distinctive fruit is a rounded, prickly ball that looks like the medieval weapon mace. All parts of the plant are poisonous if ingested.

Datura wrightii

Wild sacred datura is most often found on roadsides. It does best as a garden plant with intermittent watering through the summer. It is often put in the wells of trees or other large shrubs that will be watered anyway, and that is more than sufficient even in the hottest desert areas. In milder areas it grows well on natural rainfall alone.

Good drainage is essential, particularly during its dormancy in the winter. Tubers that are kept too wet will rot and the plant will die; however, in my yard this species reseeds freely, often in the most unexpected places, far from the original plant. If you want to move a seedling of this species, do so just at the beginning of the growing season and keep it well watered until it is established.

Summer nights with the gentle fragrance of sacred datura floating over the garden are made even more memorable by the visits of white-lined sphinx moth, tobacco hornworm moth, and other hawk moths to feast on the copious nectar of the flowers. The larvae of these insects also feed on this species, although individual plants with a stronger tendency to velvety leaves rather than to sticky leaves appear to minimize this damage. These moths are the size of small birds and cruise over the plants every evening the flowers are open. Plants are generous with their bloom; dozens of blooms open each evening, making a feast for the moths and a captivating spectacle for the gardener.

Use sacred datura in a space that is large enough to accommodate its sprawling stems, but where it will be visible at night. Along a patio or other seating area, at the terminus of a trail, or in an area near a well-used doorway offer exciting opportunities.

Odd, double forms are usually sold as *Datura metel*. These selections typically have dark green leaves with a deep purple cast and are smaller and more upright than the type. The flowers are more erect as well and arise out of a huge bract that entirely covers the bud. The flowers are deep purple on the outer side of the petal and whitish lavender inside. The petals end in acute tips that fall over like spider lilies. These flowers smell wonderful, producing a deep, permeating sweetness that is most prominent in the early morning. In the hottest deserts these forms can be short lived unless they are grown in fertile, well-drained soil with consistent watering.

Dichondra argentea
Silver pony foot

FAMILY: Convolvulaceae.
DISTRIBUTION: In the United States in southeastern Arizona, southern New Mexico, and far western Texas. Widespread in Mexico from Chihuahua and Coahuila continuously to Oaxaca at elevations from 650 to 9200 ft. (200 to 2800 m).
MATURE SIZE: Rarely over 6 in. (15 cm) tall but more commonly 3 in. (8 cm) tall and spreading up to 3 ft. (0.9 m).
BLOOMING PERIOD: May to October.
EXPOSURE: Full sun or filtered shade throughout the region, but filtered sun is best in the hottest deserts.
HARDINESS: Cold hardy to at least 20°F (−7°C).

Silver pony foot is a low-growing, widely spreading perennial with thin, lax stems. The leaves are covered in fine white or silver hairs with the overall impression of a silver plant. The rounded leaves are split at the petiole, giving them the look of a rounded hoof. Often the margins are wavy.

The flowers are solitary, whitish yellow, and tiny, less than 0.25 in. (0.7 cm) long. Because they are so small and their color fades into the foliage, they are innocuous and are rarely an ornamental feature of this species.

Silver pony foot is highly adaptable to a wide range of soils provided it has sharp drainage. In rich soils or those that stay wet too long the plant declines quickly and will rot out, but when grown in soils that dry partially between waterings and are well drained, it is a fast-growing ground-cover.

Use it generously as a groundcover; the stems root as they go and can stabilize a steep or newly formed bed. The long stems also make excellent additions to hanging baskets, a practice that many northern gardeners have adopted for this plant. I have seen it planted generously in fanciful containers to mimic a bench or a table and, because it covers the underlying structure so completely, the illusion is perfect.

Ironically, its relative *Dichondra micrantha* is the best-known member of the genus in the des-

Dichondra argentea

erts; it is used frequently in shady or wet conditions where lawn grass does not grow well. It is a sad business that silver pony foot, the only truly xeric member of the genus, is infrequently used and poorly known. It is time to correct that.

Dicliptera resupinata
Foldwing, twin seed

FAMILY: Acanthaceae.

DISTRIBUTION: In the United States in southeastern Arizona and southwestern New Mexico at elevations from 3000 to 6000 ft. (900 to 1800 m). In Mexico from Sonora to Chihuahua, as well as Sinaloa, Durango, and Jalisco.

MATURE SIZE: 2 to 3 ft. (0.6 to 0.9 m) tall and as wide.

BLOOMING PERIOD: October to May.

EXPOSURE: Full sun or filtered shade in all areas.

HARDINESS: Root hardy to 20°F (−7°C), but the plant is deciduous in temperatures below freezing.

Dicliptera resupinata

Foldwing has thin, intertwined stems that create a complicated branching pattern and arise from a woody base. Leaves are 2 in. (5 cm) long, lance shaped, and prolific on the plant. They are a dusky gray-green with a deep purple cast.

Flowers have a short, fused corolla whose lobes fall away from each other like an opened mouth. The flowers are enclosed by a prominent bract and are deep purple to indigo with white nectary guides. Although less than 0.5 in. (1.5 cm) long, flowers are profuse on the plant.

The common name "foldwing" derives from the bracts that come together like the folded wing of a butterfly and fuse over the seed into a heart-shaped pod. These pods turn tan as they age and are persistent, making an attractive feature of their own.

Foldwing is a tough plant that will grow in almost any condition, but it is most attractive in areas with regular, supplemental irrigation in the summer. Any well-drained soil seems to suit it. In the deserts, plants grown without sufficient summer water lose many of the stems and become brown and sticklike over the summer. They do return to green vigor with either a deep watering or falling temperatures.

I like all the different looks that foldwing can present. In the cool weather it is a deep green, rounded perennial that fills up the space beneath a large shrub or tree. In the later winter and spring it is full of intense blue to purple flowers. Later still it has a coating of the heart-shaped, tan pods that hang like lanterns over the fading leaves as summer starts.

Use foldwing in mixed perennial plantings. It is especially effective with both succulent and desert native plantings because of its tolerance for hot, dry conditions.

Dicliptera suberecta
King's crown, velvet honeysuckle

Dicliptera suberecta (Judy Mielke)

FAMILY: Acanthaceae.
DISTRIBUTION: Uruguay.
MATURE SIZE: 20 to 36 in. (50 to 90 cm) tall and
as wide.
BLOOMING PERIOD: July to October.
EXPOSURE: Full sun, filtered shade, or morning
sun in all locations but the deserts, where fil-
tered shade is best.
HARDINESS: Cold hardy to about 15°F (−9°C).

King's crown is a more or less erect perennial
with velvety, soft, green stems. The more or less
ovate leaves are up to 2 in. (5 cm) long and occur
in widely spaced pairs up the stem. They are
dark green, sturdy, and thick with a fine blush of
hairs.

The tubular, dusky orange flowers are held in
a shortened, branched inflorescence that appears as an axillary whorl of flowers.
Each flower is enclosed by a prominent green bract.

This South American relative of our foldwing grows best in fertile, well-
drained soil with a thick layer of mulch in the summer. Regular summer watering, similar to that for salvias, is important to keep the species vigorous and
blooming through the summer. In the deserts it grows weakly in poorly drained
soils, without sufficient enrichment, or in full sun with no protection.

Plants that are leggy or worn from the winter can be pruned in the early spring
to improve their form. Plants that have suffered heat damage may be pruned in
late September or October.

More widely used in the humid South than in the Southwest, King's crown
is nevertheless a sturdy perennial for the region. The soft, hairy leaves and the
bright orange flowers are a welcome addition to the summer-flowering garden.
Place it where it will not be brushed often as the brittle stems break easily. This
is a good species for shady or semishady perennial gardens or for use in a large
container. Hummingbirds are strongly attracted to the tubular, orange flowers.

Dyschoriste linearis

Dyschoriste linearis
Snake herb, narrow-leaf snake herb

FAMILY: Acanthaceae.
DISTRIBUTION: In the United States from south central Oklahoma into central, western, and southern Texas, continuing into Mexico in Coahuila at elevations from 40 to 2300 ft. (12 to 690 m).
MATURE SIZE: 6 to 18 in. (15 to 46 cm) tall and spreading up to 2.5 ft. (0.8 m) wide.
BLOOMING PERIOD: April to July.
EXPOSURE: Full sun to filtered shade except in the deserts, where filtered shade or morning sun is preferred.
HARDINESS: Cold hardy to at least 10°F (−12°C), root hardy to much lower temperatures.

Snake herb is a short, erect, multistemmed perennial that will spread from rhizomes to form a small colony. The leaves are narrow and range from spatulate to linear depending on their location on the plant. They are 0.5 to 1.0 in. (1.5 to 2.5 cm) long and are crowded up the stems.

The flowers are held in axillary clusters of up to three flowers and are surrounded by leafy bracts. The corolla is 0.5 to 1.0 in. (1.5 to 2.5 cm) long and ranges from lavender-blue to purple or a light purple marked with white nectar guides.

Snake herb grows best on alkaline soils with sharp drainage. Rocky soils are fine, and the plant is well suited for growing in rocky crevices or small spaces between boulders. Water regularly in the deserts through the summer, although within its range and in milder areas of the region, only intermittent deep watering is needed during the summer. Plants are often semideciduous to fully deciduous in the winter, and spring back to growth with the first warm weather.

This is one of a large number of promising perennials for the future. It has some difficulty with the driest and hottest locations in the deserts, but with filtered shade and the same attention you would give a salvia, it makes a fine ornamental for the region. The light lavender flowers are a welcome addition to a summer garden.

Encelia californica
Bush sunflower

Encelia californica

FAMILY: Asteraceae.

DISTRIBUTION: In the United States from the southern coastal counties of California and the desert regions of California and Arizona into Baja California in Mexico at elevations below 2000 ft. (600 m).

MATURE SIZE: 3 to 4 ft. (0.9 to 1.2 m) tall and as wide.

BLOOMING PERIOD: February to June.

EXPOSURE: Full sun in all areas.

HARDINESS: Cold hardy to 27°F (−3°C) and recovers from damage; however, dies at 20°F (−7°C).

Bush sunflower is a dense shrubby perennial with narrowly ovate, green, smooth leaves that are 1.0 to 2.5 in. (2.5 to 6.4 cm) long. Flowers are daisy-like with bright yellow rays and dark brown disks. They are solitary on tall stalks above the foliage.

Care for bush sunflower is the same as for all members of the genus: rocky, well-drained soils that are not heavily enriched, deep, infrequent watering during the winter growing season, and minimal summer watering.

Bush sunflower strongly resembles brittlebush (*Encelia farinosa*), particularly *E. farinosa* var. *phenicodonta*, which also has brown disks. *Encelia californica* is distinguished by its green, smooth leaves and solitary flowering heads.

Bush sunflower is not nearly as common an ornamental as brittlebush, but it is a lovely, rounded plant. It is outstanding blended into a native plant garden or into naturalized plantings of wildflowers, or used as a complimentary planting in a dry succulent garden. The regular form is tidy and formal, making it an effective choice for a boundary or border.

Encelia farinosa

Encelia farinosa
Brittlebush, incienso

FAMILY: Asteraceae.
DISTRIBUTION: In the United States in the deserts of southwestern Utah, southern Nevada, California, and Arizona at elevations below 3000 ft. (900 m). In Mexico in Sonora and Sinaloa as well as Baja California.
MATURE SIZE: 3 to 5 ft. (0.9 to 1.5 m) tall and as wide.
BLOOMING PERIOD: February to May, although bloom may begin as early as December in the hottest deserts.
EXPOSURE: Full sun in all areas.
HARDINESS: Cold hardy to 20°F (−7°C).

Brittlebush has a collection of freely branching stems that rise from a woody base. The 2-in. (5-cm) leaves are more or less triangular, gray-green with a fine film of white hairs that provide the white cast so typical of this species. The leaves, however, are quite variable over time and under different growing conditions. With ample water, they lose most of the white, hairy coating and become both greener and softer. These leaves photosynthesize rapidly, releasing water freely. With increasing drought, the leaves increase the amount of protective hairs and become almost pure white. These leaves are both smaller and firmer and have a significantly reduced rate of transpiration.

Flowers are held on branched stalks high above the foliage. The rays are bright, clear yellow and the disks are typically yellow, although var. *phenicodonta* has dark disks. Flowering heads are 1.0 to 1.5 in. (2.5 to 4.0 cm) across.

A truly extraordinary desert perennial, brittlebush must be grown in alkaline, sharply drained soils that receive only enough water to keep the plant fit. When provided too much water, this species can grow to huge dimensions with large, floppy, green leaves—losing all of its character and charm. Even in the deserts, plants thrive on natural rainfall, and only minimal supplemental irrigation is needed to prolong the bloom or keep plants from becoming completely dormant.

Under natural conditions, brittlebush loses most of its leaves in the summer and for all practical purposes is dormant. During this time, leaves are pure white, often curled, and brittle. To keep the plant from becoming quite this dry, water it monthly in the summer.

This is arguably the most beautiful native Sonoran perennial. The tight regular form of the plant with its ghostly white foliage and intense yellow flowers is the hallmark of spring in the Sonoran Desert. In good years, you are blinded by so much yellow; it appears out of crevices, in cracks, and over boulders; jumps out from behind rocks; and turns in the path, under trees, and over your head on steep trails.

In the garden brittlebush brings in all manner of wildlife while requiring only minimum of care. Flowers are a source of nectar for both butterflies and native bees. Painted lady butterflies are known to use it as a larval food plant.

When grown too well, creating leaves that are soft and pliable, the plant may be invaded by aphids during the spring. These pests are quickly removed either by strong jets of water or by hand.

As a garden plant, brittlebush provides a strong reminder of the natural desert. It blends well with other dry growing perennials, and even while dormant it is handsome. Mix brittlebush into the background of wildflower plantings or intermingle it with dry succulents for added structure and textural contrast.

A good deal of confusing information suggests that chemicals washed from the leaves may be toxic to certain, undoubtedly native, annuals, but I have never seen this phenomenon have a meaningful effect in a garden situation.

Encelia frutescens
Bush encelia, green brittlebush

FAMILY: Asteraceae.
DISTRIBUTION: In the United States in deserts of Southern California, central and southern Nevada, southern Utah, Arizona, and southwestern New Mexico at elevations up to 4500 ft. (1370 m).
MATURE SIZE: 1.5 to 5.0 ft. (0.5 to 1.5 m) tall and 3 to 4 ft. (0.9 to 1.2 m) wide.
BLOOMING PERIOD: March to October, with heaviest bloom in spring.
EXPOSURE: Full sun even in the hottest regions.
HARDINESS: Cold hardy to 0°F (−18°C).

Bush encelia is a greener version of the familiar brittlebush (*Encelia farinosa*) with the same regular rounded form and numerous branches rising from a semi-woody base. The leaves are rough, up to 1 in. (2.5 cm) long, and contrast with the whitish stems. They are more or less ovate.

Flowers are 0.5 in. (1.5 cm) wide and look like little buttons on the tall stalks. Rayless, the disks are yellow and the heads are solitary on the long, thin stalks.

Bush encelia prefers to grow in well-drained, alkaline soils with only modest fertility or added amendments. Water deeply at irregular intervals during the growing season, and once or twice a month in the deserts during the summer.

Bush encelia contrasts well with other desert perennials, including its close relative brittle-bush. The deep green color of the leaves makes a sturdy background for wildflower or other annual plantings, succulent gardens, or smaller perennials. This plant is tough enough to be grown in full or reflected sun, or in areas that will not receive regular irrigation, and its cold tolerance greatly expands the range of areas where it can be planted.

Encelia frutescens

Engelmannia peristenia
Cut-leaf daisy, Engelmann daisy

Synonym: *Engelmannia pinnatifida*.
FAMILY: Asteraceae.
DISTRIBUTION: In the United States from southwestern New Mexico and Colorado to Nebraska, Oklahoma, and south through most of Texas. In Mexico in northern Chihuahua, Coahuila, Nuevo León, and Tamaulipas.
MATURE SIZE: 1.5 to 3.5 ft. (0.5 to 1.1 m) tall and as wide.
BLOOMING PERIOD: February to November, but most prolific in May.
EXPOSURE: Full sun or filtered shade.
HARDINESS: Cold hardy to at least 15°F (−9°C).

Engelmann daisy grows as a multistemmed, sturdy perennial from an enlarged taproot. The stems are upright and numerous.

Leaves are deeply lobed and up to 6 in. (15 cm) long. They are coated with coarse hairs and are dark green. Basal leaves form a low rosette, but the flowering stalks are leafy as well.

The flowering head is over 1 in. (2.5 cm) wide and is composed of seven to eight ray flowers that are light yellow. The disk flowers are golden yellow.

Engelmann daisy grows in well-drained, alkaline soils on a wide variety of water regimens. Drought tolerant in its range, it will grow taller and bloom longer with modest supplemental watering.

This species is virtually unknown in the deserts but is more common in Texas, particularly in native themed gardens. Engelmann daisy is an exuberant plant with vivid flowers that make a strong statement when used generously or as a backdrop for a perennial garden.

Engelmannia peristenia

Epilobium canum
California fuchsia, hummingbird trumpet

Synonyms: *Zauschneria californica*, *Z. californica* subsp. *latifolia*, *Z. latifolia*.
Family: Onagraceae.
Distribution: In the United States from Oregon south to California and Arizona east to southwestern New Mexico at 4500 to 7000 ft. (1370 to 2100 m), much lower elevations elsewhere. In Mexico in northern Sonora and Baja California.
Mature size: 1 to 3 ft. (0.3 to 0.9 m) tall and as wide.
Blooming period: July to November.
Exposure: Filtered shade or morning sun in all regions, full sun only along the coast.
Hardiness: Cold hardy to 20°F (−7°C), but there is great variability depending on the origin of the plants. Recovery is quick after minor cold damage.

Epilobium canum

California fuchsia has two distinct forms. The most commonly grown ornamental form is an herbaceous plant with numerous brittle stems arising from the base. Plants are rhizomatous and spread quickly. The leaves are oval or broadly lanceolate and rise up the entire length of the stem; they are covered with fine hairs and feel velvety to the touch.

The other form has stems that rise from a semiwoody base. The leaves are linear to lanceolate and thin, in some forms almost needlelike. This form grows upright, while the former is more or less crawling.

Flowers are tubular and 1.5 to 2.0 in. (4 to 5 cm) long. They range in color from scarlet red to red-orange with both pink and white forms occasionally found.

The taxonomy of this group can be bewildering. A blizzard of names, varieties, subspecies, and forms has been proposed over the years. Currently, all forms are in this species, with four recognized subspecies. In the ornamental trade, particularly outside the deserts, considerable interest has been shown in selections for color and form. Some of the most widely grown include 'Ghostly Red', with fuzzy, gray-green leaves and fuzzy, red flowers; and 'Solidarity Pink', with somewhat larger, pink flowers and hairy, linear leaves. Gray-leaved forms are popular and include 'Catalina', introduced by Mike Evans of Tree of Life

Nursery in California. The latter is an erect plant with a woody base, thin, gray leaves, and narrow orange-red flowers. 'Everett's Choice' is a shorter plant, 6 to 12 in. (15 to 30 cm) tall, with small, gray leaves and red flowers, and 'Silver Select' is a mat-forming, dwarf selection with silver foliage that is much like the green-leaved 'Etteri'. In addition, European selections with different names match most of these forms.

California fuchsia grows best in the hottest deserts in filtered shade in a fertile, well-drained soil. Plants grow and expand during the spring and early summer, during which time it is important to keep them regularly watered. Although often considered a fall bloomer, California fuchsia can begin to bloom during the summer. Fall bloom is the most prolific and reliable.

Most forms, particularly the herbaceous ones, retain their dead leaves on the stems as they grow. This can become unsightly over the season, and a hard prune in the early spring will clean all of it out and reinvigorate the plant. For many years a planting at the Desert Botanical Garden was in effect mowed to within inches of the ground every February; this practice greatly improved both the vigor of the plants and their blooming.

I have grown the woodier, needle-leaved versions in my garden in Phoenix and found them to be shorter lived and less reliable than the herbaceous ones. Growers in milder areas find the exact opposite, with the gray-leaved, woodier forms being highly reliable.

Ericameria laricifolia
Turpentine bush

FAMILY: Asteraceae.
DISTRIBUTION: In the United States in Southern California, western Arizona, and far western Texas at elevations from 2000 to 8200 ft. (600 to 2500 m). In Mexico in northeastern Sonora.
MATURE SIZE: 3 ft. (0.9 m) tall and 4 ft. (1.2 m) wide.
BLOOMING PERIOD: September to November.
EXPOSURE: Full sun even in the hottest deserts.
HARDINESS: Cold hardy to at least 5°F (−9°C).

Turpentine bush is named for the imbedded deposits of resin on its branches and leaves that result in its distinctive pungent aroma. Leaves are 0.5 in. (1.5 cm) long, narrowly linear, and deep green.

Ericameria laricifolia (Mountain States Wholesale Nursery)

The flowers are clustered into terminal heads and have few to no rays and more or less upright disk flowers. Both rays and disks are bright golden yellow and so profuse that the plant transforms to a golden ball when in full bloom.

Grow turpentine bush in rocky or other well-drained soils. It is not necessary to make the soil too fertile; in fact, very rich soils will rot out the plant. Water infrequently, even in the hottest deserts, to keep the tight, rounded form that is so lovely in this species. Overwatered plants tend to flop or fall from the middle. In the deserts, water once or twice a month in the summer, more often during the spring growth and flowering. In milder areas, water much less frequently. Turpentine bush has a regular, symmetrical form, but if pruning is needed prune lightly in early spring.

This is an outstanding choice for a low or informal border or hedge. It is tough enough to grow in any native garden or to be mixed with succulents where it can take the dry conditions but offers vivid textural contrast. Plant a group to fill up a difficult hot spot or a west-facing corner. It makes an interesting companion planting with the similar damianita (*Chrysactinia mexicana*) because they bloom at different times of the year with such similar foliage.

Erigeron karvinskianus
Santa Barbara daisy, Mexican daisy

FAMILY: Asteraceae.

DISTRIBUTION: In Mexico from at least Guerrero, Jalisco, and Oaxaca. Naturalized widely through Europe and the United States.

MATURE SIZE: 8 to 16 in. (20 to 41 cm) tall and 24 to 36 in. (60 to 90 cm) wide.

BLOOMING PERIOD: February to June, occasionally reblooms in the fall.

EXPOSURE: Filtered sun or morning sun in all areas except the coast, where full sun is best.

HARDINESS: Cold hardy to at least 10°F (−12°C).

Erigeron karvinskianus

Santa Barbara daisy gets its unlikely name because it became known to most Western gardeners through growers from that area of California. This charming species has tiny, linear leaves that look like threads along the stems. The stems branch intricately to form a semi-woody base. The entire effect is of a billowy cushion.

Flowers are daisylike with the peculiar flat heat so distinctive to this genus. Countless small white rays are crammed into rows and are so uniform that they appear to have been pruned into shape. They often have a blue or pink cast, and in many forms the flowers fade to pink. The disk is yellow.

While Santa Barbara daisy is not particular about soils, it does best in lightly amended, well-drained soils. Water it regularly during the flowering season, and keep up weekly watering in the summer in the hottest deserts. The plant routinely declines, becoming semideciduous in the hottest part of the summer, but revives when the weather cools. Cut it back severely in the early winter to improve its form and reinvigorate the plant.

When I first knew this species, it was simply called 'Profusion'. That name refers to a selection of the species that is somewhat more floriferous than the type. An Australian horticulturist, Brian Jackson, has introduced 'Spindrift', which is a dwarf, growing only 8 in. (20 cm) tall and spreading 12 in. (30 cm). This charming selection is coated with white flowers that fade to a rich pink.

The closely related fleabane daisy (*Erigeron divergens*) can be difficult to distinguish from Santa Barbara daisy. Native to a huge range from British Columbia and North Dakota to northern Chihuahua west to Baja California, fleabane daisy is well adapted to dry, hot conditions. It is generally an annual, but occasionally will grow as either a biennial or a perennial. This is one of ways to distinguish the species: Santa Barbara daisy is much more likely to be perennial than this species. Fleabane daisy is hardy to at least 5°F (−15°C), perhaps more depending on its origins, and enjoys the same cultural conditions as Santa Barbara daisy.

All members of the genus are excellent attractants to butterflies. The diminutive size and spreading form of Santa Barbara daisy make it a great choice to hang over a large container, along a wall or raised bed, or to fill in a sunny corner. It is particularly useful in a mixed container planting with succulents where it provides good color contrast to their stark, rigid forms.

Eriogonum fasciculatum
Flat top buckwheat, California buckwheat

FAMILY: Polygonaceae.
DISTRIBUTION: In the United States in southwestern Utah, southern Nevada, southeastern California, and Arizona at elevations below 4500 ft. (1370 m). In Mexico in Baja California.
MATURE SIZE: 1 to 3 ft. (0.3 to 0.9 m) tall and spreading 2 to 4 ft. (0.6 to 1.2 m) wide.
BLOOMING PERIOD: February to May.
EXPOSURE: Full sun even in the deserts.
HARDINESS: Cold hardy to 15°F (−9°C).

Flat top buckwheat has numerous branches that rise from a semiwoody base. The stems, leaves, and blooming stalk are all covered in fine, whitish hairs.

Leaves are 0.5 in. (1.5 cm) or less in length and are arranged in groups along the stem. They are gray to gray-green with a whitish cast to the underside.

Flowers are held on long stalks above the foliage. While individual flowers are tiny, the entire head is up to 2 in. (5 cm) across. Flowers are white but are enclosed in conspicuous pink to reddish bracts. The bracts are persistent long after the bloom is spent and give the plant a two-tone flowering.

Four varieties of this species are recognized, but var. *poliofolium* has both the largest distribution in nature and in horticulture. While the other varieties are difficult to distinguish one from another, var. *fla-voride* from Baja is distinctive for its yellow-green foliage.

California native plant growers have done a great deal of selection and occasional hybridization with this species and its close relatives. A few more or less prostrate selections are available, such as 'Dana Point', 'Prostrata', 'Theodore Payne', and 'Wildwood'. All look much like the type (and each other) but with a more relaxed, even prostrate, growth habit.

Flat top buckwheat is a splendid choice for a hot, dry location. It can take any amount of sun or reflected heat and will thrive on minimal supplemental irrigation through the summer even in the hottest deserts. The flowers are abundant on the plant and make it look like a snow fall in spring. Nicest of all, the showy, colorful bracts remain for months and offer a complete change of color, from white to pinky rust, through the summer. Flat top buckwheat is a compact, almost round plant that blends well in the dry garden with cacti or as an addition to a mixed planting of native perennials and shrubs. Use it generously to get the most benefit from the bloom and to provide some structure to an otherwise bleak area.

Eriogonum fasciculatum

Eriogonum wrightii
Shrubby buckwheat, Wright's buckwheat

FAMILY: Polygonaceae.

DISTRIBUTION: In the United States in Southern California, western and southern Nevada, Arizona, southwestern New Mexico, and western Texas at 3000 to 6500 ft. (900 to 1980 m) in elevation. In Mexico in Baja California south to Aquascalientes.

MATURE SIZE: 1.5 to 2.0 ft. (0.5 to 0.6 m) tall and as wide.

BLOOMING PERIOD: July to October.

EXPOSURE: Full sun even in the deserts.

HARDINESS: Cold hardy to 0°F (−18°C).

Eriogonum wrightii (Wynn Anderson)

Shrubby buckwheat is a sturdy plant with numerous intertwined stems. It looks dense enough to hold your weight. The 0.5-in. (1.5-cm) leaves are deep green with a silvery cast on the underside formed by mats of fine hairs.

The tiny flowers are clustered into 1- to 2-in. (2.5- to 5-cm) heads at the ends of long, naked stalks. Flower color is white or pink with showy pinkish bracts.

In my area, shrubby buckwheat is uncommon, but I cannot imagine why. This extremely attractive and entirely sturdy perennial can be much more attractive out of flower than its close and more commonly used relative, flat top buckwheat (*Eriogonum fasciculatum*). Shrubby buckwheat is just as drought tolerant as flat top buckwheat but much more cold hardy.

Plant shrubby buckwheat generously to form a loose hedge or casual border. Intermingled with native plants or annual wildflowers it will provide year-round interest and structure. It also helps soften a dry succulent garden.

In the hottest deserts, water it once or twice a month to keep it in good condition. Natural rainfall in the winter is usually sufficient for good growth. Grow it in soils with excellent drainage; even rocky soils are acceptable.

Like all buckwheats, shrubby buckwheat is an excellent choice to attract butterflies; both larvae and adults use it for food.

Euphorbia antisyphilitica
Candelilla, wax spurge

FAMILY: Euphorbiaceae.

DISTRIBUTION: In the United States in far western Texas, barely into southern New Mexico. In Mexico from eastern Chihuahua through Coahuila to northern Zacatecas and western San Luis Potosí, eastern Durango, and Nuevo León at elevations from 1000 to 4300 ft. (300 to 1290 m).

MATURE SIZE: 1 to 3 ft. (0.3 to 0.9 m) tall and 1 to 2 ft. (0.3 to 0.6 m) wide.

BLOOMING PERIOD: Intermittent bloom from April to September depending on rainfall.

EXPOSURE: Full sun even in the deserts.

HARDINESS: Cold hardy to 15°F (−9°C).

Euphorbia antisyphilitica

Candelilla grows up as a congested forest of thin, gray-green stems. The stems are covered with wax, an adaptation to minimize water loss in their desert home. This waxy coating creates a mottled blush on the stems.

The leaves are less than 0.25 in. (0.7 cm) long and infrequently seen. You can own the plant a long time before you even notice it has leaves.

Flowers are minute and held in round clusters directly on the stem. They are waxy and cup shaped, white with a rosy-red throat. Most of the flowers are male with one or two females in the group.

Candelilla needs well-drained, even rocky soils that are not too rich. Too much shade or water makes the plants weak and floppy. Water no more than every other week in the summer in the hottest regions, much less often where the summers are milder or there is reliable summer rain.

The wax of the stem has been rendered for years to serve a wide array of uses. It is valued in food products, candle and soap productions, for ointment, floor polish, waterproofing, and many other uses. Sadly, its popularity has impinged on its natural abundance and the species is much reduced in both geographic range and numbers.

Euphorbia rigida

As an ornamental, candelilla makes a splendid addition to any hot, dry location. The numerous stems are attractive and provide a soft texture that contrasts well with the hard edges of cactus, agave, or yucca. The plant is tough enough to grow on the edge of the garden or any place that cannot be regularly watered. It will grow well in large pots as long as the drainage is superb.

Euphorbia rigida
Gopher plant, rigid spurge, silver spurge

Synonym: *Euphorbia biglandulosa*.
FAMILY: Euphorbiaceae.
DISTRIBUTION: Mediterranean region from Morocco to Portugal, east to Turkey and Iran.
MATURE SIZE: 1 to 2 ft. (0.3 to 0.6 m) tall and spreading 2 to 3 ft. (0.6 to 0.9 m) wide.
BLOOMING PERIOD: February to May.
EXPOSURE: Partial or filtered shade in all but the mildest climates, where full sun is possible.
HARDINESS: Cold hardy to 10°F (−12°C).

Gopher plant has more or less upright stems that fall along the ground as they lengthen. Each stem is crowded with linear, 1.5-in. (4-cm) leaves that have an acute to rounded tip. The thick, nearly succulent leaves spiral up the stem. They often show a rim or cast of pink, which in some individuals is quite pronounced.

Flowers are tiny and creamy yellow, but they are held within large chartreuse bracts. The flowers and the brilliant bracts are borne in tight, rounded clusters toward the ends of the stems.

Grow gopher plant in somewhat fertile, but well-drained soils. In the deserts it requires regular watering during the summer, but in milder climates it is quite drought tolerant and thrives on benign neglect.

This species is similar to *Euphorbia myrsinites* which grows in gardens throughout the warm climates of the world. It can be distinguished by its more erect stems, its stiff, rounder leaves (especially at the tip), and its smaller stature.

Gopher plant is a great curiosity. You have to love the commanding color to use it. It is best in generous numbers so that it makes a significant show; otherwise, it only looks gaudy. Use it where it can spread out and fill a corner, or spill over a small wall or large container.

Evolvulus glomeratus
Blue daze

FAMILY: Convolvulaceae.
DISTRIBUTION: Brazil and Paraguay. Naturalized in Florida and the West Indies.
MATURE SIZE: 6 to 12 in. (15 to 30 cm) tall and spreading more than 2 to 4 ft. (0.6 to 1.2 m) wide.
BLOOMING PERIOD: March to November.
EXPOSURE: Filtered sun or morning sun in all areas, as well as deeper shade in the hottest deserts.
HARDINESS: Cold hardy to 20°F (−7°C).

Blue daze is a lovely, soft mounding plant that spreads its long, slight stems generously in the garden. The leaves are variable from deep green to light grayish green, depending on the amount of hairs on the leaves.

The leaves are ovate to elliptic, 1 in. (2.5 cm) long and profuse. The open, cup-shaped flowers are about 1 in. (2.5 cm) across and range from light blue to deep blue. They are axillary and solitary, opening for only one day each, but they are prolific, and the series of flowering lasts for many weeks.

The name "blue daze" is confusing. A cultivar named 'Blue Daze' is so commonly offered and the forms and names have so mingled that now the species is typically known and sold with the common name of "blue daze." It is a dazzling species; in the sun it is a tighter mound, in the shade it spreads out.

Evolvulus nuttalianus (syn. *E. pilosus*) looks very similar and is often confused with *E. glomeratus*. It is native from the Midwest to Texas. Although rare in horticutlure, it might be a fine choice for Texas gardeners in particular.

Blue daze grows in almost any well-drained soil but fails quickly in wet or waterlogged soils. It prefers locations with low humidity in the winter, and in all areas should be grown on the dry side in the winter. Many gardeners grow it as annual, not only because of its limited cold tolerance but also because of its propensity to rot out over the winter if it receives too much moisture.

Grow blue daze where you need a pop of color in a dark spot. Because of its trailing habit it is spectacular in a hanging basket or in a large container where it gracefully falls over the sides. It is frequently grown in large hanging containers with many plants so an entire, blue ball is created. The effect is stunning.

Evolvulus glomeratus

Gaillardia aristata
Blanket flower, firewheel, brown-eyed Susan, Indian blanket

FAMILY: Asteraceae.

DISTRIBUTION: Throughout the northwestern United States east to North and South Dakota, and south along the western side of the Rockies.

MATURE SIZE: 6 to 18 in. (15 to 46 cm) tall and 12 in. (30 cm) wide, but up to 24 in. (60 cm) tall with the flowers.

BLOOMING PERIOD: April to October in most areas. In the deserts, heaviest bloom is in the spring and early summer, with a repeat bloom in the fall.

EXPOSURE: Full sun in all areas, but filtered shade in the deserts prolongs bloom.

HARDINESS: Cold hardy to −10°F (−23°C).

Blanket flower has lanceolate leaves that are cut with deep, widely spaced lobes. The leaves are covered with downy hairs and are dark green to gray-green and up to 3 in. (8 cm) long.

Flowers are showy 2- to 3-in. (5- to 8-cm) heads with long rays that are deep red-brown at the base and yellow along the tip like a wheel with a rim of yellow. Disks are dark brown. The extent and location of the red and yellow vary greatly, and some pure yellow forms are known.

Blanket flower appreciates a fertile, well-drained soil, and while it will grow in rocky soils, it is rarely as vigorous. In the hottest deserts do not allow plants to dry out completely. In milder areas this species is considered drought tolerant. Avoid overhead watering when possible; it mars the foliage and can provide a haven for leaf fungal infections. Flowering is extended dramatically by continuous deadheading of the spent flowers. Cut the entire plant back in the late summer or early winter to rejuvenate it for the following year. Individual plants live only two to three years but may reseed freely in most areas.

Gaillardia aristata

Blanket flower is perhaps the easiest perennial I have grown. I plant it from seed in the fall, but you can buy small plants if you prefer. I love to watch the seedlings bloom; they can be so different in flower color and form from year to year. In some years I have had plants with nearly tubular rays; in other years, yellow or red strongly dominates the color scheme.

Some growers offer named selections of this species. A few of the more readily available include 'Bijou', a dwarf from Rocky Mountain populations with bright yellow tips that is 12 in. (30 cm) tall and cold hardy; 'Fanfare' with tubular rays, a riot of red and strong yellow; and 'Indian Yellow' and 'The Sun', pure yellow forms with reddish disks.

Hybrids between this species and the annual species *Gaillardia pulchella* are known as *G. ×grandiflora*. The 'Goblin' series is one selection from this hybridization with a stunning blend of colors, but it is not a reliable perennial in the deserts. Go for the old-fashioned species. You will never be sorry. Butterflies flock to blanket flower, and it also makes a fine cut flower.

Gaura lindheimeri
Gaura, wandflower

Family: Acanthaceae.
Distribution: In the United States in Louisiana and southern and eastern
   Texas at elevations below 4000 ft. (1200 m).
Mature size: 2 to 3 ft. (0.6 to 0.9 m) tall and as wide, up to twice as tall with
   flowering stalks.
Blooming period: May to October, often earlier in the hottest deserts.
Exposure: Full sun or filtered shade in all areas.
Hardiness: Cold hardy to at least 0°F (−18°C).

Gaura is a loosely branched perennial with 2- to 3-in. (5- to 8-cm) oblong leaves.
The leaves are glossy green, often with reddish undertones, and may have widely
spaced, fine teeth.

Flowers are held on tall, loosely branched stalks that can be up to 4 ft. (1.2 m).
Individual flowers are 0.5 to 1.0 in. (1.5 to 2.5 cm) long and in bud are enclosed
in a deep pink bract. When opened, the corolla is white to pale pink and fades to
pink. Flowers open intermittently along the stalk so that, while there may not be
a great number of flowers at one time, the bloom extends over a long time.

Gaura is best grown in well-amended, well-drained soils. In areas that are
hot and dry or in soils that are not abundantly fertile a generous application of
mulch in the summer is helpful. Within its native range, gaura grows well with
no supplemental water. Plants should be left in place once established; they have
a long taproot that makes transplanting difficult and often unsuccessful.

The use of gaura as an ornamental has had a rise-and-fall history. In the
beginning, selections were made chiefly based on better or longer flowering and
whether they were closer to pure white. In 1995 Oregon nurseryman Baldassare
Mineo introduced 'Siskiyou Pink', which was an early pure pink cultivar.
Since then, a veritable explosion of gaura cultivars and selections has erupted.
'Siskiyou Pink' is recognized as having all pink flowers that fade to white and
foliage that is strongly marked with red. 'Whirling Butterflies', another of the
more or less older selections, is a name used to describe plants with somewhat
larger-than-average flowers on somewhat shorter stalks. Both names have been
misapplied, misused, and abandoned with a carelessness that is both stunning
and repetitious. True versions are easy to recognize; many inferior plants masquerade under these names.

An Australian breeder, Howard Bently, has developed a line of selections that
are lovely and distinctive. 'Crimson Butterflies' grows into a tight 18- to 24-in.

Gaura lindheimeri

(46- to 60-cm) tall plant with dark rose-red flowers and foliage and stems that are dark red as well. The flowering stalks are short, barely rising over the foliage. 'Sunny Butterflies' has similar stature, but the foliage and stems are not as red, the flowers are pink, and the foliage gray-green with a white edge. 'Blushing Butterflies' is the same size with soft pink flowers and dark green leaves.

'Passionate Pink', another selection from Baldassare Mineo, has darker pink flowers above reddish-green foliage. Both it and a white upright selection known as 'So White' are tall, 30 in. (76 cm) and 48 in. (120 cm), respectively. Many of these upright forms are the offspring of an older selection, 'Dauphin', that is rigidly upright, over 4 ft. (1.2 m) tall, and bears pink flowers that fade to white.

Many more selections and names exist, but the trend is definitely toward tighter, more compact plants with shorter flowering stalks as well as longer or more persistent flowering. A dozen or more selections are currently under evaluation around the country, and gardeners can expect to see many of them come to the market soon.

Gaura mixes well with a wide array of other perennials or shrubs. Its light texture is welcome against hard edges such as walls or fences, and its long blooming period makes it valuable to extend the season in a bed. Plant generously to get the most impact from the high wands holding the delicate flowers.

Glandularia bipinnatifida

Glandularia bipinnatifida
Plains verbena, Dakota vervain

Synonym: *Verbena bipinnatifida* var. *bipinnatifida*.

FAMILY: Verbenaceae.

DISTRIBUTION: In the United States in a wide swath from Wyoming, Colorado, and South Dakota south to Oklahoma, Missouri, Texas, and Louisiana and west to Arizona and New Mexico at elevations from 5000 to 10,000 ft. (1500 to 3000 m). In Mexico in Chihuahua, Coahuila, Nuevo León, Durango, and San Luis Potosí south to Oaxaca.

MATURE SIZE: Stems 6 to 18 in. (15 to 46 cm) tall that then fall and spread up to 24 in. (60 cm) wide.

BLOOMING PERIOD: March to October.

EXPOSURE: Full sun or filtered sun, with protection from afternoon sun in the deserts.

HARDINESS: Cold hardy to 0°F (−18°C).

Plains verbena is a mat-forming species with narrow leaves, 1.0 to 1.5 in. (2.5 to 4 cm) long. The leaves are separated into distinct lobes that are cut again, giving them a fernlike appearance. Leaf color is variable from soft, gray-green to bright green.

The purple flowers are tiny and crammed into a rounded head that is 0.5 in. (1.5 cm) wide. They continue to grow up the flowering stalks and what began as a rounded flower head may end the season looking like an elongated thumb.

Plains verbena prefers alkaline soils that are rocky or otherwise extremely well drained. Its mat-forming habit makes it useful as both a groundcover and a ground stabilizer on gentle slopes or in rocky areas subject to erosion. It is a short-lived plant, usually about three years, but it reseeds freely and will remain in the garden for many years.

Glandularia gooddingii
Goodding's verbena, desert vervain

Synonym: *Verbena gooddingii.*
FAMILY: Verbenaceae.
DISTRIBUTION: In the United States in Southern California, Nevada, and Utah to Arizona, New Mexico, and western Texas at elevations below 5000 ft. (1500 m). In Mexico in Baja California and Sonora.
MATURE SIZE: 12 to 24 in. (30 to 60 cm) tall and spreading up to 15 in. (38 cm) wide.
BLOOMING PERIOD: February to April, continuing to October in milder areas.
EXPOSURE: Full sun in all areas, but filtered shade or morning sun is best in the deserts.
HARDINESS: Cold hardy to at least 10°F (−12°C).

Goodding's verbena is a mat-forming species with 1- to 2-in. (2.5- to 5.0-cm) leaves that are broadly ovate and barely lobed. Leaves are a soft, mossy green covered with fine hairs.

Flowers are tiny and are held in dense heads that are 0.5 to 1.0 in. (1.5 to 2.5 cm) and range in color from pale lavender to pink. They are also gently fragrant.

In milder areas this verbena is drought tolerant and grows with little extra care. In the hottest deserts it grows best with regular irrigation while in bloom. Watering frequency can be reduced to two or three times a month in the summer. Provide a lightly enriched soil with excellent drainage for best results. Tight soils that retain moisture too long will rot out this verbena.

Glandularia gooddingii

Goodding's verbena is told from its near relatives by the wider, less fernlike leaves. It provides a good contrast to more linear or hard-edged plantings. Use it mixed with dry garden species such as cacti or agaves, or blend it with a perennial planting for early spring color. Butterflies are strongly attracted to this species as they are to almost all verbenas.

The trailing nature of many verbenas, this one included, makes them good subjects where they will hang over a wall or drape out of a large pot. While this is a beautiful look, this species will not take the reflected heat of a hot wall in the hottest deserts.

This short-lived perennial of two to three years is not as aggressive about receding as are either plains verbena (*Glandularia bipinnatifida*) or moss verbena (*G. pulchella*). It will need to be renewed every few years. It can also be planted successively for two or three years, thereby allowing an overlap in the life span of the plants.

Glandularia pulchella
Moss verbena

Synonyms: *Verbena pulchella*, *V. pulchella* var. *gracilior*, *V. tenuisecta*.
Family: Verbenaceae.
Distribution: South America, especially Argentina. Naturalized throughout warm regions of the United States.
Mature size: 6 to 12 in. (15 to 30 cm) tall and spreading 2 to 4 ft. (0.6 to 1.2 m) wide.
Blooming period: February to June in all areas, continuing throughout summer in milder areas or in shady desert locations.
Exposure: Full sun, filtered shade, or deep shade.
Hardiness: Leaves are damaged and die back at 25°F (−4°C), but the plant is cold hardy to 15°F (−9°C) and recovers quickly in warm weather.

Glandularia pulchella

Moss verbena is easily recognized by its deep green, finely cut leaves and sprawling habit. The 1-in. (2.5-cm) leaves are deeply cut into lobes, each of which is further incised leaving the leaf to look like filigree. The sprawling stems arise from a central, semiwoody base, and although leaves are congested at the nodes, the nodes are widely spaced.

Flowers are deep purple, occasionally white, tiny, and held in dense, rounded 1-in. (2.5-cm) heads. It is common to find flowers that are bicolored or heads that have both colors.

This is one of the easiest verbenas to grow. Moss verbena will grow in almost any type of soil from rocky to clay, alkaline or not, richly amended or not. It grows best and more lushly with lightly amended, well-drained soil. Watering requirements are equally broad. Plants, even in the deserts, grow on minimal summer watering. With regular summer water, plants continue to bloom and look green and vibrant; without it they shrink into a curled, dormant brownish state. Moss verbena grows well on ambient rainfall in the winter in the deserts, and in all areas the frequency of watering will determine size and in most cases vigor.

Moss verbena reseeds freely, even aggressively, if the conditions are good. I find it is easy to remove unwanted plants by pulling them out in the early spring keeping the ones that fell in a good spot. Because individual plants can get large, unruly, or faded by the end of the summer, pulling out the decrepit and favoring the new seedlings is a good way to maintain a consistent patch.

Although it is common, I am a fan of this verbena. It is so effortless, so pretty, and so forgiving that it is hard to say a bad thing about it. It grows all over my yard in every conceivable condition. I will admit that in the early spring I get tired of removing some of the seedlings, but then high maintenance is often the price of beauty.

Moss verbena makes a good addition to a sparse newly planted area where it fills in the blank spaces quickly. It is also useful to fill in an odd corner or niche that is in need of some color. Because of its sturdiness to dry conditions, it mixes well with succulents. Its small root system and trailing nature make it a natural for a hanging basket or to crawl out of a raised planter.

Heuchera sanguinea
Coral bells, alum root

FAMILY: Saxifragaceae.

DISTRIBUTION: From southern Arizona and New Mexico in the United States at elevations between 4000 and 8000 ft. (1200 to 2440 m) south into Mexico.

MATURE SIZE: 8 to 10 in. (20 to 25 cm) tall and spreading 12 to 15 in. (30 to 38 cm) wide.

BLOOMING PERIOD: March to October, although there is a wide variation based on the selection or cultivar.

EXPOSURE: Filtered shade or deep shade.

HARDINESS: Cold hardy to at least 0°F (−18°C).

Coral bells grows abundant leaves from a woody base. The leaves are nearly round, 2 to 3 in. (5 to 8 cm) wide, often with ruffled or wavy margins. Their abundance and uniformity create the familiar mound or rounded shape. Leaves are deep green, but there is much variation, particularly in selections and cultivars.

The bell-shaped flowers are held 20 to 24 in. (50 to 60 cm) above the foliage on a loose raceme. Flower color ranges from pink to red and white.

Coral bells requires outstanding drainage and attention to its watering needs. Too much water or tight soils causes quick rot of the roots. While it has excellent tolerance to the heat of summer in most areas, it has difficulty with the

extreme heat of the hot-
test deserts, even in the
shade. Water coral bells
regularly throughout the
year; it has only minimal
drought tolerance. Soils
need to be fertile with
sharp drainage, and con-
tinued applications of
compost and/or mulch
are beneficial.

Numerous selections
of this species exist, as
well as hybrids both with
the more widely distrib-
uted *Heuchera rubescens*
and the California native
H. maxima. Color selec-
tions include 'Snow
Angel' and 'June Bride',

Heuchera sanguinea

both of which have white flowers; 'Firefly' with dark red flowers; and 'Raspberry
Regal' with large rosy-red flowers and deep green foliage. Color selections with
different names have been around since the late 19th century, and while many of
those selections may still be grown, they no longer carry their old names. One
of the most popular hybrids (in this case with *H. maxima*), 'Santa Ana Cardinal'
was one of numerous cultivars created by Dale Emery of Santa Barbara Botanic
Garden. It forms 3- to 4-ft. (0.9- to 1.2-m) clumps with 2-ft. (0.6- m) stalks of
rosy-red flowers

Coral bells is outstanding in mass plantings under oaks or other sturdy trees.
Use it generously to increase the impact of its small delicate flowers.

While I find coral bells irresistible for its beauty, it has yet to live successfully
in my Phoenix garden. Good friends in California have provided me many trials, but I cannot vouch for them in my area from personal experience; however,
where summers are mild but moderately dry, coral bells is a gorgeous addition
to the garden.

Hibiscus coulteri

Hibiscus coulteri
Rose mallow, Coulter's hibiscus

FAMILY: Malvaceae.

DISTRIBUTION: In the United States in south-western Texas, southern New Mexico, and southern Arizona from 1500 to 4000 ft. (460 to 1200 m) in elevation. In Mexico in northern Baja California, Sonora, Coahuila, Durango, northern Zacatecas, and Nuevo León.

MATURE SIZE: 3 to 4 ft. (0.9 to 1.2 m) tall and as wide.

BLOOMING PERIOD: April to September, especially in response to moisture.

EXPOSURE: Full sun or filtered sun in all areas.

HARDINESS: Cold hardy to about 20°F (−7°C).

Rose mallow grows a few sturdy stems from a semiwoody base. The 1-in. (2.5-cm) leaves toward the base of the stem tend to be entire or rounded. The leaves higher up the stem are lobed into three sections, almost like a halberd, and are strongly toothed along the margins. Both types of leaves are deep green and widely spaced on the plant.

Flowers are solitary and axillary, occasionally terminal, and 2 in. (5 cm) across. They are yellow to whitish yellow with a deep rose-red throat.

The plant requires excellent drainage but will grow in almost any type of soil. Water intermittently through the summer in the hottest deserts to maintain a steady bloom. In areas with regular summer rainfall, water only during protracted dry spells.

Rose mallow is irresistible when in bloom and nearly invisible when it is not. The plant is so insubstantial, filmy almost, that it works best to blend it with other perennials of similar culture to maximize the lovely bloom.

This species is a charming choice for a small perennial planting where its flowers will be highly visible. It is so drought and heat tolerant that it can be mixed into native plantings or used in areas of the garden that will not receive regular irrigation.

Hibiscus martianus

Heartleaf hibiscus, heartleaf rose
  mallow

Synonym: *Hibiscus cardiophyllus*.
Family: Malvaceae.
Distribution: In the United States
  in southern and western Texas. In
  Mexico in Coahuila, Chihuahua,
  Durango, San Luis Potosí, Nuevo
  León, Tamaulipas, Hidalgo, and
  Puebla below 5600 ft. (1700 m) in
  elevation.
Mature size: 1 to 3 ft. (0.3 to 0.9 m)
  tall and as wide.
Blooming period: May to
  November.
Exposure: Filtered sun or morning
  sun in all areas, as well as full sun
  in mild areas.
Hardiness: Cold hardy to 20°F
  (−7°C).

Hibiscus martianus

Heartleaf hibiscus is a multistemmed plant with a semiwoody base. The leaves
are ovate to triangular with a soft feel, the result of the fine, grayish hairs. The
margins are gently serrated and leaves are 1.25 to 2.75 in. (3 to 7 cm) long.

Flowers are solitary, bright red, and 2 to 3 in. (5 to 8 cm) across. The flowers
are prolific and bloom more or less continuously through the season.

The plant grows in any soil but is sensitive to good drainage. Heavy clay soils
or waterlogged soils will cause it to rot and die quickly. Plants are semideciduous to fully deciduous in the winter, although in frost-free areas they may retain
many of their leaves. Although fairly drought tolerant, particularly in its native
range, it should be watered regularly in the hottest deserts during the summer.

Heartleaf hibiscus is so stunning it makes a dashing statement in any mixed
planting. Hummingbirds are strongly attracted to it, so place it where you can
enjoy their visits. So much color in partial or full shade is welcome in hot, dry
gardens and using heartleaf hibiscus generously just increases the fun.

Justicia brandegeeana

Justicia brandegeeana
Shrimp plant

FAMILY: Acanthaceae.
DISTRIBUTION: Mexico.
MATURE SIZE: 2 to 3 ft. (0.6 to 0.9 m) tall and spreading up to 6 ft. (1.8 m) wide.
BLOOMING PERIOD: September to November in the deserts, although there may be a short spring bloom. In milder areas, bloom is throughout the summer.
EXPOSURE: Filtered sun or morning sun only in the deserts, full sun or filtered sun in milder climates, particularly coastal California.
HARDINESS: Leaves are damaged at 25°F (−4°C), but the plant is hardy to 10°F (−12°C) and recovers quickly from cold damage.

Shrimp plant is a weak-stemmed perennial whose brittle green stems support widely spaced lanceolate leaves. Leaves are 1.0 to 1.5 in. (2.5 to 4.0 cm) long and thin.

Flowers are held in terminal, axillary clusters. Although the tubular corolla is white, it is almost entirely enclosed in large, overlapping, showy bracts that range in color from pink to deep burnt orange. The bracts provide the resemblance to a shrimp's tail and the common name.

I have grown this plant in all kinds of conditions. It is incredibly resilient to soil conditions, growing equally well in fertile, well-drained soils and rocky, native soils. Salty soil or water causes the leaf edges to darken and dry out. Deep irrigation is the best prevention as well as a short-term cure for this condition.

Although shrimp plant grows with modest irrigation and short dry spells, it does best with regular summer irrigation. A heavy mulch helps maintain soil moisture.

The species has a number of named selections, many of which are redundant. A form with white variegated foliage and deep red bracts is known by the horrid name 'Mutant', but similar plants show up in other locations with other names. 'Fruit Salad' has bright chartreuse bracts, white flowers with a pink lip, and green foliage. 'Yellow Queen' and 'Chartreuse' both have bright chartreuse bracts and entirely white flowers.

Because of its sprawling habit, shrimp plant is a fine choice for an out-of-the-way corner or place that needs to be filled up. Use it under woody shrubs or small trees, in the wells of fruit trees, or as part of a mixed perennial planting. Hummingbirds are strongly attracted to its flowers.

Justicia californica
Chuparosa

FAMILY: Acanthaceae.

DISTRIBUTION: In the United States in southeastern California and southwestern Arizona at elevations below 2500 ft. (800 m). In Mexico in Baja California, Sonora, and northwestern Sinaloa.

MATURE SIZE: 3 to 4 ft. (0.9 to 1.2 m) tall, occasionally to 6 ft. (1.8 m), and spreading from 3 to 12 ft. (0.9 to 3.7 m) wide.

BLOOMING PERIOD: October to May.

EXPOSURE: Full sun even in the deserts.

HARDINESS: Leaves and stems can be damaged at 28°F (−2°C), and the plant dies to the ground at 20°F (−7°C) but recovers quickly once the weather warms.

Chuparosa is a fine-stemmed plant that often appears to have no leaves. The small leaves, less than 1 in. (2.5 cm) long, are bright green, but deciduous in both cold and dry conditions.

Flowers are clustered in axillary groups at the ends of the stems. They are thin, tubular, up to 1 in. (2.5 cm) long, and bright red to red-orange.

In nature, chuparosa grows in sandy washes and gullies, and this is a good indication of the conditions under which it thrives. Grow it with excellent drainage and lightly amended soils, and it will thrive. With too much shade, rich soils, or poor drainage, it quickly becomes chlorotic and suffers from root rots.

This species is often slow to start after transplant, but once it is established grows quickly to the dimensions listed above. Although extremely drought tolerant, chuparosa has better form and color if it is watered every two to three weeks through the summer.

Justicia californica

A few selections from gardens in California have never become common: from Theodore Payne Foundation a yellow form with good color called 'Tilden', and from Rancho Santa Ana Botanic Garden a charming bicolored form called 'Tequila Sunrise'. Both are lovely and highly superior to the faded yellow form that is both unnamed and unremarkable but is frequently found in the trade.

Hummingbirds are especially fond of this species and seek it out whenever it is planted in the garden. We, too, can enjoy it. The flowers are edible and taste like cucumbers.

Chuparosa is a fine choice for a native wildflower planting, as a softening influence on a dry succulent garden, or to complement a pool or patio planting. Placing it near a seating area will offer many hours of delightful spying on the hummingbirds for which it is named.

Justicia candicans
Red justicia, Arizona water willow

FAMILY: Acanthaceae.

DISTRIBUTION: In the United States in southern Arizona and New Mexico at elevations from 1500 to 3500 ft. (460 to 1100 m). In Mexico in Sonora, Sinaloa, and western Chihuahua.

MATURE SIZE: 3 to 4 ft. (0.9 to 1.2 m) tall and as wide.

BLOOMING PERIOD: November to April, but intermittently throughout the year.

EXPOSURE: Filtered shade or morning sun in the deserts, full sun or light shade elsewhere.

HARDINESS: Cold hardy to at least 20°F (−7°C).

Red justicia is an erect plant whose countless tan to brown stems become woody at the base. The pale green, ovate leaves are covered in fine hairs and end in an acute tip. Leaves range from 1 to 3 in. (2.5 to 8.0 cm) long and are deeply congested along the stem.

Justicia candicans (Mary Irish)

The flowers are in axillary clusters in the top half of the stems. Each one is almost entirely enclosed in bright green, threadlike bracts with the 1-in. (2.5-cm) tubular, deep red-orange flowers peeking out.

This plant grows best in fertile, well-drained soils with a deep layer of mulch on the roots. It is able to accept a wide range of watering regimens, but to maintain the best form and continued flowering it must be watered regularly through the summer, particularly in the deserts.

Pruning is difficult to time and perform on this plant. Although the plant can occasionally be sheared to the ground if necessary, it takes a full season of growth to return to its best form. It is much better and less traumatic to the looks of the plant to prune out old stems from the base to both reduce the height of the plant and to tidy it up. Light pruning along the edges or the top will increase the plant's density. Although pruning can be done at any time, fall is the best time because it is the beginning of a long growing season for this species.

I cannot imagine why this species is not in everyone's backyard. It is the single most reliable blooming desert plant that I know of—it seems always to be in bloom. Hummingbirds love it, more than most other justicias save chuparosa.

When I first started growing and selling desert and arid-adapted perennials, red justicia carried the name *Justicia ovata* but that was quickly corrected to

J. candicans. The old name still crops up from time for this species and is frequently listed as a synonym, but the confusion is worse than just synonymy and the reluctance of some nurseries to adapt to the shifting winds of taxonomy.

The true obsolete name for this species (and therefore a name that can claim synonymy) is *Jacobinia ovata*, having long ago given way to *Justicia candicans*. The plant currently named *Justicia ovata* grows in swamps in the southeastern United States and has purple to blue flowers; it could never be confused with this species.

The color of red justicia is as restless as a sunset. In the morning light it is red, nearly scarlet. In the fading light of the late afternoon, the flowers transform into an eerie burnt orange with the vibrancy of flame.

Red justicia blends with almost any perennial planting. Because of its size and dense form it can be used as an informal hedge to line a walkway or patio area. Its dense form fills up a large container or raised bed. Hummingbirds are wild for it, so place it where they can be viewed and enjoyed.

Justicia spicigera
Mexican honeysuckle

FAMILY: Acanthaceae.
DISTRIBUTION: Throughout Mexico into South America.
MATURE SIZE: 2 to 3 ft. (0.6 to 0.9 m) tall and spreading to 5 ft. (1.5 m) wide.
BLOOMING PERIOD: February to October, but most prolific in late spring.
EXPOSURE: Full sun in all areas but the deserts, where filtered shade is best.
HARDINESS: Leaves are damaged at 24°F (−4°C), but the plant is root hardy to
    at least 20°F (−7°C) and recovers quickly.

Mexican honeysuckle is a loosely branched perennial with green to light brown stems. The leaves may be covered with fine hairs or entirely smooth. They are yellow-green, ovate to elliptic with an acute tip, thin, and 1 to 3 in. (2.5 to 8.0 cm) long.

Flowers are in terminal clusters with few individuals. They are tubular and bright orange with a green bract.

Plants vary widely in form; some are upright and semishrubby, and others are sprawling and lax. Regardless of the form, this perennial benefits from a hard prune in late winter or early spring to reinvigorate the plant and to tidy up any winter damage.

Mexican honeysuckle grows best, especially in the deserts, in fertile, well-drained soils. It is not tolerant of highly salty conditions; salt burn is a common late-summer problem in the deserts but can be mitigated by frequent deep irrigation. Water this species weekly throughout the summer in the deserts and during prolonged dry spells in summer rainfall areas to maintain good health and form and a strong bloom.

Justicia spicigera

This species has quickly become popular in much of the low desert, and I must admit I wonder why. The shade of orange is garish and difficult to use, and I am not attracted to the combination of the yellowish leaves and orange flowers. It is, however, a great favorite with hummingbirds. Because it sprawls and crawls so well, it will quickly fill up a shady spot in the garden.

Lantana montevidensis
Trailing lantana, weeping lantana

FAMILY: Verbenaceae.
DISTRIBUTION: Brazil, Uruguay, and Argentina. Naturalized in the United States in California, Texas, Louisiana, Alabama, Georgia, and Florida, through Central America and the West Indies.
MATURE SIZE: 18 in. (46 cm) tall and spreading up to 6 ft. (1.8 m) wide.
BLOOMING PERIOD: March to October.
EXPOSURE: Full sun in all areas, as well as filtered shade in the deserts.
HARDINESS: Leaves will freeze at 32°F (0°C), but the plant is root hardy to around 25°F (−4°C).

Lantana montevidensis

As the name suggests, trailing lantana is a low-growing perennial with extended stems that allow it to spread over a wide area. The stems are thin and semiwoody, especially toward the base, and feel rough.

Leaves are 1.0 to 1.5 in. (2.5 to 4.0 cm) long, lanceolate with a dimpled or quilted surface. The surface is covered with sharp hairs giving it a rough, irritating touch. Leaves often have a pungent aroma when crushed.

Flowers are tiny and held in rounded heads that are 0.5 in. (1.5 cm) wide or less. They range in color from deep purple to lavender or white.

Like all lantanas, this species loves the heat and will bloom throughout the hottest part of the summer even in the hottest deserts. It is not particular about soil, growing in rough, rocky native soil or fine garden soil, but does best with moderate, regular watering throughout the summer. It is at least partially, if not fully, deciduous in the winter and survives well on natural rainfall during that time. Leaves will turn purple to brown-purple at the slightest frost but recover quickly when temperatures warm.

Where whiteflies are common or severe, they can damage or defoliate the plant in large infestations. Otherwise this species is not bothered by most disease or pest problems.

Trailing lantana makes a charming ground cover. Use it to fill odd or difficult spaces or let it hang over a raised planter. It is a graceful, long-flowering choice for a hanging pot. In congenial locations, it forms enough of a mat to be an excellent groundcover.

A few named selections are known: 'White Lightning', which is white; 'Imperial Purple', which is purple with a prominent white eye; and 'Lavender Swirl', which has flowers that begin white and fade to purple or lavender with all colors on the plant at once.

Numerous named hybrids with the shrubby and commonly grown *Lantana camara* are available. Many have retained the crawling habit of trailing lantana and include 'New Gold', which is a sterile, garish gold-yellow; 'Silver Mound', a lovely, but not often used, cultivar with white flowers and a golden eye; 'Lemon Drop', which has yellowish white flowers; and 'Malan's Gold', with yellow variegated foliage and deep rose-red flowers. Some of these hybrids are short shrubby plants, including the extremely heat resistant 'Athens Rose', with flowers that begin magenta and fade to rose, and the 'Patriot' series, which has a wide range of color including reds, oranges, pinks, and corals, and numerous others.

In gardens, the genus *Lantana* is sadly restricted to these two species, and occasionally *L. horrida* in Texas, but dozens of outstanding uncommon or rare species in the trade could be much more widely used. Two in particular come to mind. *Lantana trifolia*, the popcorn lantana, is familiar to many southern gardeners. This delightful perennial has long, linear, deep green leaves and small, purple flowers. The glory of the species is the large purple fruit that is long persistent on the plant. Another species, *L. mexicana*, also has deep green leaves topped by small white flowering heads that tend to elongate out the flowering stalk as it ages. This species is excellent in filtered shade in the desert and makes a great addition to dry, perennial gardens.

Lavandula dentata
French lavender

FAMILY: Lamiaceae.
DISTRIBUTION: Algeria, Arabian Peninsula, Balearic Islands, Morocco, southern and eastern Spain, Tenerife, and Yemen.
MATURE SIZE: 2 to 3 ft. (0.6 to 0.9 m) tall and nearly as wide.
BLOOMING PERIOD: February to April in the deserts, but throughout summer in milder climates.
EXPOSURE: Full sun even in the deserts.
HARDINESS: Cold hardy to 20°F (−7°C).

French lavender is a shrubby perennial with many sturdy stems growing from a woody base. Stems often become larger and firmly woody as they age.

Lavandula dentata

The leaves are 1.0 to 1.5 in. (2.5 to 4.0 cm) long, deep green to gray-green, with well-defined crimps along the margin. They are powerfully aromatic with the familiar lavender fragrance.

Flowers are held on tall, naked, square stems high above the foliage and range in color from deep indigo to pale lavender and sometimes white. The flowers are held within the bracts, and a few flowerless bracts are erect at the top of the spike like a feather in a hat.

Like many natives of the Mediterranean, French lavender is a winter- or cool-season grower that needs a dry summer to thrive. It prefers an alkaline, rocky or exceptionally well-drained location. Such a site is not difficult to provide in the deserts, but in areas with regular summer rain, sharp drainage is extremely important. I have grown this species with and without irrigation, and it does fine either way. When grown without regular irrigation in the deserts, it should be watered intermittently through the summer, perhaps once every two to three weeks. My solution for plants like this is to place them near a source of water; that is usually sufficient to meet their watering needs.

Pruning lavenders can be trying. Prune only if necessary and then only in the fall as they begin to grow. It is best to take small amounts at the ends if you want to tidy up the plant or make it fuller. Hard or severe pruning to the woody stems can result in a plant taking years, if ever, to regrow and recover. Never prune French lavender in the late spring or the summer; the exposed areas easily sunburn, and because the plant is virtually dormant in the summer, it doesn't recover well.

Many forms are known, chiefly based on flower color, but 'Goodwin Creek Gray' has much grayer, almost white, foliage. This beautiful selection provides a bright spot in any dry garden.

Lavandula multifida
Fern-leaf lavender

FAMILY: Lamiaceae.
DISTRIBUTION: Spain, Portugal, and Italy.
MATURE SIZE: 12 to 18 in. (30 to 46 cm) tall and
   spreading 3 to 4 ft. (0.9 to 1.2 m) wide, but 3
   to 4 ft. (0.9 to 1.2 m) tall with the flowering
   stalks.
BLOOMING PERIOD: February to April is the
   heaviest bloom; however, it may begin as
   early as October and often has intermittent
   bloom in the summer.
EXPOSURE: Full sun or filtered shade in the deserts, full sun elsewhere.
HARDINESS: Cold hardy to at least 25°F (−4°C).

Lavandula multifida

Fern-leaf lavender has a knotty heritage. The true
species has gray-green foliage marked by coarse
but sparse hairs, and is lobed so deeply it resem-
bles fern; however, a form variously known as *Lavandula multifida* var. *canariensis*, *L.* 'Multifida', or *L.* 'California' has lobed gray-green leaves without the
hairs, is common in California horticulture, and is the form sold in the region.

By whatever name, this is an extraordinary perennial for hot, dry gardens.
The numerous stems are so closely held that you think you could walk over the
mounded plant. It has a tendency to become wider as it matures.

The leaves are gray-green and deeply lobed; they are indeed fernlike. Leaves
are 2 to 4 in. (5 to 10 cm) long and vary along the stems in both shape and size.

The flowers are held on long, naked, square stalks up to 12 in. (30 cm) above
the foliage and are so numerous that they hide the foliage when in full bloom.
Flowers are in congested terminal racemes and are deep blue to indigo. They are
not particularly fragrant and last on the plant for weeks.

Fern-leaf lavender prefers well-drained, alkaline soils that are not too
enriched. Water weekly in the summer to maintain good form and to encourage summer flowering, but take care not to overwater the plant or it will rot and
develop a floppy, loose appearance.

Prune the spent flowering stalks anytime, but only prune the stems in the early
spring or early fall, and then only if damaged. This lavender has excellent natural form and rarely needs pruning just for shape.

Lavandula stoechas

Lavandula stoechas
Spanish lavender

FAMILY: Lamiaceae.
DISTRIBUTION: Southwestern Europe, Near East, and North Africa.
MATURE SIZE: 17 to 36 in. (43 to 90 cm) tall and half as wide.
BLOOMING PERIOD: April to June, occasionally all summer.
EXPOSURE: Full sun even in the deserts.
HARDINESS: Cold hardy to 5°F (−15°C).

Spanish lavender is a compact perennial with numerous, short stems from a woody base. The leaves are deep gray-green, narrow, and linear. The smooth margins roll toward the middle, giving the leaf an even more needlelike appearance.

Flowers are held on flowering stalks up to 8 in. (20 cm) over the foliage. The tubular flowers are embedded within the bracts. At the end of the stalk many showy but flowerless bracts form a colorful tuft. Flowers and these bracts are deep purple, almost black.

Provide regular irrigation during the winter growing season, but water sparingly through the summer. Deep soaks once or twice a month are sufficient. Spanish lavender rarely needs pruning to improve its tight form, but any pruning should be done in the fall just as growth is resumed.

It is important to be careful about mulch with lavenders. Light applications of organic mulch annually, in the early fall, are all the fertilization they need. The mulch should never be deep or allowed to run up the stems of the plants.

Countless color forms and selections of this species are available, particularly in Europe, Australia, and New Zealand. A large number of cultivars from hybridization with the similar *Lavandula viridis* also are known. Many of these forms have larger flowers, and the colors range from light purple-pink to magenta and rose, as well as shades of lavender and purple.

Leonotis nepetifolia
Lion's ear

FAMILY: Lamiaceae.
DISTRIBUTION: Tropical and subtropical Africa.
Naturalized throughout warm regions of the
world including the United States from Texas
and the Gulf Coast states to North Carolina.
MATURE SIZE: 3 to 8 ft. (0.9 to 2.4 m) tall and 3 to
4 ft. (0.9 to 1.2 m) wide.
BLOOMING PERIOD: March to October.
EXPOSURE: Filtered shade or morning sun in all
areas, as well as deep shade in the deserts.
HARDINESS: Cold hardy to 28°F (−2°C).

Leonotis nepetifolia

In most regions where winter freezes are common,
this large herbaceous perennial is an annual that
vigorously reseeds itself. In the deserts and other
warm mild winter areas, it is perennial, returning
year after year from running root stocks.

Lion's ear has numerous, erect, square, rough-textured stems with widely
spaced pairs of leaves. The leaves are more or less triangular, 2 to 5 in. (5 to 13
cm) long. They are deep green to yellowish green, rough to the touch with a
serrated margin.

Flowers are held in densely congested whorls up the stem. During the blooming season the stem continues to grow, and ever more flowering heads are assem-
bled up its length. Each flower is coated with fine hairs, making it velvety to the
touch. The tubular 1- to 2-in. (2.5- to 5-cm) flowers range from a pale apricot
to deep, burnt orange. They are surrounded by a dark green leafy calyx. These
whorls are so tightly packed that they are almost round and the stems rise directly
from the middle of it all.

Two other members of the genus are found horticulturally in the region from
time to time. Lion's tail (*Leonotis leonurus*) is common in California and other
warm regions. The plants have the same form with numerous erect, hairy stems
but rarely grow over 3 ft. (0.9 m) tall. The long leaves are linear and narrow.
Flowers are the same tubular, velvety orange in whorls, but the set has fewer
flowers and has a more open, flattened appearance.

Leonotis menthifolia has the same general growth style but grows a bit shorter, in some areas only to 2.5 ft. (0.8 m) tall. The leaves are gray-green and lobed much like mint leaves. The orange flowers are held in whorls that are much more open than the others, almost like a flattened wheel around the stem.

I have grown all three from time to time and find that lion's ear is the easiest to grow in the deserts. In fact, if you grow it too nicely it becomes a pest, which has happened in benign areas like Hawaii. This species prefers to grow in soils of low fertility with minimal watering. Some of my plants are in deep shade at the back of a large perennial bed trying to find sun through a redbud, a creosote, and a palm; there they bloom and grow sensationally. They are so tall you have to put them in the back of something, both to get the most effect from their flowering and to prevent them from overwhelming the rest of the beds. They are not often watered on purpose.

The other two species were much shorter lived for me and resented being in too much sun. Both of them were better in rich beds with fertile, well-drained soils. They, too, can run away from you in benign climates or with too much water.

Both hummingbirds and butterflies are strongly attracted to this group of African perennials.

Lobelia cardinalis
Cardinal flower, scarlet lobelia

FAMILY: Campanulaceae.

DISTRIBUTION: Widespread throughout the eastern and central portions of the United States, west to the mountains of Texas, New Mexico, Arizona, Southern California, and Nevada at elevations from 2000 to 7500 ft. (600 to 2290 m). Also in northern and eastern Mexico, including Baja California, south to Panama.

MATURE SIZE: 2 to 6 ft. (0.6 to 1.8 m) tall, including the flowering stalks.

BLOOMING PERIOD: April to September, but highly variable depending on elevation and conditions.

EXPOSURE: Filtered shade or deep shade in the deserts, filtered shade in milder areas, full sun only in the mountains or where plants are kept consistently wet.

HARDINESS: Cold hardy to at least 0°F (−18°C).

Cardinal flower has numerous herbaceous stems which are covered with alternate, linear, deep green leaves that are 3 to 6 in. (8 to 15 cm) long.

Flowers are held on tall spikes above the foliage. The narrow tube is divided into two small lobes and three larger ones that are spread widely from the throat. They are deep scarlet red with the pale, often white, stamens extending beyond the lobes.

Cardinal flower is another choice for shady, moist areas or ponds. It performs poorly, becoming chlorotic and weak, when grown without a rich, highly organic soil and permanent moisture. If growing it in sunnier locations provide deep mulch to the roots to prevent it drying out. The subspecies *graminea* is grown throughout the West and occurs naturally in wet seeps, canyons, and mountains valleys, which explains its preference for cool, shady, moist sites.

This species is short lived; three to four years is common. Lift it every few years in the early spring or fall, discard the oldest stems, and replant the young shoots. This will maintain the clump much longer. It can also be propagated by laying a stem on the ground and holding it in place; the plant will root from the leaf nodes.

Lobelia cardinalis (Judy Mielke)

Use cardinal flower near or at the edges of a pond, in a dark, moist corner of a courtyard, or beneath a dense tree like citrus. It is astounding when planted in large numbers so that it fills the site. The flowers are highly attractive to hummingbirds and make fine cut flowers.

Lobelia laxiflora
Mexican lobelia, drooping lobelia

FAMILY: Campanulaceae.

DISTRIBUTION: In the United States in southern Arizona at elevations from 4000 to 5000 ft. (1200 to 1500 m). In Mexico in the southern half of Baja California, through Oaxaca and San Luis Potosí south into Central America.

MATURE SIZE: 2 to 3 ft. (0.6 to 0.9 m) tall and as wide.

BLOOMING PERIOD: April to September, but may bloom intermittently throughout the year.

Lobelia laxiflora

EXPOSURE: Full, but not reflected, sun or filtered shade in all but the deserts, where filtered shade or deep shade is preferred.

HARDINESS: Cold hardy to 10°F (−12°C).

Mexican lobelia is a loose collection of herbaceous stems from a semiwoody base. It spreads readily from rhizomes. The species varies widely over its range, but the forms that do best and are most commonly offered in the region are from var. *angustifolia*.

The leaves are linear with a sharp tip, dark dusky green, and 4 to 5 in. (10 to 13 cm) long.

Flowers are held on tall spikes above the foliage. They are tubular and are red, sometimes yellow, with a yellow throat. The amounts of red and yellow vary greatly from one individual to the next.

Mexican lobelia performs well in a wider range of conditions in the garden than its close relative, cardinal flower (*Lobelia cardinalis*). If kept well watered and heavily mulched, it will grow in full sun, even in the deserts; however, it is often easier to care for and requires less water if grown in light, filtered shade. It does best in fertile soils that are well amended with organic matter and are well drained.

Cutting it back in the late winter or early spring will help reinvigorate the plant. After lifting the plant, you can easily separate newer shoots to replant and keep it good condition, or have gifts for your gardening friends.

Outside the deserts, and especially in the Mediterranean climate of Southern California, it has a tendency to become invasive. This is not the case in the inland deserts.

Use Mexican lobelia in a shady garden to fill in a corner of a bed or an area that needs a lift of color. Its long blooming period and showy flowers let it light up an otherwise dull or uninteresting spot. Hummingbirds are strongly attracted to the flowers.

Lotus rigidus
Desert rock pea, shrubby deer vetch

FAMILY: Fabaceae.

DISTRIBUTION: In the United States in southeastern California, Arizona, southern Nevada, and southwestern Utah below 5000 ft. (1500 m) in elevation.

MATURE SIZE: 1.5 to 3.0 ft. (0.5 to 0.9 m) tall and nearly as wide.

BLOOMING PERIOD: March to May.

EXPOSURE: Full sun or filtered shade.

HARDINESS: Cold hardy to 0°F (−18°C).

Lotus rigidus (Mountain States Wholesale Nursery)

Deer vetch is a deceptive plant with thin, wiry stems and sparse leaves that make it look like a green wisp in the garden. Leaves are tiny, 0.5 in. (1.5 cm) long, and composed of three to five even smaller oblong leaflets. The leaves are both sparse on the plant and ephemeral, dropping at the first sign of drought.

Flowers are pea shaped with a curving hood and an elongated banner. They are from 0.5 to 1.0 in. (1.5 to 2.5 cm) long and begin bright yellow with orange nectar guides and age to dull orange. Flowers at all ages on the plant give an individual a multicolored look.

Deer vetch grows best in dry, rocky conditions with only intermittent supplemental water in the summer. If winter rainfall is insufficient to maintain leaves and flowers, supplement with deep soaks. Even without the leaves the plant has a delicate, twiggy look that blends well with succulents or provides interest when backed up by a boulder or wall.

Malvaviscus arboreus var. drummondii

Malvaviscus arboreus var. drummondii
Turk's cap, bleeding heart

Synonym: *Malvaviscus drummondii*.
FAMILY: Malvaceae.
DISTRIBUTION: In the United States in the Gulf Coast states and in Texas in the western Edwards Plateau and through the Rio Grande Valley. Widespread in Mexico and the West Indies, including Cuba.
MATURE SIZE: 3 to 4 ft. (0.9 to 1.2 m) tall and up to 5 ft. (1.5 m) wide.
BLOOMING PERIOD: May to November, but year-round in frost-free areas.
EXPOSURE: Full sun or filtered shade in all areas but the deserts, where only filtered shade is possible.
HARDINESS: Cold hardy to 20°F (−7°C) and recovers quickly from damage.

Turk's cap is an open-branched perennial with stems rising from a semiwoody base. In the southern parts of its range or in frost-free areas it can grow into a 10-ft. (3-m) shrub. It is rarely this tall within the region, however.

Leaves are large, 4 to 6 in. (10 to 15 cm) long, and range from dark, dusky green to dull green with fuzzy to rough surfaces. Most leaves are roughly heart shaped with wavy or slightly toothed margins.

The flowers are vivid red and the corolla lobes are wrapped around the long extended pistil. The style is surrounded near its base by clustered, stalkless anthers. In most forms the flowers are held upright, but in others the flowers fall gracefully. White- and pink-flowering forms are also available.

Turk's cap is a splendid choice for the shade in any dry garden. It will grow in almost any type of soil from rocky, alkaline ones to the thick clays of the Gulf Coast. It is equally accepting of a wide array of watering regimens. In the deserts, it should be watered regularly through the summer but needs much less frequent watering during the winter. In areas with regular summer rainfall, it may need supplemental irrigation only during extended dry spells.

Turk's cap can extend long stems from time to time that have only a few leaves. These stems can be cut back anytime during the hot weather to tidy up the plant or encourage a tighter form. Because the plant is somewhat cold tender, avoid pruning it in the late fall or winter.

It is always a delight to find plants that bloom exuberantly in the dry shade, and Turk's cap is one of the best. Use it in the back of a shady bed to form a background for shorter species. Mix it with other perennials and shrubs in a garden designed to attract hummingbirds, which are strongly drawn to the flowers.

Melampodium leucanthum
Blackfoot daisy

FAMILY: Asteraceae.

DISTRIBUTION: In the United States from Colorado and Kansas to Arizona, New Mexico, and Texas at elevations from 1700 to 8000 ft. (520 to 2440 m). In Mexico in northern Sonora, Chihuahua, and Coahuila.

MATURE SIZE: 6 to 12 in. (15 to 30 cm) tall and spreading 12 to 18 in. (30 to 46 cm) wide.

BLOOMING PERIOD: March to October.

EXPOSURE: Full sun or filtered shade in all areas.

HARDINESS: Cold hardy to 0°F (−18°C).

This tidy, nearly round plant is small, but its profuse bloom makes a grand display in the garden. The leaves are gray-green, softly hairy, and 0.5 to 1.5 in. (1.5 to 4.0 cm) long. They are linear and may have either straight or wavy margins, often with shallow lobes.

The flowering heads are 1 in. (2.5 cm) across with less than a dozen white ray flowers and bright yellow disk flowers. They rise on small stalks and cover the foliage when in full bloom. Plants look like a white bouquet in the ground and as an added bonus have a delicate, sweet fragrance.

Blackfoot daisy is a hardy plant that likes to grow quite dry; it performs best in alkaline, rocky soils. Failing that, grow it in perfectly drained soils. Water carefully and sparingly, even in the deserts. Overwatering is the premier reason for failure with this species. In the summer, water two or three times a month in the deserts; that is sufficient to keep plants fit. Water much less frequently where there is regular summer rainfall. Plants are not long lived, typically living four to

Melampodium leucanthum

five years, but reseed in congenial circumstances thereby maintaining the planting over a longer time.

Prune occasionally in the late winter to tidy up the plant, or in the late spring to remove spent flowers. Otherwise, this is a remarkably carefree perennial for a dry garden.

The tidy form and small stature make this species a good choice to mix with smaller succulents or annual wildflower plantings. Use it as a loose border, or plant it generously to fill a dry, hot corner. Butterflies are strongly attracted to this species, making it a charming addition to a dry butterfly garden.

Mimulus cardinalis
Crimson monkey flower

FAMILY: Scrophulariaceae.
DISTRIBUTION: In the United States throughout the mountains of California, Oregon, Utah, Nevada, northern and central Arizona, and western New Mexico. In Mexico in the mountains of Sonora, Sinaloa, and Chihuahua at elevations from 2000 to 8500 ft. (600 to 2600 m).
MATURE SIZE: 10 to 30 in. (25 to 76 cm) tall.
BLOOMING PERIOD: March to October.
EXPOSURE: Filtered shade to deep shade throughout the region.
HARDINESS: Cold hardy to below 0°F (−18°C).

Stems are coarse and covered with fine straight hairs. The deep green stalkless leaves are obovate to oblong with a widely serrated margin. Flowers are bright scarlet, up to 2 in. (5 cm) long, and enclosed with a narrow, green, hairy bract. Rare yellow forms exist in nature but these have not made it into horticulture.

Every desert garden has an odd, wet spot, often in the shade. If you don't have one, you might want to create such a place just to have this exquisite streamside species and its relative, yellow monkey flower (*Mimulus guttatus*). Crimson monkey flower must have its roots wet all the time to thrive and prefers not be in full or unrelieved sun. Hummingbirds are strongly attracted to it.

Mimulus cardinalis

Mimulus guttatus
Yellow monkey flower

FAMILY: Scrophulariaceae.
DISTRIBUTION: In the United States from Washington to North and South Dakota, then south to New Mexico and Arizona at elevations from 500 to 9500 ft. (150 to 2900 m).
MATURE SIZE: 1 to 2 ft. (0.3 to 0.6 m) tall and spreading at least that wide.
BLOOMING PERIOD: March to August.
EXPOSURE: Filtered shade or deep shade throughout the region.
HARDINESS: Cold hardy to at least 10°F (−12°C).

In nature, yellow monkey flower is often only annual, but with regularly watering and a mild winter climate, it becomes perennial. As the stems rise and then quickly fall over, the plant roots along, covering larger areas than the size of the plant might suggest.

Leaves are oval with a wavy, slightly toothed margin. In some individuals the leaf is deeply lobed. Both smooth-leaved and fine, hairy leaved forms are known.

Flowers are held on 6- to 8-in. (15- to 20-cm) flowering stalks. The calyx is prominent and bell shaped while the corolla is tubular with the top two lobes erect

Mimulus guttatus

and the lower three widely spreading. Flowers are bright yellow, often with red dots on the lobes or throat, and the throat is congested with yellow hairs.

Yellow monkey flower relishes a location that is consistently moist, rich with organic material, and in light sun. In these situations it will bloom continuously through the summer and light up dark spots well. Use it near a pond, in a dark spot beneath citrus or other dense trees, or anywhere the conditions can be maintained. Because it spreads so readily, yellow monkey flower is a fine choice to fill in an odd corner under a deep overhang or where a wall makes dense shade.

Mirabilis jalapa
Four o'clock, marvel of Peru

FAMILY: Nyctaginaceae.
DISTRIBUTION: Tropical South America. Widely cultivated and naturalized throughout the tropical areas of Central and South America, as well as moderate climates in Mexico and the southern United States.
MATURE SIZE: 2 to 3 ft. (0.6 to 0.9 m) tall and as wide.
BLOOMING PERIOD: April to November.
EXPOSURE: Full sun to filtered shade throughout the region, but filtered shade or even deep shade is best in the deserts.
HARDINESS: Leaves and stems can be damaged at 24°F (−4.5°C), but the plant recovers quickly in spring.

Plants grow from a large tuberous black root and as they age send up ever wider, green succulent stems. The lanceolate leaves are 2 to 4 in. (5 to 10 cm) long, thin, and deep green.

Flowers are clustered within a spreading involucre and bloom in a wide array of colors from pink to magenta, white, and yellow. They derive the common name "four o'clock" from the habit of opening in the late evening, staying open through the night. On cloudy days flowers remain open all day.

Four o'clock will grow in any kind of soil from native, unamended soils to lush garden soils. It is surprisingly drought tolerant. I water it only when I remember or think of it and it thrives in my garden. Even in the hottest deserts with virtually frost-free winters, four o'clock is at least partially deciduous in the winter. By the time the weather cools, the leaves become so decrepit that I usually cut the entire thing down rather than look at it.

The round black seeds form throughout the summer as the succession of bloom continues, and four o'clock will reseed freely where conditions are favorable. I don't find the seedlings easy to relocate, but this species reseeds so

Mirabilis jalapa

freely that I suggest you grow it from seed planted in the spring where you want the plants to grow.

I brought a pure white strain with me from a neighbor's garden when I left New Orleans. I planted it as a sentimental gesture and was astounded at the plants' ease of care, bountiful summer flowering in the hottest part of the summer, and toughness to desert conditions. The flowers have a delicate sweet fragrance that is magnified on warm, humid nights. I let them go almost wild in a shady bed near the house, where they provide both shade for tender winter growing succulents and a magnificent night show in the summer.

Two principal strains are widely available from seed. 'Jingles' is a somewhat smaller plant with flowers that bloom in a wide array of colors, often on the same plant. 'Broken Colors' also flowers in a wide array of colors, but each flower is splashed erratically with magenta. Packages of mixed color seeds are available wherever seed are sold.

If you find a single color you like and want to maintain it, you should keep a sharp eye on the flowers and pull out any that aren't that color. After a year or two, if you are persistent in removing the "wrong" color, you will have the one you want permanently. This is how my neighbor finally got her white strain and why I won't let another color in my garden dilute it.

Mirabilis multiflora

Mirabilis multiflora
Showy four o'clock, Colorado four o'clock

FAMILY: Nyctaginaceae.
DISTRIBUTION: In the United States from California to Colorado south to Arizona, New Mexico, and Texas at elevations from 2300 to 7500 ft. (690 to 2290 m). In Mexico in Baja California.
MATURE SIZE: 1 to 3 ft. (0.3 to 0.9 m) tall and spreading up to 3 ft. (0.9 m) wide.
BLOOMING PERIOD: April to September.
EXPOSURE: Full sun or filtered shade in all but the hottest deserts, where filtered shade or morning sun is needed.
HARDINESS: Cold hardy to 0°F (−18°C).

Showy four o'clock has loose, unbranched stems that rise from a swollen, pithy root. As the stems elongate and spread, the plant forms a low, gentle mound.

The leaves are firm, almost leathery, ovate to rounded, sometimes heart shaped with an acute tip. They range in color from deep green to blue-green and may be either smooth or sticky.

The flowers occur both in the axils of the leaves or terminal to the stem and may be either solitary or in small dense clusters. The corolla is greatly reduced or missing, but the showy, colorful bracts create the stunning floral display. These papery, bright bracts are colored rose, red, or magenta.

In the hottest deserts, showy four o'clock is a plant for the shade or where it is sheltered from the western sun. It grows best in soils that are perfectly drained, even sandy or rocky soils.

Showy four o'clock is stunning growing alongside a boulder, peeking from under the rocks at the edge of pathway, or finding a tiny hole in the pavement near a doorway or patio edge. Plants are winter deciduous, disappearing entirely until the warm days of the spring bring them back to life.

Odontonema tubiforme
Firespike

Synonym: *Odontonema strictum*.

FAMILY: Acanthaceae.

DISTRIBUTION: From southern Mexico to
Panama at elevations from sea level to 4600 ft.
(1400 m). Naturalized in the United States in
Florida.

MATURE SIZE: 3 to 6 ft. (0.9 to 1.8 m) tall and as
wide.

BLOOMING PERIOD: Late summer through fall,
but may continue all winter in frost-free areas.

EXPOSURE: Filtered shade or deep shade.

HARDINESS: Leaves and stems are damaged or
die at 24°F (−4°C), but the plant is root hardy
to about 16°F (−9°C).

Odontonema tubiforme

The numerous thin, green stems rise from a rhizomatous base. The deep green 4- to 8-in. (10-
to 20-cm) leaves are lanceolate, glossy, with a wavy margin and a hard, crisp
texture.

Flowers are held in a large spike high above the foliage. Each 1-in. (2.5-cm)
flower is a thin, scarlet tube with a tiny opening at the end. The shiny flowers
look as if they were dipped in wax.

Use firespike anywhere that the sun will not hit it directly, particularly in the
deserts. It grows in any kind of soil from rich clay to rocky, native soil. It is
best to provide some supplemental water in the summer, but firespike is remarkably drought tolerant once established. I mix my firespike among four o'clock
(*Mirabilis jalapa*) because both species like the same amount of shade, tolerate
the same casual watering scheme, and firespike blooms when the four o'clock is
cut back for the winter. It is an excellent plant for dry shade, a situation in any
garden that can be deeply challenging.

Finding this species in the desert was a surprise from the past. I knew it well
from New Orleans and Florida where it is a great favorite and a more or less old-
fashioned, pass-along plant. It is grown there into small, colorful hedges.

While I still worked at the Desert Botanical Garden, a dear volunteer came in and handed me a large handful of a plant he had found at his new house growing under a huge pine. He wanted to know its name and when I told him he thought I was a genius, but I thought it was the oddest coincidence to find this long-forgotten favorite from another place and time, here in the desert. I took his donation; the plants grew quickly and easily from cuttings, and a few of them are at home in my desert garden. The volunteer is now sadly gone but those firespikes left him forever in my garden.

Firespike flowers are highly attractive to hummingbirds. The species also attracts queen and many other butterfly species into the garden.

Oenothera caespitosa
Tufted evening primrose

FAMILY: Onagraceae.
DISTRIBUTION: In the United States from Washington and Montana south through Colorado, northern New Mexico, Arizona, and western Texas at elevations from 4000 to 7000 ft. (1200 to 2100 m), sometimes higher. In Mexico in Chihuahua and Baja California.
MATURE SIZE: 8 to 12 in. (20 to 30 cm) tall and 24 in. (60 cm) wide.
BLOOMING PERIOD: April to August.
EXPOSURE: Full sun even in the deserts, where filtered shade is also tolerated.
HARDINESS: Cold hardy to at least 0°F (−18°C).

Tufted evening primrose is a ball of a plant that may be solitary or consist of several rosettes, or heads, that are tightly congested on a nearly invisible stem.

The leaves are lanceolate with sinuous margins that are occasionally distinctly lobed. The leaves are up to 6 in. (15 cm) long and are deep green to gray-green with widely spaced teeth and a prominent midvein that is white or cream, frequently with a pink or reddish tinge. Plants from the northern portions of the range have smooth leaves, while those from the southern part of the range have fine hairs on the surface, making them fuzzy to the touch. Most plants sold in this region have fine velvety leaves. In the coldest areas, plants are deciduous; in warmer regions, they are merely winter dormant.

Flowers are large, up to 6 in. (15 cm) long, white, and fragrant. Often several open at once practically covering the plant. Flowers open late in the day and remain open for only one night. Spent flowers fade to a soft rose-purple.

Tufted evening primrose grows in any well-drained soil, and although quite drought tolerant when mature, continues to bloom through the summer with biweekly summer watering. When grown in full sun in the deserts, it may need watering more frequently during the hottest part of the summer.

Oenothera caespitosa

Tufted evening primrose is a perfect species around which to build a desert night-flowering garden. The slight perfume of the flowers draws in hawk moths and other night pollinators. The crisp form provides excellent contrast to other night-flowering species such as the sprawling sacred datura (*Datura wrightii*), tall four o'clock (*Mirabilis jalapa*), and the rigid upright night-blooming cereus (*Cereus hildmannianus*).

Oenothera macrocarpa
Yellow evening primrose, fluttermill, Missouri primrose

SYNONYM: *Oenothera missouriensis*.
FAMILY: Onagraceae.
DISTRIBUTION: In the United States from Nebraska, Oklahoma, and Illinois south to Mississippi, Tennessee, and northern and central Texas.
MATURE SIZE: 4 to 18 in. (10 to 46 cm) tall and 2 ft. (0.6 m) wide or more.
BLOOMING PERIOD: April to August.
EXPOSURE: Full sun or filtered shade in its range, but filtered shade or deep shade in the deserts.
HARDINESS: Cold hardy to at least 0°F (−18°C).

Yellow evening primrose grows from a woody base with long extended stems. The leaves are narrow and lanceolate with finely toothed margins. They are 2 to 4 in. (5 to 10 cm) long.

The night-opening flowers are bright yellow, with a long, narrow tube up to 4 in. (10 cm) long and 3.5 in. (9 cm) across. The flower buds are marked with pink before they open.

Yellow evening primrose grows best in fertile, well-drained soils. In the deserts, grow it in filtered or deep shade and mulch the roots heavily to keep them cool.

Cut it back severely in the early spring to reinvigorate it and remove any winter damage.

Yellow evening primrose forms a colorful groundcover in the well of dense trees or fills a troublesome dark corner. In cold climates it is deciduous in the winter, but in most of this region it is merely winter dormant.

Oenothera macrocarpa

Oenothera speciosa
Mexican evening primrose, pink evening primrose

Synonym: *Oenothera berlandieri.*

FAMILY: Onagraceae.

DISTRIBUTION: In the United States from Kansas and Missouri south to eastern Texas. Widely cultivated in many areas and naturalized from California to Virginia as well as throughout northeastern Mexico in Coahuila, Chihuahua, Nuevo León, and Zacatecas.

MATURE SIZE: 8 to 24 in. (20 to 60 cm) tall and spreading 1 to 4 ft. (0.3 to 1.2 m) wide.

BLOOMING PERIOD: March to July.

EXPOSURE: Full sun or filtered shade in all areas.

HARDINESS: Cold hardy to 0°F (−18°C).

Mexican evening primrose spreads its thin, weak stems quickly from a rhizomatous base. Leaves are obovate to lanceolate and 1.5 to 4.0 in. (4 to 10 cm) long with widely spaced, sinuous lobes. Leaves may be smooth or hairy and often have undersides or margins tinged with red.

The delicate cup-shaped flowers are 1.0 to 1.5 in. (2.5 to 4.0 cm) across and last only one day. Delicately scented, they range in color from deep pink to pale pink, rarely white, and often with darker venation on the corolla. They are so thin that the flower seems translucent, but that fragility belies the great toughness of this species.

Mexican evening primrose will grow in any soil from deep, clay soils to rocky, unamended desert soils. In most areas, including the deserts, it is best to grow it as dry as possible to prevent its aggressive spreading and reseeding. When watered regularly it remains evergreen, while it is summer dormant when grown under drier conditions.

This species is an excellent groundcover, particularly for erosion control. Use it to fill up a dry corner, provide spring color to a hot area, or

Oenothera speciosa

as part of a mixed wildflower planting. It has been used occasionally as a lawn replacement and works well in areas where there is no foot traffic. This type of use requires regular and consistent watering to keep the plants green. To maintain such a planting, mow Mexican evening primrose in the early spring and fall to keep it tidy.

Named selections of this species show up from time to time. 'Pink Petticoats' is pink with a pleasant fragrance; 'Roseum' and 'Rosea' are both pale pink; 'Siskiyou' has 3-in. (8-cm) pink flowers on somewhat smaller plants; 'Woodside White' has petals that are whiter than average. Frankly these differences are minute; most plants of whatever name look pretty much the same except 'Woodside White'.

This species was long sold as *Oenothera berlandieri*, and although that name is no longer valid, plants are still offered under it. Someone, somewhere, decided that if the name was changed to *O. speciosa*, it must really mean *O. speciosa* var. *berlandieri*, a name that has never had any botanical standing.

Oenothera stubbei (Wynn Anderson)

Oenothera stubbei
Saltillo evening primrose

FAMILY: Onagraceae.
DISTRIBUTION: Mexico from Chihuahua to
Nuevo León.
MATURE SIZE: 5 to 8 in. (13 to 20 cm) tall and
spreading up to 6 ft. (1.8 m) wide.
BLOOMING PERIOD: May to September.
EXPOSURE: Filtered shade in the deserts, full sun
in less harsh conditions.
HARDINESS: Cold hardy to 10°F (−12°C).

Saltillo evening primrose is a low-growing species
that rises from a tuberous root. The long stems
are interrupted by 3-in. (8-cm) long, deep green
leaves that cluster together to resemble a rosette.

The yellow flowers are up to 2 in. (5 cm) long
with a long tube.

This species does best when protected from
afternoon sun, especially in the deserts. Provide a well-drained but enriched soil.
In the hottest part of the summer, water about once a week, especially in the hottest deserts.

I first grew this species a long time ago in the rough beds in the front yard
where the soil is unamended, the watering intermittent, and the sun intense. The
species was introduced to the area under the name "Baja primrose." It subse-
quently turned out that the plants were not of this species but of the coastal
native *Oenothera drummondii*. Those first plants seduced me with their name, but
they died the first summer. The true *O. stubbei*, now grown in the region, is much
better suited to the deserts. It does best with some shade, especially protection
from the western sun of the hottest deserts, and with regular summer irrigation
and a moderately fertile soil.

Saltillo evening primrose is a lovely yellow-flowering groundcover. Use it
generously to form a wide-spreading cover, although it is not as aggressive as
some of its kin.

Pavonia lasiopetala

Rock pavonia, rose mallow, Wright's mallow

FAMILY: Malvaceae.

DISTRIBUTION: In the United States only in
central and southern Texas. In Mexico in
Coahuila and Nuevo León.

MATURE SIZE: 1 to 3 ft. (0.3 to 0.9 m) tall and as
wide.

BLOOMING PERIOD: March to November.

EXPOSURE: Filtered shade or light shade.

HARDINESS: Cold hardy to at least 10°F
(−12°C).

Pavonia lasiopetala

Rock pavonia has numerous irregular stems
growing from a woody base. The leaves are dark
green, more or less three lobed, with serrated
margins, and covered with minute white hairs that
are rough to the touch. Leaves range from 1.0 to
2.5 in. (2.5 to 6.4 cm) long.

The 1.5-in. (4-cm) pink flowers open in the morning and close in the afternoon heat. They are solitary in the leaf axils.

Grow rock pavonia in fertile, alkaline, well-drained soils. In the deserts, water
it weekly in the summer, but in its natural range it grows well on natural rainfall
except during a prolonged dry spell.

Rock pavonia is a short-lived perennial, lasting three to six years in the garden. The seeds germinate readily and cuttings are easy. It is an exceptionally
attractive perennial for dry gardens throughout the region.

This species has a rangy branching habit. Tip prune with scissors or your fingers intermittently through the early spring to encourage a denser, tighter plant.
This will also encourage a longer and more prolific bloom. Although evergreen,
rock pavonia is not a winter-flowering species and could be blended with other
more colorful winter-flowering species, such as red justicia (*Justicia candicans*),
to hide it while it is out of flower.

Penstemon baccharifolius

Penstemon baccharifolius
Rock penstemon, cut-leaf penstemon

FAMILY: Scrophulariaceae.
DISTRIBUTION: In the United States in Texas along the Edwards Plateau and southeastern Trans-Pecos at elevations from 2000 to 7000 ft. (600 to 2100 m). In Mexico in Coahuila.
MATURE SIZE: 1.5 to 3.0 ft. (0.5 to 0.9 m) tall and 1 to 2 ft. (0.3 to 0.6 m) wide.
BLOOMING PERIOD: June to September.
EXPOSURE: Full sun, filtered shade, or morning sun throughout the region.
HARDINESS: Cold hardy to 5°F (−15°C).

Rock penstemon is a loosely branched perennial that may be semiwoody with age. The ovate to oblanceolate leaves are 1 to 2 in. (2.5 to 5.0 cm) long and may be entire or partially serrate. They are a deep green and in some individuals are covered with fine hairs.

The flowers are widely spaced on thin stalks in a spreading panicle. Flowers are up to 1 in. (2.5 cm), tubular, and have open, flaring lobes at the tip. Colors range from scarlet to coral. In some populations the corolla tube is partially rimmed with white.

This is one of the few penstemon species that will bloom reliably through the summer in the hottest deserts. It is a handsome perennial with its serrate leaves, tan stems, and red flowers. Prune it hard in the early spring to maintain its tidy, mounded form. Over time plants can become woody and lose many lower leaves, so this annual cleanup keeps the plant attractive.

Rock penstemon, as the name implies, needs superb drainage to grow best. It is highly susceptible to root rots when grown in soils that are too wet or too rich.

Use rock penstemon in any location that needs some summer color, mixing it with other perennials or succulents. It adds summer blooming to a hummingbird garden.

Penstemon barbatus
Scarlet bugler, beardlip penstemon

FAMILY: Scrophulariaceae.

DISTRIBUTION: In mountains and canyons of Utah and Colorado south through Arizona, New Mexico, and Texas in the United States and through Mexico south to Oaxaca.

MATURE SIZE: 1 to 2 ft. (0.3 to 0.6 m) tall and 1 ft. (0.3 m) wide.

BLOOMING PERIOD: April to September.

EXPOSURE: Full sun or filtered shade throughout the region, although filtered shade is preferred in the hottest deserts.

HARDINESS: Cold hardy to at least 0°F (−18°C).

Penstemon barbatus (Wynn Anderson)

Scarlet bugler is a bundle of delicate stems. The leaves are glossy green, linear, and 2 to 3 in. (5 to 8 cm) long but very narrow.

The flowers are tubular, thin, and held in a loose raceme up the leafy flowering stalk. Flowers are bright red or scarlet, although red-orange and pinkish forms are known.

The plant's fragile appearance, however, is deceptive since in nature this species occurs in a wide range of habitats and conditions and in the garden it is equally versatile. Scarlet bugler will tolerate almost any soil as long as it has good drainage. It thrives in fertile, well-drained garden soils as well as in native, unamended rocky soils. Plants grown in sweeter conditions grow larger and often continue to bloom more regularly through the summer. Outside the hottest deserts, this species is a reliable rebloomer through the summer when kept deadheaded. In the deserts, it is a good spring bloomer often with a repeat in the fall.

This species has some fine cultivars and selections, most of which are not commonly grown in the region. 'Navigator' and 'Cambridge' series are probably of hybrid origin. In the former, plants grow up to 18 in. (46 cm) tall and bloom in pinks, lavenders, and purples. In the later, the color of the blooms is much the same, but the plants have gray-green foliage and are only 12 in. (30 cm) tall.

Penstemon cardinalis (Wynn Anderson)

'Bashful' is a 12-in. (30-cm) plant with flowers that range from pastel coral to salmon pink, often on the same flower. 'Elfin Pink' has a compact habit with numerous stems rising from the base. Flowers, as expected, are pink. This selection is widely praised for its ability to withstand both heat and humidity. 'Prairie Dusk' is a hybrid between this species and *Penstemon strictus*. It has large, deep purple flowers and does best in higher elevations and cooler climates.

Penstemon cardinalis
Cardinal beardtongue, cardinal penstemon

FAMILY: Scrophulariaceae.
DISTRIBUTION: In the United States in mountains of southern New Mexico and in the Guadalupe and Davis Mountains of western Texas at elevations from 7000 to 9000 ft. (2100 to 2740 m).
MATURE SIZE: Blooming stalks 24 to 30 in. (60 to 76 cm) tall.
BLOOMING PERIOD: May to June.
EXPOSURE: Full sun in all areas but the hottest deserts, where filtered shade is preferred.
HARDINESS: Cold hardy to at least 20°F (−7°C).

Cardinal penstemon is a handsome upright penstemon that is a show stopper when well grown. Leaves are obovate to spatulate, occasionally ovate, with distinct petioles. The leaves are usually smooth and green, but some have a bluish cast. In most populations the leaves are thick and firm.

Flowers are held in groups of two or three up the stalk. They are tubular, not widely opened at the tip, and rich scarlet red. Golden hairs nearly obstruct the base of the tube.

This handsome penstemon needs excellent drainage and minimally amended soils to thrive. Even in desert areas it does not require more than incidental supplemental watering to survive through the summer. In other areas, water only during protracted dry spells. Once growth resumes in the fall, the plant can be given regular watering.

Like the flowering stalks of most penstemons, those of this species can be pruned anytime after flowering is complete to tidy up the plant. Plants continue to grow for months after flowering from a basal set of leaves but eventually become virtually dormant for the summer.

Use cardinal penstemon to accent any wildflower or perennial planting. The tall spires of red are a vivid contrast to smaller, rounded forms such as blackfoot daisy or chocolate flower. It can also be a part of a larger grouping or form the back of a perennial border. Hummingbirds are wild for it, and, as is true for most penstemons, using it generously will encourage many of these beautiful jewels into your garden.

Penstemon cobaea
Showy beardtongue, wild foxglove

FAMILY: Scrophulariaceae.

DISTRIBUTION: In the United States from Kansas to Ohio, south to Mississippi and Arkansas, and central and eastern Texas. Naturalized in other parts of western United States, including New Mexico and Arizona.

MATURE SIZE: Basal growth 4 to 6 in. (10 to 15 cm) tall and as wide, with flowering stalks 1.0 to 1.5 ft. (0.3 to 0.5 m) tall.

BLOOMING PERIOD: April and May.

EXPOSURE: Full sun in all but the hottest deserts, where filtered shade or morning sun is best. HARDINESS: Cold hardy to at least 0°F (−18°C).

Showy beardtongue has elliptic to lanceolate leaves that vary from 1 to 4 in. (2.5 to 10.0 cm) long. They are glossy green and lustrous with fine teeth along the margins.

Flowers are held in congested panicles, almost whorls, along the stem. Each flower is about 1 in. (2.5 cm) long but is shaped like a wide inflated tube. The lobes flare widely at the ends. Flowers range in color from pale pink-lavender to deep lavender, and most show prominent purple nectar guides. The large flowers are spectacular and are mildly fragrant.

Showy beardtongue grows best in a fertile, well-drained soil. Regular watering, even in the summer, is required, especially in the deserts. Showy

Penstemon cobaea

beardtongue blooms later than most desert species, so it is just beginning when the first frantic rush of spring flowering is finished.

I first grew this unlikely penstemon because it was given to me. It quickly became one of my favorites. I planted it together with Hill Country penstemon (*Penstemon triflorus*), and the resulting hybrids that come up on their own are delightful. Showy beardtongue is nowhere near as common as I think it could be in dry gardens. It offers gardeners in this region a chance to continue the penstemon blooming season. It is also one of the few penstemons that does well in the shade.

Penstemon eatonii

Firecracker penstemon, Eaton's penstemon

FAMILY: Scrophulariaceae.

DISTRIBUTION: In the United States in eastern California, southern Nevada and Utah, southwestern Colorado, northeastern New Mexico, and central and eastern Arizona at elevations from 2000 to 7000 ft. (600 to 2100 m).

MATURE SIZE: Flowering stalks 1 to 3 ft. (0.3 to 0.9 m) tall.

BLOOMING PERIOD: May to June.

EXPOSURE: Full sun even in the deserts, or filtered shade.

HARDINESS: Cold hardy to at least 10°F (−12°C).

Firecracker penstemon has stems that are either erect or gracefully looping toward the ground. The leaves are 3 to 4 in. (8 to 10 cm) long and are a deep green with a glossy texture. They are oblong to spatulate at the base but lanceolate with an acute tip on the flowering stalk. Stems have a blush of red to red-purple along their length.

Flowers are 1 in. (2.5 cm) long and narrowly tubular. They are brilliant red, often drooping or hanging on the stalk.

Penstemon eatonii

   This exquisite penstemon is one of the hardiest for desert gardeners. It thrives in rocky, well-drained sites in full sun. Soils that are too rich or too wet will kill this species. It is especially sensitive to these conditions in the summer. Even in the deserts, water plants carefully in the summer; once a month or less is usually sufficient.

   Penstemons from the deserts grow in the cooler temperatures of the fall and winter, flower in the spring, and nearly wither away into dormancy during the summer. This can make them a challenge for gardeners unfamiliar with their habits. It takes restraint to keep from watering these species too much in the blistering summers, but they only need enough water to keep them from literally shriveling up and blowing away.

   The reward of good cultivation is the brilliant sprays of scarlet flowers in the spring. Add this penstemon to any dry perennial planting or wildflower bed, or mingle it among dry-growing cacti and agaves. Nestled up against a rock it is right at home with the cool mulch its roots favor but the heat that it demands.

   Like many penstemons, particularly the desert species, this one is short lived but reseeds well in a congenial location. Plant it in the fall for best results; spring planting often leaves too little time for plants to establish before going dormant for the summer and thus can result in large losses.

Penstemon palmeri

Penstemon palmeri
Scented penstemon, Palmer's penstemon

FAMILY: Scrophulariaceae.
DISTRIBUTION: In the United States in eastern California, southern Utah, Arizona, central and western New Mexico, and central and northern Arizona from 4000 to 7000 ft. (1200 to 2100 m).
MATURE SIZE: Basal growth 8 to 12 in. (20 to 30 cm) tall, flowering stalks 3 to 5 ft. (0.9 to 1.5 m) tall.
BLOOMING PERIOD: March to September.
EXPOSURE: Full sun or filtered shade.
HARDINESS: Cold hardy to at least 0°F (−18°C).

Scented penstemon can be a commanding plant in the garden. The leaves are large, 3 to 4 in. (8 to 10 cm) long or more, gray-green, in some individuals blue-green, and firm. Leaf margins are markedly toothed, and each leaf clasps around the sturdy, upright stem.

The 1- to 2-in. (2.5- to 5-cm) flowers are much inflated and the tips are nearly round with a wide opening. The flowers are pink to pinkish white with noticeable nectar guides.

This extraordinary penstemon can be difficult in the hottest parts of the region. It may grow well for one gardener and not at all for another, or die out in one season. Summers are particularly difficult; it needs plenty of summer watering in the deserts, but unless that is coupled with excellent drainage, the plants will rot out. It is not nearly so tricky in milder areas or high-elevation gardens.

Years ago when I first moved into our present house, Howard and Marie Gentry were our neighbors. He had long retired from botany but still had some projects underway at their farm in Riverside, California, one of which was growing this penstemon for the cut flower trade. That project succeeded and although both of them are now gone, the farm and penstemons are still going strong.

Scented penstemon was a great choice for a cut flower with its huge, pink flowers, delicate fragrance, and long, sturdy stems. When you find it in the wild, it is a shock—such a stunning beauty arising out of rock and rubble in the mountains. Entire hillsides can be in flower in good years, and the scene is breathtaking. Now if only I could figure out how to get them to live longer than a year in my garden.

Penstemon parryi
Desert penstemon, Parry's penstemon

Penstemon parryi

FAMILY: Scrophulariaceae.

DISTRIBUTION: In the United States in central and southern Arizona as well as in Mexico in the state of Sonora at elevations from 1500 to 4000 ft. (460 to 1200 m).

MATURE SIZE: Flowering stalks 3 to 4 ft. (0.9 to 1.2 m) tall and often as wide.

BLOOMING PERIOD: February to April.

EXPOSURE: Full sun even in the deserts.

HARDINESS: Cold hardy to 15°F (−9°C).

Desert penstemon is a multistemmed perennial that arises from a low basal growth. Leaves are linear, gray-green to blue-green with a smooth or slightly toothed margin.

Flowers are held on tall stalks above the foliage, and even though the basal set is small and sometimes sparse, each plant can have many stems. The flowers are 1 in. (2.5 cm) long and tubular with flared lobes that are more or less radial so the end looks like a wheel. The flowers are bright pink with darker nectar guides that extend to the lip of the corolla.

Desert penstemon grows best in well-drained, preferably rocky, soils that are only lightly amended, if at all. When grown in richer soils or with too little light, plants are floppy and often die out quickly. This species, like firecracker penstemon (*Penstemon eatonii*), is sensitive to overwatering in the summer, although some supplemental watering is what keeps it perennial. In the hottest areas, water once a month during the summer. In milder areas or where there is regular summer rainfall, water only during a protracted dry spell.

Many penstemons are sold as seed; however, this one is among the most reliable to start from seed and is planted in the fall. Individual plants make a prolific amount of seed, which can be saved for future use. Desert penstemon reseeds freely, especially in rocky soils or gardens with a rocky mulch, so even though individual plants are short lived, there are so many progeny it hardly matters.

Grow this penstemon in wildflower plantings, mingling it with a rich array of spring-flowering annuals. It is also a superb choice to fill in the spaces around winter-dormant perennials or bulbs and provides both color and contrast to a dry succulent garden. Plant in exuberant numbers for the most satisfying results, and stand back; hummingbirds go to war over this species.

Penstemon pseudospectabilis

Penstemon pseudospectabilis
Canyon penstemon

FAMILY: Scrophulariaceae.
DISTRIBUTION: In the United States in the desert mountains of eastern California, southern Utah, western Arizona, and southern New Mexico at elevations from 2000 to 7000 ft. (600 to 2100 m). In Mexico in northwestern Sonora.
MATURE SIZE: Flowering stems 3 to 4 ft. (0.9 to 1.2 m) tall and 2 to 3 ft. (0.6 to 0.9 m) wide.
BLOOMING PERIOD: March to May.
EXPOSURE: Full sun or filtered shade.
HARDINESS: Cold hardy to at least 10°F (−12°C).

Canyon penstemon is a robust species with several stems from its basal growth. Leaves are blue-green, markedly serrated, and clasped around the stems.

Flowers are up to 2 in. (5 cm) long, narrowly tubular, and vivid pink. They tend to one side of the stalk and often are pointed downward.

Canyon penstemon grows best in moderately enriched, well-drained soils. It appreciates regular watering when it is actively growing and flowering, but should be kept on the dry side during the summer. It can be short lived, often only annual, in the hottest regions, but watering every other week through the summer helps keep it perennial.

This is a beautiful penstemon to plant generously around a patio or pool, or within a large, mixed wildflower planting. Because of its need for intermittent water during the summer, it can be mixed with agaves or yuccas in a semidry succulent garden and is a wonderful addition to a rock garden.

Penstemon spectabilis
Showy penstemon, royal beardtongue

FAMILY: Scrophulariaceae.

DISTRIBUTION: In the United States in Southern California and in Mexico in northern Baja California at elevations from 600 to 6000 ft. (180 to 1800 m).

MATURE SIZE: Flowering stems 2 to 4 ft. (0.6 to 1.2 m) tall.

BLOOMING PERIOD: April to June.

EXPOSURE: Full sun throughout the region, as well as filtered shade or morning sun in the deserts.

HARDINESS: Cold hardy to 0°F (−18°C)

Penstemon spectabilis

Showy penstemon has oblanceolate to ovate leaves that are 2 to 3 in. (5 to 8 cm) long. They are smooth and gray-green with a serrated margin and clasp the stems.

The flowers are 1 in. (2.5 cm) long and are lavender to blue with a whitish blush in the interior of the corolla.

This lovely desert penstemon is one of the few blue-flowered penstemons that can stand up to the rigors of the high heat and dry soils of the deserts. For that reason I am constantly astounded at how seldom it is used in the region and why it is not better known. It certainly should be.

Grow showy penstemon in any type of soil that is well drained, including rocky or native soils. Water carefully in the summer, just enough to keep the plant from drying out completely, but not so much as to rot it out. In the hottest areas, water every two weeks during the summer, and in areas with regular summer rainfall, water during protracted dry spells.

Mix this blue-flowering penstemon with wildflower plantings or other gardens to extend the flowering season. It can grow dry enough to be blended with dry succulent gardens or used in areas that do not receive regular irrigation.

Penstemon superbus

Penstemon superbus
Coral penstemon, superb beardtongue

FAMILY: Scrophulariaceae.
DISTRIBUTION: In the United States in southeastern Arizona and southwestern New Mexico at elevations from 3500 to 6000 ft. (1100 to 1800 m). In Mexico in northeastern Sonora and northwestern Chihuahua.
MATURE SIZE: Flowering stems 1 to 4 ft. (0.3 to 1.2 m) tall, some individuals to 6 ft. (1.8 m).
BLOOMING PERIOD: April to June.
EXPOSURE: Full sun in all areas, filtered shade in the deserts.
HARDINESS: Cold hardy to at least 15°F (−9°C).

Coral penstemon is a princely plant with its long, up to 4-in. (10-cm), bluish-green leaves and soaring flowering stalks. Leaves are elliptic to lanceolate and are 1 to about 5 in. (2.5 to 12.0 cm) long. Stems add to the attraction; along with the leaves, they are often tinged with purple.

Flowers are held in tight clusters at the nodes on the leafy flowering stalk and are 0.75 in. (2.0 cm) long with a narrow tubular shape that ends with widely flared lobes. Colors range from rosy red to scarlet, but deep carmine or coral is most common.

Coral penstemon is a breathtaking choice in any perennial garden. Because of its size it works best in either a solitary planting against a wall or a small spot that it will entirely fill in. When mixed with other perennials or in a mixed planting, it needs to be given plenty of room or moved to the back.

This penstemon grows in any kind of soil with good drainage but is one of the few penstemons that will accept regular summer watering and a light organic mulch on the roots. Consider using it as the background of a summer-flowering perennial garden, where the extra water will not be harmful to it.

Like many penstemons, this one hybridizes freely when grown with other species. Some of these hybrids, especially those with desert penstemon (*Penstemon parryi*), have been sold for a long time in the Phoenix area. They are excellent plants, with the sturdy stems of this species, the graceful floral shape of desert penstemon, and a huge range of pink to rosy-red colors. In general, they are shorter than coral penstemon but much more robust than desert penstemon.

Penstemon triflorus
Hill Country penstemon, Heller's beardtongue

FAMILY: Scrophulariaceae.
DISTRIBUTION: In the United States only in the Edwards Plateau region of Texas.
MATURE SIZE: Flowering stems 1.5 to 2.0 ft. (0.5 to 0.6 m) tall.
BLOOMING PERIOD: April and May.
EXPOSURE: Full sun in its native range, filtered shade or morning sun in the deserts.
HARDINESS: Cold hardy to 10°F (−12°C).

Hill Country penstemon has glossy, green leaves that have widely spaced fine teeth along the margin. Leaves are 2 to 3 in. (5 to 8 cm) long and firm.

Flowers are held to one side of the stalk in either pairs or threes. The 1.5- to 2-in. (4- to 5-cm) long corolla is narrowly tubular with flaring lobes. The exterior is a rosy red to purple pink, and the interior is whitish with prominent nectar guides.

This species is a recent introduction into desert gardens by Mountain States Wholesale Nursery but has been used widely in Texas for some time. It is

Penstemon triflorus

perhaps the finest and easiest penstemon to grow in the hottest deserts save the two natives, firecracker and desert penstemon (*Penstemon eatonii* and *P. parryi*). Hill Country penstemon grows and blooms much better in shaded locations than either of these two species. It is tolerant of any soil that is well drained, reseeds freely, and has a sturdy reliability that all gardeners treasure.

Mix Hill Country penstemon with other penstemons to extend the blooming season. It begins a full month later than the other desert species. This species also provides long season beauty to shadier perennial plantings, as a massed planting beneath large, light shade trees.

I first grew it with foxglove penstemon (*Penstemon cobaea*). They made a fine pair, but this species lasted a few years longer than the former. The two hybridized to create a colony of lovely mauve-purple progeny that are even better than their handsome parents. I wish more gardeners would blend closely related species like penstemons in wild abandon and see what results from these natural crossings.

Perovskia atriplicifolia
Russian sage

FAMILY: Lamiaceae.
DISTRIBUTION: Afghanistan, Pakistan, and eastern Iran.
MATURE SIZE: 3 to 4 ft. (0.9 to 1.2 m) tall and as wide.
BLOOMING PERIOD: April to September, most profusely in the deserts in late spring and again in fall.
EXPOSURE: Morning sun or light filtered shade in the hottest areas, full sun elsewhere.
HARDINESS: Cold hardy to −20°F (−29°C).

Russian sage is an upright plant with a woody base and widely spaced branches. Leaves are deeply lobed, especially toward the base of the stem, and vary from gray-green to silver. They are 2 to 3 in. (5 to 8 cm) long and up to 1 in. (2.5 cm) wide.

The small, tubular, deep blue flowers are carried on branched blooming stalks held more than 1 ft. (0.3 m) above the foliage. The entire effect is of a silvery blue haze in the garden. Plants are rhizomatous and may spread gently as they mature into wider clumps.

Russian sage grows well in almost any soil as long as it has excellent drainage. It has remarkable heat, sun, and cold tolerance, making it one of the few perennials that can be used just about anywhere from the low deserts to the mountains.

Perovskia atriplicifolia

The light gray-green foliage of Russian sage blends well with deeper green species such as salvias, plumbago, or evergreen shrubs, where the airy form and delicate flowers can be shown to best advantage. Consider planting it generously; massing enhances the effect of the tiny blue flowers. Because of its great tolerance to heat and drought, it can also be mixed with succulents or other dry gardens. Russian sage is winter dormant in cold climates, which means it disappears for the winter, but in the milder parts of the region it is merely semideciduous and out of flower.

Nearly all plants offered are widely considered hybrids between this species and *Perovskia abrotanoides*. 'Blue Haze' has nearly entire leaves and sky blue flowers, and 'Blue Mist' likewise features light blue flowers. 'Blue Spire', the most common form, has dark, nearly violet, flowers and is easily confused with 'Longin' from Kurt Bluemel of Maryland, which has gray-green leaves that are nearly entire and a habit that is definitely spreading. 'Little Harvest' from Herbert Oudshoom of Holland is a dwarf form growing to 2 ft. (0.6 m). The charming 'Filagren' from German horticulturist Ernst Pagels is an upright plant with deeply dissected, silvery foliage.

Phlomis fruticosa

Phlomis fruticosa
Jerusalem sage

FAMILY: Lamiaceae.
DISTRIBUTION: Along the Mediterranean Sea, in Albania, and Yugoslavia to Greece, Turkey, Lebanon, Syria, Italy, and Sicily at elevations from sea level to 3000 ft. (900 m).
MATURE SIZE: Flowering stalks 3 to 4 ft. (0.9 to 1.2 m) tall and 2 to 3 ft. (0.6 to 0.9 m) wide.
BLOOMING PERIOD: March to May in the deserts, but intermittently through summer in milder regions.
EXPOSURE: Filtered sun or morning sun in the deserts, full sun or filtered sun elsewhere.
HARDINESS: Cold hardy to 25°F (−4°C), sometimes more.

Jerusalem sage grows from a dense basal set of leaves that are crowded along the branches. The gray-green leaves have many fine hairs on the underside that make it appear white or silvery and give it a velvety touch. Leaves are 2 to 3 in. (5 to 8 cm) long.

Flowers are held in dense whorls on leafy stalks above the foliage. The calyx is large and green with a tubular corolla that is bright sulfur yellow, sporting a prominently hooded upper lobe.

Jerusalem sage grows best in well-drained soils. In the deserts, it grows well in native, unamended soil or in garden soil with excellent drainage. Jerusalem sage needs minimal summer watering, even in the deserts, and elsewhere is best grown dry.

Known in British horticulture for over 400 years, this fine ornamental is widely regarded wherever it is cultivated. It can be grown anywhere in the region with ease. The tidy shape and brilliant flowering stalks accent the back of any perennial planting. Because of its ease of culture and need to grow dry, Jerusalem sage blends well with succulents, winter-flowering bulbs, and other Mediterranean or dry climate perennials.

A sturdy hybrid form is known variously as 'Edward Bowles' (introduced by Hilliers in England), 'Grande Verde' (from San Marcos Growers in California), and 'Lemon Swirl'. It is believed to be a hybrid between this species and *Phlomis russeliana*. This hybrid is larger than the type, with leaves up to 6 in. (15 cm) long and 3 in. (8 cm) wide. Flowering stalks and flowers are also somewhat larger than the type. The hybrid is commonly sold, although many times the cultivar name is abandoned and the plant is sold as simply Jerusalem sage.

Many European selections are virtually unknown in the West, but the French form 'Crispy' with undulate margins and the English 'Speckles' variegate form might be of special interest.

A number of other beautiful members of this genus would be worthy species for a dry garden. Many of them are uncommon in the region outside of California. They include the purple-flowering *Phlomis lanata* and *P. purpurea*, as well the rarer *P. samia*. *Phlomis russeliana* is a rhizomatous species with large leaves and buttery yellow flowers that fade to creamy white. The stunning *P. italica* has silvery leaves with lilac-pink flowers and is not often offered.

Phyla nodiflora
Frogfruit, turkey tangle fogfruit

FAMILY: Verbenaceae.
DISTRIBUTION: South America. Widely naturalized in warm parts of the world including the United States in the Gulf Coast states and Florida.
MATURE SIZE: Rarely over 3 in. (8 cm) tall but up to 2 ft. (0.6 m) wide.
BLOOMING PERIOD: March to May, often reblooming in the fall.
EXPOSURE: Full sun or filtered shade in all areas.
HARDINESS: Cold hardy to at least 15°F (−9°C).

Frogfruit is a mat-forming species that rises mere inches from the ground. The leaves are obovate or spatulate and 1.25 to 2.5 in. (3.0 to 6.4 cm) long.

Flowers are Lilliputian lantana-like blooms. The white to yellowish individual flowers have orange throats and are crammed together into a rounded head. Flowers tend to age to a shade of lavender or purple, and the entire head is less than 0.5 in. (1.5 cm).

Although naturalized, this species is so extensive that three varieties are recognized. Var. *longifolia*, found in southern Texas and the coast of Mexico to the western coast of South America, has leaves that are uniformly elongate and up to

Phyla nodiflora

2.25 in. (5.7 cm) long. Var. *reptans* occurs sporadically through the range as far north as northern Texas and has thinner, rougher leaves with widely spaced teeth. Var. *rosea* is widely naturalized as far north as North Carolina and forms dense mats with minute, rough leaves. In Mediterranean gardens, this species and most likely var. *rosea* are used as a lawn substitute.

Frogfruit grows in any type of soil but needs good drainage to thrive. In the hottest deserts, it should be watered somewhat regularly through the summer, but in summer rainfall areas it needs supplemental irrigation only during protracted dry spells.

An excellent choice for a low, dry garden groundcover, frogfruit is frequently seen planted among stones. I know a charming planting where it was planted among the risers of a stone stairway. The incredibly small flowers are highly attractive to butterflies, and the plant makes a delightful choice in a large container or raised bed planted to attract these delicate visitors.

Plumbago scandens
White desert plumbago, leadwort, doctorbush

FAMILY: Plumbaginaceae.

DISTRIBUTION: Widespread throughout tropical Americas. In the United States in southern Arizona, western and southern Texas, and southern Florida at elevations from 2500 to 4000 ft. (800 to 1200 m). It is found throughout Mexico including Baja California.

MATURE SIZE: Usually 2 to 4 ft. (0.6 to 1.2 m) tall and as wide, but varies greatly. Forms in the tropics grow to 10 ft. (3 m) tall .

BLOOMING PERIOD: May to September, but intermittently year-round in the warmest regions.

EXPOSURE: Full sun, filtered sun, or morning sun throughout the region, although filtered shade is best in the deserts.

HARDINESS: Cold hardy to 15°F (−9°C).

White desert plumbago is a tidy rounded plant with countless, wiry interwoven stems. The 3-in. (8-cm) leaves are bright, glossy green, turning a deep burnished red in the winter. They are more or less lanceolate and are widely spaced up the stems.

Plumbago scandens

The flowers are small, about 0.75 in. (2 cm) across, with a thin tube that ends in five flat, flared lobes. They are bright white, occasionally lavender. Although the flowers are held in clusters at the ends of the stems, they open sequentially so they appear more solitary than they are. The calyx is covered with sticky glands that glisten when light hits them.

White desert plumbago grows best in well-drained, somewhat fertile soils. In the deserts it thrives on weekly watering to retain its handsome shape and maintain the bloom. In areas with more reliable summer rainfall, it may take only intermittent supplemental watering. Although it is extremely drought tolerant, its principal adaptation to drought is to become more or less deciduous during dry times and that may not be desirable in the garden.

This is a difficult plant to prune because of the enormous number of small, thin stems. It is best to give it ample room to spread and avoid frequent pruning. Every few years it can be sheared to 1 to 2 ft. (0.3 to 0.6 m) tall in the late winter to reinvigorate it and return it to a more tidy form. Prune as early as possible because it takes a while for the plant to recover from a hard prune.

Many authors note that contact with the roots causes mild to severe dermatitis in susceptible people, so handle any transplanting with care.

I am always delighted by this species for its many faces. In the winter the deep red of the leaves provides a welcome note of color in the garden and contrasts spectacularly with the pure white flowers. Later as the leaves green up, it becomes another plant altogether—full of fresh spring greenery and gentle white flowers. It blooms a long season, even in the deserts, and that, too, makes it even more welcome in any perennial planting.

White desert plumbago blends well with all other dry garden perennials, but I like it in the back of the bed where its density can form a backdrop. Use it around pools and patios for its lovely colors, and to fill in a troublesome or dull spot.

Poliomintha maderensis

Poliomintha maderensis
Mexican oregano, Madrean rosemary

FAMILY: Lamiaceae.
DISTRIBUTION: Endemic to central Coahuila in Mexico at 7900 ft. (2400 m).
MATURE SIZE: 3 to 4 ft. (0.9 to 1.2 m) tall and as wide.
BLOOMING PERIOD: May to July, with intermittent bloom through the summer and fall.
EXPOSURE: Full sun or filtered shade throughout the region, although filtered shade or morning sun is best for the deserts.
HARDINESS: Cold hardy to at least 10°F (−12°C).

Mexican oregano has numerous square brown stems rising from a semiwoody base. Stems may either be rigidly erect or fall in a graceful cascade, often the result of the weight of the flowers.

Leaves are held on thin reddish pedicels in clustered pairs along the main stem and the branches directly attached to it. The linear leaves are 1.0 to 1.5 in. (2.5 to 4 cm) long and have smooth margins. As the leaves approach the end of the stem they become smaller. They have a pungent, oregano smell and taste.

Flowers are packed into axillary clusters at the ends of the stems, often so dense that it causes the stem to fall over. Each flower is encased by a green calyx with sharp tips and is up to 1.5 in. (4 cm) long. The corolla is tubular with the upper lobes split into three and the lower fused together. The flowers are variously colored on the same plant, from deep purple to pale lavender. Both the pistil and the anthers are purple.

Mexican oregano will grow in any well-drained soil. I have known it in rich, well-amended garden soils, in rocky sites, and in rugged native soils, and in all cases it looked excellent.

Time any pruning carefully. Plants bloom on the ends of the current year's branches, and pruning too late can interrupt good flowering. I think it is best to prune it either in the late winter just as it begins to grow and at least two months before bloom, or in early fall. It has a graceful natural form and does not need annual pruning, but every few years it helps to prune it hard to bring back its attractive form and clear out any dead wood.

I first saw this species at the Desert Botanical Garden when one of the researchers brought it up from Mexico and planted it as part of an experimental farm then in operation. I came on after the farm operation was abandoned and this species was growing, entirely on its own, under a huge, spreading mesquite. I was so impressed that I took cuttings and began to spread it around the garden and occasionally sell it. Not long after that, other growers, particularly Greg Starr of Tucson and Ron Gass of Phoenix, began to offer it from plants they had collected in Mexico. It has never become as popular or common as it deserves to be.

The luscious wands of purple and lavender flowers come later in the spring when the riotous spring bloom is fading and before the tropicals of summer have taken up flowering. Hummingbirds are mad for it, and in my yard it is the cause of countless hummingbird territorial wars.

Poliomintha maderensis was first known in the region as *P. longiflora*. The latter name continued for a while until it was made clear that *P. maderensis* has purplish flowers and could not be mistaken for the red-orange flowering *P. longiflora*.

Psilostrophe cooperi
Paper flower, white-stemmed paper flower

FAMILY: Asteraceae.
DISTRIBUTION: In the United States from southeastern California to southwestern Utah, southern Nevada, western Arizona, and southwestern New Mexico from 2000 to 6500 ft. (600 to 1980 m) in elevation. In Mexico in northern Sonora and Baja California.
MATURE SIZE: 1.0 to 1.5 ft. (0.3 to 0.5 m) tall and as wide, sometimes up to 3 ft. (0.9 m) across.
BLOOMING PERIOD: March to September, occasionally into October.
EXPOSURE: Full sun even in the deserts.
HARDINESS: Cold hardy to at least 15°F (−9°C).

Paper flower is a multistemmed, clump-forming perennial whose stems and branches are covered with felty white hairs. Plants are usually erect or gently leaning.

The linear gray-green leaves are 1 to 2 in. (2.5 to 5 cm) long. They are covered with fine white hairs when young but lose that covering as they age.

Psilostrophe cooperi

The 1-in. (2.5-cm) flowering heads are solitary on thin stalks above the foliage. Only three to four bright yellow ray flowers surround the yellow disk flowers.

This lively, yellow-flowering perennial lights up any mixed planting with its profuse, long lasting bloom. Paper flower will grow in a wide range of soil types but requires excellent drainage. Weekly watering in the deserts or during protracted dry spells in milder areas will maintain the bloom longer and more prolifically.

Paper flower is named for the bright yellow ray flowers that turn whitish tan when they are spent and remain on the plant for months. This charming effect gives the plant two full flowerings—one yellow, the other whitish—throughout the spring and summer.

Psilostrophe tagetina
Woolly paper flower, paper flower

FAMILY: Asteraceae.
DISTRIBUTION: In the United States from Kansas and Oklahoma south through Texas and west to New Mexico and eastern Arizona at elevations from 4000 to 7000 ft. (1200 to 2100 m).
MATURE SIZE: 2 to 3 ft. (0.6 to 0.9 m) tall and as wide.
BLOOMING PERIOD: March to June, and again from October to December in the deserts.
EXPOSURE: Full sun in all areas as well as filtered shade in the deserts.
HARDINESS: Cold hardy to −20°F (−29°C).

Woolly paper flower is a multistemmed plant with hairy or tufted stems and non-woody branches. The leaves are ovate to spatulate, and the entire plant is more herbaceous than shrubby.

Flowers are clustered in heads at the ends of the branches. Each head consists of usually three to four ray flowers, which, like the disks, are bright yellow.

This species and its nearly identical relative, paper flower (*Psilostrophe cooperi*), may be difficult to distinguish without a close inspection. This species tends to be more herbaceous than shrubby, has ovate rather than linear leaves, and has flowers in a loose cluster rather than being solitary on the stalk. Because of its stunning cold tolerance, woolly paper flower is recommended in many arid, but colder, climates, while paper flower is the more xeric species and is better suited for the hottest desert regions. Both species are grown widely and are often confused one for the other.

Woolly paper flower blends well with any array of perennials or wildflower plantings. Butterflies are

Psilostrophe tagetina

strongly attracted to both species, which are handsome additions to any butterfly garden.

Ratibida columnifera
Mexican hat

FAMILY: Asteraceae.
DISTRIBUTION: Throughout the central, southern, and western United States.
MATURE SIZE: 2 to 3 ft. (0.6 to 0.9 m) tall and 1 to 2 ft. (0.3 to 0.6 m) wide.
BLOOMING PERIOD: April to September, but April to June in the deserts.
EXPOSURE: Full sun or filtered shade in all areas.
HARDINESS: Cold hardy to 0°F (−18°C).

Mexican hat begins as a low-growing mound with long spatulate leaves that are deeply lobed. In some individuals the lobes are so thin that the leaves look compound or fernlike. The basal leaves are deep green, up to 3 in. (8 cm) long, and have a rounded tip. They form a dense mound. As the season progresses and blooming begins, long leafy blooming stalks begin to elongate. The leaves along these blooming stalks are lighter green, and the lobes are very narrow.

Ratibida columnaris

The flowering stalk is composed of an elongated 1- to 1.5-in. (2.5- to 4-cm) long head of brown disk flowers that are surrounded at the base by yellow ray flowers. It looks like a thimble with a skirt, although it must have looked like a hat to whoever gave it the common name. Rays are usually yellow but they can be marked by various amounts by brownish red as well.

Mexican hat will grow in almost any soil that is fairly well drained, at least never boggy or consistently wet, and favors disturbed or newly turned areas. It is an outstanding perennial for a new garden or an area that needs a quick lift.

Although sold as transplants, this species grows quickly and reliably from seed and will reseed throughout the garden in the most unlikely places. In my garden I leave the seedlings that come up in favorable spots and remove the ones that are not so well placed. After one initial purposeful planting I have never been without a few of this wonderful species.

Mexican hat blends well into any wildflower or annual planting. Because it blooms later and longer than most annuals, it will continue the beauty of an annual planting for a long time. It makes a charming addition to a butterfly planting.

Rosmarinus officinalis
Rosemary

FAMILY: Lamiaceae.
DISTRIBUTION: Throughout the region surrounding the Mediterranean Sea.
MATURE SIZE: 3 to 4 ft. (0.9 to 1.2 m) tall and spreading up to 6 ft. (1.8 m) wide, depending on the variety.
BLOOMING PERIOD: January to April.
EXPOSURE: Full sun in all areas.
HARDINESS: Cold hardy to 15°F (−9°C).

Rosemary is familiar to many gardeners throughout the world with its sturdy, ultimately woody stems that can be upright, spreading, or prostrate. The stems are soft and deep green initially, becoming thick and woody with age.

Leaves are 0.5 to 1.0 in. (1.5 to 2.5 cm) long, leathery, and deep green. Most have fine hairs on the underside that give them a silvery cast. The leaves are intensely aromatic, often smelling of pine or with a sharp, distinctive pungency.

Flowers are small and tubular and held closely in axils of the leaves. They are commonly blue but can range from an intense dark blue to blue-violet with pink or white forms also known.

Rosemary is extremely drought tolerant even in the deserts. This was brought home to me vividly when I first moved to the deserts. I entered a modest restaurant in an even more modest part of Phoenix and took a quick about-face when I realized that the small perennial lining the walkway was rosemary. I had struggled for years to grow a few twigs of rosemary in New Orleans and could hardly believe it was so common that it occurred in this setting.

Rosmarinus officinalis

Rosemary grows best in rocky or very well drained soils without excessive watering. In areas where it receives too much water or receives it too regularly, it becomes soft, floppy, and overly large, and eventually rots out, typically from the middle; however, this perennial will take a great deal of abuse. In the hottest deserts it should be kept dry during the summer when it is not actively growing and watered just enough to keep it from becoming decrepit. This usually means supplemental watering once a month at most.

Prune lightly throughout the growing season to keep plants tidy and dense. Old woody stems do not resprout if they are cut back, a trait this species shares with many Mediterranean perennials such as lavender and artemisias, so regular pruning is a more successful way to keep the plant in good shape.

Rosemary is not only delicious as a culinary herb but also makes a graceful perennial in the garden. Use it to hang over a hot wall, to line a walkway or staircase where it will be touched often to release its seductive fragrance, or in locations with strong reflected heat such as near pool decking. I like to mix rosemary with other Mediterraneans and with winter-flowering bulbs because they all like the same culture and are at their best in the benign desert winter. Rosemary also makes a splendid backdrop for low, colorful perennial plantings.

Untold numbers of selections and varieties of this long-cultivated species are available. If you are growing this herb for use in the kitchen, taste the variety before you buy it. All varieties do not taste precisely the same. 'Tuscan Blue' is one of the most commonly offered; it is upright with dark blue flowers. A prostrate form without a proper name is also seen frequently.

Ruellia brittoniana
Mexican petunia

FAMILY: Acanthaceae.
DISTRIBUTION: Mexico. Naturalized throughout the southern United States from Texas to Florida and South Carolina.
MATURE SIZE: 3 ft. (0.9 m) tall and as wide.
BLOOMING PERIOD: March to November, with heaviest bloom in summer even in the deserts.
EXPOSURE: Full sun to filtered shade in all areas, as well as deep shade in the hottest deserts.
HARDINESS: Leaves and stems will freeze at 32°F (0°C), but the plant is root hardy to 24°F (−4°C) and recovers quickly.

Mexican petunia has numerous, upright herbaceous stems. It spreads rapidly from a network of underground stems. In locations with ample water it can become a subtle herbaceous hedge.

Leaves are up to 4 to 6 in. (10 to 15 cm) long, deep green, and are heavily marked along the veins, the edge, and the pedicel with purple. The width of the leaves varies greatly from nearly 1 in. (2.5 cm) wide to barely one-fourth as wide.

The flowers are thin and crinkled, looking like wet paper, with a tubular corolla that ends in wide, flared lobes. The 2-in. (5-cm) wide flowers are axillary and range in color through shades of purple, pink, and white. Although each flower opens and dies in a day, the flowers are so prolific that once the plant begins to flower it appears to never go out of bloom.

This species is one of the toughest and most reliable of all summer-flowering perennials for the entire region. In areas or gardens with reliable summer water it can become a pest and quickly spread more than you might wish. Although it can seed like crazy around the place, it never shows up in places lacking consistent water.

Mexican petunia and its forms and selections grow best in fertile, well-drained soil with modest summer watering. You can keep the spreading nature of the species under control by how much you water it. In the hottest deserts, Mexican petunia blooms reliably even in deep shade and can be a welcome addition to such difficult locations.

All forms, but especially the taller ones, can become dreary looking at the end of the winter. Shear to within a few inches of the ground in early spring to rejuvenate the plant.

A number of named and unnamed forms are available and there is often abundant confusion about them. In general, the "tall" or typical species form comes in three colors: purple, pink, and white. Neither the purple nor the white have widely accepted names, but the pink is called 'Chi Chi'. It was found in the late 1980s by horticulturist Scott Ogden in McAllen, Texas. He asked for and received a piece of the plant and took it to Austin,

Ruellia brittoniana

where the Native Texas Nursery began to grow it for sale. When asked what to call it, Scott says he replied, "It is sort of chichi pink," and the die was cast.

Most gardeners are now familiar with the dwarf forms of the species, particularly the abundant and delightful 'Katie'. The leaves of these forms are crammed onto the stem, leaving almost no room between the nodes. 'Katie' was first noted by employees of a now-defunct nursery in Conroe, Texas, that was owned by the late Lynn Lowery. It first began life as 'Nolan's Dwarf' and you will still occasionally see it for sale by that name. Katie Ferguson bought the nursery from Lowery and when she became ill, the name was transferred to 'Katie' to honor her and her friendship with Lowery.

Pink and white dwarf forms have a bewildering mass of names, but none of them seem to have stuck and been accepted the way 'Katie' has. The white form is just as short and tidy as 'Katie', sending out trailing stems that root along the ground. The pink form becomes a mound 12 to 16 in. (30 to 41 cm) tall over time.

The tight mounding habit of the pink form makes it useful as an addition to a perennial bed or mixed planting. The low-growing, spreading habit of 'Katie' and the white form make them useful to line pathways and walkways or to surround beds.

A variegated form called 'Strawberries and Cream' has yellow netted foliage and pink flowers. It was found by Scott Rivers and is grown chiefly by nurseries in the eastern United States and England. I have never been a great fan of variegate forms, and this one has done nothing to change my mind.

Ruellia malacosperma
Softseed wild petunia

FAMILY: Acanthaceae.
DISTRIBUTION: Southern and southeastern Mexico south through Central America to at least Ecuador. Naturalized throughout the southeastern United States including Florida.
MATURE SIZE: 3 to 4 ft. (0.9 to 1.2 m) tall and as wide.
BLOOMING PERIOD: March to October, but year-round in the warmest areas.
EXPOSURE: Full sun or filtered shade in all areas.
HARDINESS: Root hardy to at least 10°F (−12°C) and recovers quickly.

Softseed wild petunia is similar in many respects to the widely grown Mexican petunia (*Ruellia brittoniana*) with upright, numerous, herbaceous stems spreading readily from rhizomes.

The leaves are deep green, broadly lanceolate or linear, with an acute tip. They are 2 to 4 in. (5 to 10 cm) long and are thick up the entire stem.

Flowers are up to 2 in. (5 cm) long with a tubular corolla that ends in a widely flared lobe. Although each purple or light lavender flower lasts only a day, the flowers are so prolific that the plant appears to be in permanent bloom throughout the summer.

This species is best known by its white-flowered form, one version of which was found in the Rio Grande Valley of Texas by horticulturist Scott Ogden and grown for sale by Native Texas Nursery in Austin. Another known as 'White Flower Form' came from Lynn Calhoun of Texas and is grown by Plant Delights Nursery in Raleigh, North Carolina. Both forms have long, wide, deep green leaves without the prominent purple veins or leaf edges of Mexican petunia.

Although purple is the common flower color, forms with white flowers are grown most frequently in the region. The only drawback to this species is that the flowers fail to fall off the plant, remaining as brown reminders of past bloom. I leave every seedling that comes up in my yard until it blooms, looking for the one that will flower without this trait.

Softseed wild petunia is an effortless addition to any perennial planting for its deep green color and soothing white flowers. I am partial to white flowers in the summer; I find them restful and calming. Use softseed wild petunia generously where you need color in either shade or filtered sun. In the hottest deserts it grows in any amount of sun as long as it receives some protection from the afternoon sun. This species reseeds even more aggressively in the garden than Mexican petunia, but it only finds a home where a reliable source of water occurs.

Ruellia peninsularis
Desert ruellia

FAMILY: Acanthaceae.
DISTRIBUTION: In Mexico in Sonora and Baja California.
MATURE SIZE: 2.0 to 4.5 ft. (0.6 to 1.4 m) tall and 3 to 4 ft. (0.9 to 1.2 m) wide.
BLOOMING PERIOD: May to October.
EXPOSURE: Full sun even in the hottest deserts.
HARDINESS: Stems can be damaged at 26°F (−3°C), but the plant recovers rapidly from mild winter damage.

Ruellia malacosperma

Desert ruellia has pale, nearly white stems that are firm and almost woody. It straddles the line between what might be considered a small shrub or a largish perennial.

The small 1- to 1.5-in. (2.5- to 4-cm) long leaves are gray-green, smooth, and sparse so that the contrast with the stem is apparent.

Flowers of this species are similar to all ruellias, with a tubular corolla that flares into wide, flattened lobes. The flowers are deep royal purple and are most prolific in the spring.

Desert ruellia is easy to grow in the roughest conditions of the hottest desert. It requires excellent drainage but grows well in rocky, native soils with only intermittent deep waterings through the summer. I have known plants that were

Ruellia peninsularis (Mary Irish)

grown with ample summer water, and they were enormous and overwhelming and seemed entirely out of character for this rugged desert native. Even in the hottest deserts this species can thrive with only minimal summer watering; where rainfall exceeds 10 in. (250 mm) per year, plants rarely need watering.

Use this tough perennial in areas of the garden that do not receive regular irrigation. It can be mixed with other desert shrubs or succulents or used to soften and relieve the hard edges of cacti. It is also a good choice to backup a planting of native perennials.

The similar *Ruellia californica* has leaves that are glandular and rough to the touch as opposed to the smooth leaves of this species. Much confusion exists in the trade regarding these species, and you can buy either one carrying either name.

Russelia equisetiformis
Coral fountain, firecracker plant, fountain plant

FAMILY: Scrophulariaceae.
DISTRIBUTION: In southern Mexico south through Guatemala. Naturalized in the United States in central and southern Florida.
MATURE SIZE: 3 to 6 ft. (0.9 to 1.8 m) tall and 4 to 6 ft. (1.2 to 1.8 m) wide.
BLOOMING PERIOD: Year-round in warm climates, but most prolific in late spring and fall.
EXPOSURE: Full sun or filtered shade in all areas but the deserts, where filtered shade is best.
HARDINESS: Stems can be damaged below 25°F (−4°C), but the plant recovers quickly.

Coral fountain has countless fine, angular, green stems that rise up directly from the base and then fall over when they are about half their final length. The leaves are so minute that they look more like scales. For most of the year, leaves are not present on the stems.

The flowers are vivid orange to orange-red tubes that are about 1 in. (2.5 cm) long. Flowers hang from thin pedicels and are profuse on the plant. They are often so thick that you cannot see the stems.

Coral fountain needs a fertile, well-drained soil to thrive. While it is tolerant of any amount of heat, it needs to be regularly watered through the summer.

Because of its grasslike form, this perennial is exquisite when planted in mass or used to fill in corners or nooks. It can be dramatic as an accent in a large pot or raised bed that will enhance the effect of the graceful fall of the stems. Hummingbirds flock to it, and it makes sense to plant it where you can watch their daily rituals.

I first knew this species in New Orleans, where it was a reasonably common ornamental. Frequently it was planted at the entry to a house. It was a great surprise to me to find how well it did

Russelia equisetiformis

in the deserts and is yet another example of species that roam around the warmer parts of the country without much regard for the wide differences in conditions as long as the temperature is warm enough for them. A yellow-flowered form occurs but I find it insipid; the color just does not hold up well to the light green foliage.

The similar *Russelia polyedra* is native to Sonora, Mexico, and is much more adapted to drought, although it has more consistent summer flowering with regular watering. It is rarely found for sale, but it probably should be considered.

The exquisite *Russelia coccinea* of southern Mexico and Central America is not well known in the region. Its leaves are larger, up to 0.5 in. (1.5 cm), and are much darker green. The flowers are scarlet rather than red-orange, and when in congenial circumstances the stems will extend 6 to 10 ft. (1.8 to 3.0 m).

Ruta graveolens

Ruta graveolens
Rue

FAMILY: Rutaceae.

DISTRIBUTION: Southern Europe and North Africa, although reported to be extinct in the wild. Naturalized widely in North America and Balkan Europe.

MATURE SIZE: 2 to 3 ft. (0.6 to 0.9 m) tall and as wide.

BLOOMING PERIOD: April to June, but through the summer in areas outside the hottest deserts.

EXPOSURE: Full sun in all areas, although filtered shade is best in the deserts.

HARDINESS: Cold hardy to at least 10°F (−12°C).

Rue is a mounding perennial with soft gray-green stems that arise from a woody base. The leaves are pinnately compound and are 3 to 5 in. (8 to 13 cm) long. The leaflets are much wider at the end than the base, much like a spoon, and were in fact the origin of the image in playing cards for the suit of clubs. The leaves are a soft gray-green with a fine blush to the surface.

The flowers are held in a tall panicle up to 12 in. (30 cm) over the foliage. Individual flowers are small, 0.5 in. (1.5 cm), and have tiny cup-shaped petals, often with fringed edges. Seeds arise in the midst of the petals as a segmented ball that is prominent during flowering.

Rue has an immense cultivation history. It is recorded in the Bible and has been used and known in Europe since plants have been recorded. The list of its uses is exhaustive; it has been thought over time to cure almost everything. Rue must be treated with great care when attempting to use it either externally or internally, and it should never be used without careful understanding of its properties. Many people find the leaves cause a rash when handled during hot weather.

A gorgeous ornamental in a dry perennial planting, rue grows in almost any kind of soil but needs good drainage. It will grow equally well in sand or gravel soils and fertile, well-amended soils. Water regularly through the summer, particularly in the deserts; where drainage is poor, be careful not to overwater to prevent rotting.

Rue blends beautifully with other harder edged or deep green plants. The soft, mounding habit and the calm colors make it a lovely choice for both textural and color contrast in the garden. The charming flowers blend well with other late spring- or summer-flowering perennials including later-flowering wildflowers. Swallowtail butterfly larvae are strongly attracted to this species, making it a good addition to the butterfly garden.

Salvia apiana
White sage, bee sage

FAMILY: Labiatae.
DISTRIBUTION: In the United States in Southern California from Santa Barbara County to the Mexican border at elevations below 5000 ft. (1500 m). In Mexico in northern Baja California.
MATURE SIZE: 4 to 5 ft. (1.2 to 1.5 m) tall and as wide.
BLOOMING PERIOD: March to July, but often shortened to April to June in cultivation.
EXPOSURE: Full sun in all areas, although it will tolerate filtered sun in the hottest deserts.
HARDINESS: Cold hardy to at least 20°F (−7°C).

Salvia apiana

White sage has long wandlike stems that rise from a semiwoody base. The branches are densely covered with fine white to gray hairs.

Leaves are 2 to 4 in. (5 to 10 cm) long and are likewise smothered in fine, white hairs that give the entire plant a ghostly aspect.

Flowers are 0.5 to 1.0 in. (1.5 to 2.5 cm) long. They are held in tight clusters surrounded by prominent bracts and in a whorl or rounded head. Individual flowers are pale lavender to bright white. The flowering stalks can be enormous, up to 5 ft. (1.5 m) tall, with numerous whorls of flowers. The stalks commonly become lax and fall over with the weight of flowering.

This species has been something of a holy grail of plants during my gardening life. It first came to my attention in California, where it is both native to the chaparral hills there and often offered by native nurseries. I planted one in front of my sales area at the Desert Botanical Garden. It thrived on virtually no care as have others in that collection. This species, like many California chaparral natives, has difficulty with the warm, moist soils of summer, particularly in a container, and therefore this species has never become as common in the hottest deserts as it probably should be; however, in the ground it is magnificent. The tall fragrant wands of white flowers rising over white foliage are irresistible.

White sage grows best in well-drained soils, even those with low fertility. It strongly resents too much summer water wherever it is grown. This makes it a fine addition to any area that gets only intermittent or no summer watering, such as along a drive or in a distant corner. The flowers are lightly fragrant, but the foliage has a pungent, almost seaside aroma that will carry over the entire garden.

Several hybrids between this species and other native species are found in California. One of the most handsome is a Rancho Santa Ana selection known as 'Desperado', a hybrid with *Salvia leucophylla* that has pink-lavender flowers.

Salvia azurea var. grandiflora
Pitcher sage, blue sage

Synonym: *Salvia pitcheri*.

FAMILY: Lamiaceae.

DISTRIBUTION: Widespread in the United States through the prairie states, along the Great Lakes to the Gulf Coast and west to Texas, northeastern New Mexico, and Utah at elevations below 5000 ft. (1500 m).

MATURE SIZE: 3 to 5 ft. (0.9 to 1.5 m) tall and spreading 1 to 3 ft. (0.3 to 0.9 m) wide.

BLOOMING PERIOD: July to September.

EXPOSURE: Filtered shade or morning sun in all areas, deep shade in the deserts.

Salvia azurea var. *grandiflora*

HARDINESS: Cold hardy to 0°F (−18°C) or more.

Pitcher sage is a loose-growing perennial with few stems that may be erect but are more commonly lax. The leaves are linear and 1 in. (2.5 cm) long or less. They are gray-green and sparse on the plant.

The flowers are small, usually 0.5 in. (1.5 cm) long, and are an intense, sky blue. Flowers are arranged in loose racemes up to 6 to 8 in. (15 to 20 cm) tall.

Pitcher sage requires fertile, well-drained soil. In all areas it needs regular summer watering for best performance, although I have found that with a heavy mulch and shade, it will need no more water in my garden than other arid-adapted perennials.

This salvia is an unexpected winner for dry, hot gardens. It is hard to find good flowering species for the shade, much less species that perform so well in the summer, but pitcher sage makes a great show in those areas of the garden. The stunning color and loose growth habit make it a good choice to blend into a perennial bed or mix with other shade-flowering plants such as cupheas, ruellias, or small yuccas. Because of its loose structure it can be interplanted with sturdier plants and allowed to grow among them using other stems as a support.

Salvia canariensis
Canary Island sage

FAMILY: Lamiaceae.
DISTRIBUTION: Endemic to the Canary Islands.
MATURE SIZE: 4 to 5 ft. (1.2 to 1.5 m) tall and 3 to 4 ft. (0.9 to 1.2 m) wide, but sometimes 6 to 7 ft. (1.8 to 2.1 m) tall and about 5 ft. (1.5 m) wide.
BLOOMING PERIOD: April to June, but may continue all summer in mild areas like the California coast.
EXPOSURE: Filtered shade in the hottest areas, full sun or filtered shade elsewhere.
HARDINESS: Stems can be damaged or killed below 20°F (−7°C), but the plant recovers quickly.

Salvia canariensis

Canary Island sage is included here, despite it large size, because I accept a certain subjectivity to the designation "perennial" and believe that it is appropriate to consider the look and feel the species brings to the garden. This arresting salvia softens and highlights a planting and never shouts shrub to me.

The sturdy stems are covered with fine, long, white hairs. Leaves are 3 to 5 in. (8 to 13 cm) long and shaped like an arrowhead. They are a dusky gray-green with a smothering of fine white hairs on the underside.

Flowers are held in whorls up the tall flowering stalks and are clustered densely within each whorl. The showy, large calyx almost encloses the corolla and ranges in color from purple to rosy magenta. The corolla is tubular with prominent expanded lobes like lips and ranges in color from purple to a rich burgundy.

Plants sold in the region most closely resemble var. *candissima*. This variety is somewhat smaller than the type, with silvery white foliage and with flowers that are a dark brooding mauve color. The white hairs of the stems and the foliage are often so dense that you cannot see either the stem or the leaf surface.

Grow Canary Island sage in well-drained soils of almost any type. Some watering is necessary in summer to keep the plants vigorous, but they can be easily overwatered. In areas with regular summer rainfall or heavier soils pay close attention to good drainage. Prune Canary Island sage only to remove old flowering stalks when they are spent. New growth arises quickly after flowering, and pruning out old growth encourages quick regrowth.

Canary Island sage is especially effective in groupings or mass to accentuate its spectacular foliage and unusual flower color. It fills a corner or marks a turning in the path well. This salvia is also an excellent choice for a large container.

Plants are somewhat short lived in the hottest deserts, as are many salvias, but in congenial circumstances will reseed freely. If not, they should be replenished every three to five years or so.

Salvia chamaedryoides
Blue Chihuahuan sage

Salvia chamaedryoides

FAMILY: Lamiaceae.

DISTRIBUTION: In Mexico from Coahuila and Nuevo León to Zacatecas and San Luis Potosí at 4000 to 9000 ft. (1200 to 2740 m) in elevation.

MATURE SIZE: 2 ft. (0.6 m) tall and as wide.

BLOOMING PERIOD: April to October, but usually in spring, then ceasing in summer before resuming in fall.

EXPOSURE: Full sun in mild areas such as the coast of California, but filtered shade or morning sun elsewhere.

HARDINESS: Cold hardy to 10°F (−12°C).

Leaves are simple and gray-green and usually less than 1 in. (2.5 cm) long. Flowers are deep blue to violet, less than 1 in. (2.5 cm) long, and are held on loose terminal spikes.

Salvias in deserts or dry gardens are often a frustrating series of experiments. Lovely ones are offered, or you find them at sales or in publications, but many of these glorious species are from the highlands of eastern Mexico. While these species perform well in the milder parts of the region, such as coastal California, higher elevations, and Texas, they struggle in the hot, arid, long summers of the deserts. This is one of those species.

In milder areas grow Mexican blue sage in well-amended loamy soils with excellent drainage, and give it a little supplemental irrigation during prolonged dry spells. In the deserts, especially the hottest deserts, provide the same kind of soil, but give plants a site in filtered shade. Regular summer irrigation every four to seven days maintains good growth and form in these areas. Mexican blue sage spreads by rhizomes and can form a loose groundcover when its needs are met.

Betsy Clebsch (1997) notes in her book on salvias that this species has been in cultivation in Europe since the early 19th century, but it is a more recent addition to the horticulture of the Southwest. While a few selections of this species have been made, they are not common.

Use Mexican blue sage as part of a dry perennial garden in milder parts of the region. Its beautiful flowers complement any color scheme, and like most of their relatives, are highly attractive to hummingbirds.

Salvia clevelandii
Chaparral sage, Cleveland sage

FAMILY: Lamiaceae.
DISTRIBUTION: From Southern California at elevations below 3000 ft. (900 m) south into Baja California of Mexico.
MATURE SIZE: 2 to 5 ft. (0.6 to 1.5 m) tall and as wide.
BLOOMING PERIOD: April to June.
EXPOSURE: Full sun in all locations.
HARDINESS: Cold hardy to at least 20°F (−7°C).

Chaparral sage is a multistemmed plant that grows from a semiwoody base. The 0.5- to 1-in. (1.5- to 2.5-cm) long leaves are ovate to linear-lanceolate and are dusky green with slightly wavy margins. The leaves are rough and intensely aromatic when touched or crushed.

The flowers are up to 1 in. (2.5 cm) long and are congested into whorls along the 3- to 4-ft. (0.9- to 1.2-m) tall stalk. The flowers are a showy dark blue to purple.

Chaparral sage grows best in soils with excellent drainage but is otherwise not particular about soil type. In the hottest areas water it two or three times a month in the summer. In all other areas it does best with a dry summer.

This charming California native has been the subject of much selection and hybridization in California. Many of these are not common outside of the state, but they could be; most of them are beautiful plants.

Perhaps the best known is 'Winifred Gilman', a form originally distributed by Strybing Arboretum in San Francisco, California, but brought into greater production and prominence by California Flora Nursery of Santa Rosa. It has good cold hardiness, grows to only 3 ft. (0.9 cm) tall, and has red flowering stems, dark reddish calyx, and violet flowers.

'Allen Chickering' is a hybrid that sprang up at Rancho Santa Ana Botanic Garden and has medium dark green leaves and purple flowers. A number of named forms are almost impossible to distinguish from this hybrid form and include 'Aromas', with a lower habit, medium gray-green foliage, and lavender flowers; 'Pozo Blue'; 'Santa Cruz Dark'; and 'Whirly Blue'.

'Betsy Clebsch' was introduced by Rancho Santa Ana Botanic Garden to honor the doyenne of salvia growers. It has flowers in a wide array of light and dark purple, and even white, on the same plant.

Salvia clevelandii

Mountain States Nursery in Glendale, Arizona, introduced a hybrid between chaparral sage, *Salvia mohavensis*, and *S. dorrii* that was found in a private yard in Tucson. Known as 'Trident' it has small gray-green leaves, grows to 3 ft. (0.9 m) tall, and bears deep blue flowers. Another hybrid between *S. clevelandii* and probably *S. mohavensis* is known as 'Carl Nielsen'; it is an outstanding and dramatic plant with the stature of *S. clevelandii* and dark purple flowers. It is not currently under production in the region, but sensational representatives are growing at Arizona-Sonora Desert Museum in Tucson.

Flowering stalks are fragrant and long lasting when used either fresh or dried. While deer may browse chaparral sage from time to time, it withstands such pruning well. Use this outstanding species in any dry area that needs a good color splash in the late spring. Because of its great drought and heat tolerance, chaparral sage blends well with native plantings in areas that are only intermittently watered, or with dry growing succulents. Like most salvias, it does not last beyond 10 years, when it needs to be replaced.

Salvia coccinea

Salvia coccinea
Scarlet sage, tropical sage

FAMILY: Labiatae.
DISTRIBUTION: Origins of this species are murky, but it is thought to be native to Mexico. Naturalized throughout Mexico, South America, and the southern United States from eastern Texas to Florida and South Carolina.
MATURE SIZE: 2 to 3 ft. (0.6 to 0.9 m) tall and spreading 1 to 2 ft. (0.3 to 0.6 m) wide.
BLOOMING PERIOD: March to December, but year-round in areas with warm winters.
EXPOSURE: Full sun or filtered shade in all areas, although filtered shade is best in the deserts.
HARDINESS: Leaves and stems can be damaged at 30°F (−1°C), but the plant recovers quickly.

Scarlet sage grows initially as a low, basal set of lanceolate, paired leaves. The heart-shaped leaves are 1 to 3 in. (2.5 to 8.0 cm) long, dark green, and covered with fine hairs that are irritating when you handle them. The square stems are also covered with prominent, straight, irritating hairs.

Flowering stalks rise from the base and are leafy and up to 3 ft. (0.9 m) tall. They are frequently branched into three parts toward the end, and each branch blooms sequentially.

Flowers are enclosed by a prominent green calyx that is persistent after flowering and will cover nearly half the bloom. The tubular corolla has an upper lobe that folds over like a hood while the lower lobes are frilly, extending from the tube like a flouncy collar. Flowers are red, pink, bicolor, and white.

Scarlet sage has been grown in gardens for a long time. Thomas Jefferson included it in his extensive collection at Monticello, and it has been in warm European gardens since at least the early 19th century. This means there are numerous selections and forms with an equally large number of names, often for plants that look just the same. Some of the most common and reliable are mentioned here. 'Alba,' 'Lactea', and 'Snow Nymph' are white-flowering forms. 'Bicolor' has white upper lobes and pink lower lobes. 'Brenthurst' is a peachy pink bicolor with dark stems. 'Coral Nymph' (also called 'Cherry Blossom') has pale salmon upper lobes and pale pink lower lobes. 'Lady in Red' has scarlet flowers. 'Punicea' is purple-red with a red calyx. 'Rosea' is pink. Of these the most commonly sold in the Southwest are the dark red, 'Coral Nymph', and any of the variously named white forms.

Scarlet sage grows best in fertile, well-drained soils. In the deserts it needs regular supplemental irrigation in the summer to continue flowering through the warm weather. In areas with reliable summer rain, it grows well on natural rainfall. In fact, in some areas it can become a pest in the garden, spreading by both seed and runners aggressively. In the hottest deserts it will reseed freely with water but is rarely aggressive enough to be considered a garden pest. Amazingly, the color forms are true from seed.

Once all the flowering stalks have finished it is best to cut them back to the ground. This not only tidies up the planting but also encourages another round of blooming.

As all gardeners know, there is more life in the garden than just the plants. Birds, insects, butterflies, lizards, and a wide array of other less-visible or -cuddly life abound. When lesser goldfinch took up residence in our yard, they were first attracted to the fruit of bee bush (*Aloysia wrightii*), but later I noticed that they showed just as strong a preference for the seed of scarlet sage, particularly the exuberant red-flowering form. That is a good enough reason in my garden to keep this perennial around forever.

Use scarlet sage to fill in any area that needs an intense dose of color, particularly in the summer. It blends well with other perennials including other salvias and forms an effortless addition to any garden intended to attract hummingbirds.

Salvia farinacea
Mealy cup sage, mealy sage

FAMILY: Lamiaceae.

DISTRIBUTION: In the United States from southern New Mexico to central and western Texas at elevations from 1400 to 6000 ft. (420 to 1800 m). In Mexico in Coahuila.

MATURE SIZE: 3 to 4 ft. (0.9 to 1.2 m) tall and spreading 2 to 3 ft. (0.6 to 0.9 m) wide.

BLOOMING PERIOD: March to November, with heaviest bloom in late spring and again in the fall.

EXPOSURE: Full sun in all but the hottest deserts, where filtered shade or morning sun is needed.

HARDINESS: Foliage is cold hardy to 0°F (−18°C).

Salvia farinacea

This loose perennial has numerous stems rising from the base. The stems are generally erect, but in some areas or populations they can also be reclining or lax.

Like many species with a large range, this one shows much variation, particularly in the leaves. These are linear to ovate, with entire or serrated edges, and may have sharp, acute tips or be nearly rounded, They have variable amounts of hairiness and range from 1.25 to 3.5 in. (3 to 9 cm) long.

Flowers are crowded into a terminal cluster. The calyx is covered with whitish hairs, which in some forms are vivid and prominent. The 0.5-in. (1.5-cm) corolla ranges in color from lavender to deep violet.

This species is yet another example of a western native that has traveled around, especially to England, and come back as an ornamental plant. Mealy cup sage has been grown since the mid-19th century and is recognized chiefly for the selection 'Victoria Blue', also called 'Victoria'. This form is a short congested plant with minimal hairs on the stems and flowers, and deep blue flowers. A white version of this selection is sometimes called 'Victoria White'. Both are tender plants in the deserts and are considered annuals by most gardeners.

The well-known 'Indigo Spires' with its deep purple flowers and tall, erect spikes is reported to be a hybrid between *Salvia farinacea* and *S. longispicata*.

Bicolor forms exist, one of which is 'Strata', a 1.5-ft. (0.5-m) tall plant with silver leaves.

Fortunately, the strains that come from wilder stock are now showing up in the trade. These are considerably sturdier selections for the region. The plants grow taller and are usually coated with the fine white hairs so indicative of the species. They tend to bloom in dark lavender or violet shades.

The wilder strains of mealy cup sage tolerate any kind of soil, including rocky, unamended soils, and require only modest summer watering, even in the deserts, to thrive. In the hottest areas it is best to provide these strains with protection from afternoon sun. When grown in these conditions, mealy cup sage is intermittently in bloom throughout the year. Plants grown in the shade tend to run and flop a bit more.

The flowers are much more interesting to me in the wilder strains. The calyx looks as if it has been dipped in fine talc, which provides a stunning contrast to the deep blue of the corolla. The calyx encloses almost half the corolla, and the extended lobes are divided into a lower lip and an upper hood.

Because it will spread when grown well, use mealy cup sage to fill in a small dry corner or relieve the boredom often associated with too many green leafy plants. Its tolerance for extreme alkalinity makes it useful in areas that are only slightly amended and rocky. Supplemental irrigation in the summer helps keep the plants in flower, but it is not necessary to provide more than weekly watering during the driest parts of the summer, even in the deserts.

Salvia greggii
Autumn sage

FAMILY: Lamiaceae.

DISTRIBUTION: In the United States in western and southern Texas. Widespread in Mexico from Chihuahua to San Luis Potosí at elevations from 5000 to 9000 ft. (1500 to 2740 m).

MATURE SIZE: 1 to 4 ft. (0.3 to 1.2 m) tall and 1 to 2 ft. (0.3 to 0.6 m) wide.

BLOOMING PERIOD: March to September, but spring and fall in the hottest deserts.

EXPOSURE: Full sun to filtered shade in all areas but the deserts, where filtered shade or morning sun is needed.

HARDINESS: Cold hardy to 15°F (−9°C) with no damage, and to 0°F (−18°C) with damage from which it will recover.

This loosely branched perennial has brownish stems and glossy green, leathery leaves. Leaves range from obovate to elliptic with a rounded tip. They are usually 1 in. (2.5 cm) long on a short pedicel and have a minty fragrance when crushed. They are so closely packed around the node that they appear as a cluster.

Flowers are sparsely arranged on a 6- to 8-in. (15- to 20-cm) tall leafless stalk in a loose raceme. Each flower is surrounded by a prominent calyx that ranges in color from green to deep rosy red. The flowers have a huge color range from deep red to magenta, pink, orange, yellow, and white.

Autumn sage thrives in rich, well-amended soils with good drainage. Its water and sun requirements depend greatly on the area in which it is grown. In milder areas it can be grown in any amount of sun and with watering only during long

Salvia greggii

dry spells in the summer. In the deserts it should be grown in filtered shade or morning sun with regular, supplemental watering in the summer. In these climates, mulch is important to keep the root zone cool and to mitigate water loss.

Autumn sage is one of the most commonly grown and beloved of all salvias in the region—and with good reason. Well-grown plants are a wonderful addition to any perennial planting. This species blends beautifully with all other salvias and with most arid-adapted perennials. In the hottest deserts it was often used in extremely hot locations where it failed dramatically, but when used in less rigorous situations it is a glorious and abundant flowering perennial.

It is always wise to not become overly attached to any individual salvia. Like raising wild animals, salvias won't be with you long. As a rule they are short-lived plants and you can count on five to seven years from them, especially in the hottest areas. Therefore, when a salvia begins to languish or isn't as vigorous as it used to be and has fewer leaves or flowers, it is probably old age. Plan for the next one, either by making a cutting from your current plant, or by scouting out a new one to take its place.

In both nature and horticulture a bewildering number of hybrids exists with this species as one parent. In fact, I am never certain that most of what is sold as *Salvia greggii* is purely that. This does not, however, detract from the grace and beauty of this species in the garden. The most common hybrid forms are those with *S. microphylla*—which are discussed under that species description.

A few color forms of this species have been brought out over the years. 'Big Pink' is just as it sounds with larger-than-average pink flowers. 'Furman's Red' is one of the oldest named color forms and is a deep, rich red. 'Wild Thing' from Tom Peace of Colorado has pink flowers with a wine-colored calyx. Pat McNeal of Austin, Texas, has introduced a couple of purple forms, 'Purple Pastel' and 'Purple Haze'.

Hummingbirds are strongly attracted to this species, and a generous planting near a seating area or patio will assure an abundant number of these delightful visitors in the garden.

Salvia leucantha
Mexican bush sage

FAMILY: Lamiaceae.
DISTRIBUTION: The exact distribution of this species is poorly known, but it is known to occur in Mexico in the states of Morelos, México, Tlaxcala, and Veracruz at elevations from 7200 to 8200 ft. (2160 to 2500 m).
MATURE SIZE: 4 to 6 ft. (1.2 to 1.8 m) tall and spreading 3 to 6 ft. (0.9 to 1.8 m) wide.
BLOOMING PERIOD: March to October.
EXPOSURE: Full sun or filtered shade in all locations but the deserts, where filtered shade is best.
HARDINESS: Leaves and stems are damaged below 25°F (−4°C), but well-mulched plants are root hardy to 0°F (−18°C).

Mexican bush sage grows a low mound of basal leaves throughout most of the year. The leaves are up to 2.5 in. (6.4 cm) long and are ridged with prominent veins that make them look crimped. The upper surface is gray-green, but the underside, as well as the flowering stalks, is covered with white, woolly hairs.

The flowers are held in dense spikes or racemes on flowering stalks that can rise over 3 ft. (0.9 m) above the foliage. The calyx of the flowers is fuzzy and ranges in color from soft lavender to deep purple. The corolla is tubular and extends about 0.5 in. (1.5 cm) beyond the calyx. It is typically white but occasionally purple.

Salvia leucantha

Mexican bush sage grows in almost any garden soil, but rocky, unamended soils may cause it to become quickly chlorotic. Good drainage is essential. In most areas it requires steady summer watering. In summer rainfall areas, water during dry spells, and in the hottest deserts provide supplemental watering every four to seven days.

This garden ornamental is common in many parts of the region and has some noteworthy selections. 'Midnight' has both a dark purple calyx and deep purple flowers. Other purple-flowered selections go by a number of names but are indistinguishable one from another.

'Santa Barbara' grows 2 to 3 ft. (0.6 to 0.9 m) tall when flowering and up to 4 ft. (1.2 m) wide. The foliage is somewhat denser than typical and the rose-lavender flowers emerge from a purple calyx. It was found by Santa Barbara gardener Kathy Ann Brown and introduced by San Marcos Growers.

Often considered a fall-flowering species, Mexican bush sage may actually bloom anytime during the year. Remove the long flowering stalks once flowering is complete to encourage repeat blooming and keep the plant looking tidy. Once relieved of the old blooming stalks, plants grow quickly again to blooming size.

I have found this species to be almost effortless in a perennial garden. It can be large when in bloom, often with as many as a dozen stalks in bloom at one time, so give it plenty of room. I like the mighty spires of flowers that arise and float over the other perennials. The colors are gorgeous, regardless of the selection, and blend well with a mixed perennial planting. In the hottest areas, Mexican bush sage adds much drama to the colors of fall. Hummingbirds love it and, because it is so tall, you can easily enjoy their antics as they feed on the velvety flowers.

Salvia microphylla
Cherry sage

Synonym: *Salvia grahamii* (in part).

FAMILY: Lamiaceae.

DISTRIBUTION: In the United States in southeastern Arizona and across a wide arc encompassing the mountainous areas of the western, eastern, and central portions of Mexico.

MATURE SIZE: 3 to 4 ft. (0.9 to 1.2 m) tall and about as wide.

BLOOMING PERIOD: March to December.

EXPOSURE: Filtered sun in the hottest deserts, filtered shade or full sun in milder areas.

HARDINESS: Cold hardy to about 15°F (−9°C) for brief periods.

It can be difficult to know if you have cherry sage because it hybridizes freely in the garden, in the nursery, and in nature, particularly with autumn sage (*Salvia greggii*). The resulting selections and forms may be sold under almost any name.

Typical cherry sage has ovate leaves that are smooth, somewhat rounded at the tip, often with a crimped or slightly wavy margin. The 1-in. (2.5-cm) long leaves have a lovely aroma when crushed that isn't as minty or sharp as autumn sage.

Flowers are held in a terminal raceme with two flowers per node. The flowering stalk rises 6 to 8 in. (15 to 20 cm), sometimes more, above the foliage. The color range is impressive from pink to rose, magenta, rosy red, and scarlet, and many shades in between.

Cherry sage grows best in well-amended soil with good drainage. In the deserts it is important to provide regular summer watering and shade or filtered shade. In areas with reliable summer rains, cherry sage grows well with minimal irrigation unless there is a protracted dry period. To keep the plants tidy and dense, prune in the early spring before the first flush of growth. Thereafter, restrict pruning to taking out the blooming stalks as they finish.

You will still find plants sold as *Salvia grahamii*, the form from southern Arizona. It is often known, as is *S. microphylla*, as Graham's sage. In England, *S. grahamii* was formerly known as *S. neurepia*, and you can still find references to the latter name as either a species or a variety of *S. microphylla*.

An enormous number of color forms of cherry sage have received names. These include 'Cerro Potosi' with large, magenta flowers; 'La Trinidad Pink'

Salvia microphylla (Wynn Anderson)

with bright pink flowers; and 'San Carlos Festival' with rosy-red flowers and gray-green leaves. The fancifully named 'Berzerkeley' is a compact dwarf form growing 24 in. (60 cm) tall and up to 4 ft. (1.2 m) wide, with deep blue-green, slightly glossy foliage and deep rose-pink flowers. It was discovered as a seedling at Monterey Bay Nursery in California.

Grower Rich Dufresne introduced 'Wild Watermelon', a seedling he received from Strybing Arboretum in San Francisco. He also introduced 'Maraschino', which he considered a hybrid between *Salvia microphylla* and *S. grahamii*, but is probably more appropriately considered the result of crossing two different forms of the same species. This cultivar is well named for its cherry red flowers with deep purple notes.

A new introduction is the astounding 'Hot Lips' brought into cultivation from plants received by Richard Thomas of California from a Mexican garden. It is a brilliant bicolor with half the flower scarlet red and the other half pure white.

Many more forms are available, some of which may not be unique. In England a deep red form that has been grown a long time as 'Kew Red' has bright red flowers and is particularly vigorous.

In case all that botanical confusion was not enough, James Compton has proposed the natural hybrid swarm *Salvia ×jamensis* for a group of *S. microphylla* and *S. greggii* hybrids found in Coahuila, Nuevo León, and San Luis Potosí, Mexico. Members of this group are especially good garden plants for the hottest desert regions. *Salvia ×jamensis* thrives in the heat and low humidity of the deserts and has a longer life than most selections of either parent. Some of the named selections of this taxon include 'Cienega de Oro', which is light yellow; 'Sierra San Antonio', which is a peachy and yellow bicolor; and 'San Isidro Moon', which has pale pink flowers and a purple calyx.

A vigorous red selection is almost assuredly part of this hybrid group. Found in garden centers especially in Texas, it has no proper name, but I like to call it 'Texas Red'. The nearly identical 'Desert Red' from Desert Tree Farm in Phoenix can also be seen in the region. Both of these forms have deep, rich scarlet flowers that are larger than average.

Whichever form of cherry sage is grown, it is lovely blended into a mixed perennial bed, to accent a mixed succulent garden, or around a seating area or pool. The plants are highly attractive to hummingbirds and with their long blooming season make an excellent choice for a hummingbird garden.

Santolina chamaecyparissus
Lavender cotton, gray santolina

FAMILY: Asteraceae.
DISTRIBUTION: Spain and Morocco.
MATURE SIZE: 18 to 24 in. (46 to 60 cm) tall and 24 to 36 in. (60 to 90 cm) wide.
BLOOMING PERIOD: May to September, but May and June in the deserts.
EXPOSURE: Full sun even in the deserts.
HARDINESS: Cold hardy to 0°F (−18°C).

Lavender cotton has countless branched stems from a woody base. The stems are so thick and complicated that the plant looks impenetrable and usually forms a tight mound.

The leaves are 1.5 in. (4 cm) long, pinnately compound, and covered with short gray hairs. They look like tight miniature ferns.

Flowers are solitary on a long stalk held up to 12 in. (30 cm) high over the foliage. The bright yellow rayless flowering head is 0.5 in. (1.5 cm) across. The flowers are tightly congested in the head and resemble a flattened button on a stalk.

Lavender cotton grows best in rocky or other extremely well-drained soils with only negligible amendments. Water regularly through its fall and winter growing season, but reduce watering to a minimum through the summer even in the deserts. This Mediterranean native is best suited for hot, dry sites that are not regularly irrigated during the summer.

Lavender cotton tends to become leggy over the years. To prevent or minimize this problem, prune the plant gently each fall to retain its tidy, regular form. Spent flowering stalks may be pruned anytime after flowering is complete. The flowers dry well for use in dried arrangements.

A few selections of this species are not common outside of California but would be worthwhile in dry gardens. 'Little Ness' grows 8 to 10 in. (20 to 25 cm) tall and 12 in. (30 cm) wide. 'Pretty Carol' is 16 in. (41 cm) tall and wide and,

Santolina chamaecyparissus

similar to 'Weston', a silvery dwarf, is chiefly found in Europe. 'Lemon Queen' is likewise compact and smaller with bright lemony flowers.

Lavender cotton is a useful addition to a dry garden that needs some color relief. The calm, silvery cast of the foliage contrasts well with both the hard edges of smaller cacti and agaves, as well as species such as desert buckwheat (*Eriogonum fasciculatum*), Angelita daisy (*Tetraneuris scaposa*), and rosemary (*Rosmarinus officinalis*). Use it to line a walkway or define a bed or planting area. Because of its excellent drought hardiness, lavender cotton can be used in any garden situation that has regular supplemental irrigation.

The closely related green santolina (*Santolina rosmarinifolia*) is a short, tidy, many branched perennial of similar size. Its leaves are bright green and finely cut into short lobes, with a strong sharp aroma. The flowers are much the same as those of lavender cotton. This plant grows in the same conditions as lavender cotton and can be used anywhere that a low-growing, deep green mound would be welcome.

Scutellaria suffrutescens
Red skullcap

FAMILY: Lamiaceae.

DISTRIBUTION: In Mexico from Nuevo León and Coahuila at elevations from 5000 to 6600 ft. (1500 to 2010 m).

MATURE SIZE: 4 to 8 in. (10 to 20 cm) tall and 10 to 15 in. (25 to 38 cm) wide.

BLOOMING PERIOD: June to October.

EXPOSURE: Full sun or filtered shade.

HARDINESS: Cold hardy to at least 15°F (−9°C).

Scutellaria suffrutescens

Red skullcap is a dense collection of numerous stems that arise from a semiwoody base. The plant is tidy and often so well formed that it looks as though you could lay down on it.

The ovate leaves with rounded tips are tiny, less than 0.25 in. (0.7 cm) long. They are densely packed up the entire length of the stem.

Flowers are tubular with flared lobes at the tips. They are up to 1 in. (2.5 cm) long and range in color from rosy red to pink. Flowers are held on a flowering stalk above the foliage and are arranged up the entire stalk.

Red skullcap grows best in fertile, well-drained soils. Although it performs well in the sultry heat of central Texas and presumably in the milder parts of the region with supplemental watering only during the driest periods, it struggles in the hottest deserts.

This charming perennial is one of the many legacies of Texas horticulturist Lynn Lowery, who collected it in eastern Mexico. It is often included on lists of plants native to the Southwest. Such confusion is understandable, as the plant is an extremely common and well-performing perennial in the region despite not being strictly native. It may also have naturalized to some extent, but I haven't seen any direct evidence of that.

Red skullcap blends beautifully in a mixed perennial planting, especially with salvias and other close relatives that attract hummingbirds. Its tight form makes it useful as an informal border or to fill in space between rocks or boulders.

Scutellaria wrightii

Scutellaria wrightii
Shrubby skullcap, Wright's skullcap

FAMILY: Lamiaceae.
DISTRIBUTION: In the United States from south-western Oklahoma through central and Trans-Pecos areas of Texas, south into Mexico through Coahuila at elevations from 4600 to 7500 (1400 to 2290 m).
MATURE SIZE: 6 to 8 in. (15 to 20 cm) tall and up to 12 in. (30 cm) wide.
BLOOMING PERIOD: March to July.
EXPOSURE: Full sun to filtered shade in all areas.
HARDINESS: Cold hardy to 15°F (−9°C).

Shrubby skullcap has numerous stems rising from a semiwoody base. Stems are more or less the same size, which gives the plant a strong mound shape.

Leaves are oval to almost round and olive green. While small, 0.5 in. (1.5 cm) long, they are packed on the stem in groups that almost overlap.

The flowers are tubular with wide, falling lower lobes. Flowers are deep violet-blue with prominent white nectar guides. The plants bloom prolifically and can be coated with blooms when in full flower.

Shrubby skullcap grows best in somewhat fertile, well-drained soils. It is equally tolerant of rocky, alkaline soils that are lightly amended with organic matter.

This charming Texas native can be found readily on roadsides and occasionally in native nurseries. It has great charm and should undoubtedly be more popular both in and out of its native region. Shrubby skullcap looks good with smaller succulents, in a rock garden planting, or even in containers where its conditions are met.

Senna covesii
Desert senna

FAMILY: Fabaceae.

DISTRIBUTION: In the United States in central and southern Arizona, New Mexico, and Nevada; rarely in southeastern California. In Mexico in Baja California, Sonora, and Sinaloa at elevations below 2000 ft. (600 m).

MATURE SIZE: 1.5 ft. (0.5 m) tall and 2 ft. (0.6 m) wide in nature, but up to 3 ft. (0.9 m) tall and as wide in cultivation.

BLOOMING PERIOD: April to October, but often in response to summer rains.

EXPOSURE: Full sun in all areas.

HARDINESS: Cold hardy to at least 20°F (−7°C).

Senna covesii

Desert senna has many herbaceous stems that arise from a woody base. Stems often rebranch and form a loose, shrubby appearance.

The leaves are compound with six to eight simple, gray-green leaflets. The entire leaf is 2 in. (5 cm) long. Leaflets are covered with fine hairs that make them velvety to the touch.

The flowers are bright yellow in short terminal panicles and appear to be clustered. Each five-petaled flower is 1 in. (2.5 cm) wide.

Best grown in well-drained soils, desert senna is otherwise not fussy about soil type. It should, however, be grown with only modest watering, even in the hottest deserts. It is highly susceptible to rotting out when grown with too much water or where water frequently stands. It is a short-lived perennial but reseeds freely so ample replacements are available for any plants that die out.

In the late spring and summer, desert senna can cover disturbed roadsides of its native area, providing a burst of color during the hottest part of the year. In cultivation it will do the same, providing a welcome break in a dry, hot garden.

Desert senna looks spectacular in a mass planting along a walkway or driveway that is irregularly irrigated. Because of its drought and heat tolerance, it is a fine choice to use mixed with dry succulents to provide textural and color contrast to the planting. Many gardeners use it in a mixed annual or wildflower planting because it will continue the bloom almost year-round.

This species can be grown from plants set out in the spring or fall, or it can be directly seeded in the fall or early spring.

Butterflies and other insects are fond of the nectar, and the plant makes an important contribution to a butterfly garden. Not only does it bloom through a long season, but also it is the larval host for both sleepy orange and cloudless sulfur butterflies.

Senna lindheimeriana
Velvet leaf senna

FAMILY: Fabaceae.

DISTRIBUTION: In the United States in far southeastern Arizona, southern New Mexico, and far western Texas south into the Edwards Plateau and South Plains. In Mexico in central Chihuahua and Coahuila into southwestern Tamaulipas.

MATURE SIZE: 3 ft. (0.9 m) tall, occasionally to 6 ft. (1.8 m), and spreading 2 to 3 ft. (0.6 to 0.9 m) wide.

BLOOMING PERIOD: May to October.

EXPOSURE: Full sun in all areas.

HARDINESS: Plants freeze to the ground at 20°F (−7°C) but recover quickly.

Velvet leaf senna has numerous herbaceous stems arising from a semiwoody base. The plant has an open, loose appearance.

Leaves are pinnately compound, with four to eight pairs of leaflets, and overall up to 6 in. (15 cm) long. Each leaflet is 1 to 2 in. (2.5 to 5.0 cm) long, oblong or rounded, and especially on the underside coated with fine, velvety hairs that are soft and silvery. Leaf color varies by native region with eastern populations more silver and western ones greener.

Flowers are held in short racemes near the tips of the stems. The number of flowers in a cluster varies widely from 5 to more than 20. Flowers are about 1 in. (2.5 cm) across and bright yellow to yellow-orange.

Velvet leaf senna is one of many perennials that made a big splash in my area a few years ago and is nowhere near as common any longer. It is a reliable and sturdy summer-flowering component of any perennial planting, however, and should be used more often than it is. Although tolerant of dry soils, it does best in exceptionally well-drained alkaline soils.

In the desert regions, water two or three times a month in the summer to prolong flowering and keep plants in good condition. In its native region or in milder areas this species needs only intermittent watering during a long dry spell. Pinching back the tips makes the plant fuller and blooming more profuse.

Blend velvet leaf senna with succulents, especially larger agaves or yuccas, to accent their formal, rigid form. Plant it generously for a big summer color fiesta. It is drought tolerant enough to grow well in areas that are watered irregularly.

Senna lindheimeriana

Simsia calva
Bush sunflower

FAMILY: Asteraceae.

DISTRIBUTION: In the United States from southern New Mexico through western and southern Texas at elevations from 700 to 6000 ft. (210 to 1800 m).
In Mexico in Coahuila and rarely in parts of Chihuahua, Nuevo León, and Tamaulipas.

MATURE SIZE: 2 to 3 ft. (0.6 to 0.9 m) tall, but often much shorter.

BLOOMING PERIOD: April to October.

EXPOSURE: Full sun in all areas.

HARDINESS: Cold hardy to at least 20°F (−7°C).

Bush sunflower is not widely grown in the region; in fact, I have yet to see it used in the deserts. I am so impressed with its performance and lovely, long season

Simsia calva (Wynn Anderson)

flowering, however, that I have included it here to encourage more experimentation with this species.

This low-growing plant has a few to several stems arising from a woody root. Plant size is highly variable from tall and almost shrubby to low and mounding.

Leaves are up to 2 in. (5 cm) long and triangular. They occur in pairs at wide intervals up the stem. They are deep green with shallow undulations on the margins and a rough, scratchy feel.

Flowers are held above the foliage on stalks that can be up to 10 in. (25 cm) tall. Flowers are solitary on this stalk, and the flowering heads are 1 in. (2.5 cm) across. The ray flowers are bright yellow, and the congested disk flowers are golden yellow but often fade to a reddish hue.

Bush sunflower grows best in extremely well-drained soils; rocky ones are even better. In nature it is often found poking out of a rocky ledge. It makes a wonderful addition to native perennial plantings or as a season-extending bloomer in a wildflower planting. Because of its tolerance to rugged conditions, it blends well with succulents or can be used in areas of the garden that are not routinely irrigated.

Sphaeralcea ambigua
Globemallow, sore-eyes

FAMILY: Malvaceae.

DISTRIBUTION: In the United States from southern Nevada and southwestern Utah to southeastern California and central and southern Arizona. In Mexico in Sonora and Baja California.

MATURE SIZE: 3 ft. (0.9 m) tall and as wide, but varies greatly in cultivation.

BLOOMING PERIOD: March to May, but anytime during the year, often in response to rainfall.

EXPOSURE: Full sun even in the deserts.

HARDINESS: Cold hardy to at least 10°F (−12°C).

Globemallow has numerous stems, often over 100, arising from a semiwoody base. Stems are covered with yellowish glands and frequently have a pale yellowish or whitish cast.

Leaves are gray-green, 1.0 to 1.5 in. (2.5 to 4.0 cm) long, and divided into three lobes. Margins of the leaves may be wavy, and the surface of the leaf is often pocked or puckered.

Flowers are held in racemes or tight panicles up a stalk to 12 in. (30 cm) high over the foliage. Flowers are cup shaped and usually orange, but pink-, white-, blue-, lavender-, and purple-flowering forms exist. All of the flowers do not open at once, which greatly prolongs the bloom.

I can never get over how tough globemallow is and how lovely it is when in flower. The less you do for it the better it looks. Without a doubt, this is the one of the finest desert native perennials and deserves to have a place in any hot, dry garden.

It is important to grow globemallow lean to keep the plants vigorous and long blooming. They are best in sharply drained, even rocky, soils. Even in the hottest areas, water only infrequently during the summer. In the cooler weather of fall and winter, globemallow grows well on natural rainfall. During protracted dry spells, supplemental water will maintain the plant's vigor.

I have grown numerous species and color forms, and all are outstanding and effortless perennials. Globemallow looks wonderful blended with other dry growing perennials or as an accent along areas that do not have regular irrigation. It is a charming and colorful backdrop for wildflower plantings or in succulent gardens.

Sphaeralcea ambigua

The first spring bloom is often the most spectacular, but plants that are cut back to the base of the flowering stalk right after flowering will put on another equally prolific bloom. After a few years plants should be sheared in the fall or late winter to reinvigorate them and remove any dead stems.

The botany of this species and its numerous close kin is nearly beyond comprehension, and it is probably true that many of the beautiful color forms coming into horticulture in the deserts are hybrids between who knows how many parents. Even wild populations have many naturally occurring hybrids, and it just makes them that much more interesting to gardeners.

Sphaeralcea fendleri is a beautiful species with tall, sturdy stems and pink to pink-lavender flowers. It is occasionally offered in the region, and gardeners should seek it out. In cooler parts of the region *S. coccinea* and *S. angustifolia* are frequently offered. These two species are easy to recognize because of their leaves. In *S. coccinea* the leaves have five lobes, are finely divided, and look lacy and delicate; flowers, as the name suggests, are usually red. In *S. angustifolia* the leaves are linear, much longer than they are wide, and not divided or lobed; flowers are apricot in color. I have found both of these difficult in the hottest areas but excellent in milder areas.

Sphagneticola trilobata
Yellow dots, creeping oxeye

Synonym: *Wedelia trilobata*.
FAMILY: Asteraceae.
DISTRIBUTION: Northern South America and the West Indies. Naturalized along the Caribbean, in the United States in Louisiana and Florida, as well as in many Pacific Islands and in western Africa.
MATURE SIZE: 10 to 12 in. (25 to 30 cm) tall and spreading up to 6 ft. (1.8 m) wide.

BLOOMING PERIOD: Spring and summer most profusely, but year-round in warm climates.

EXPOSURE: Full sun or filtered shade throughout the region, although filtered sun or shade is best in the hottest deserts.

HARDINESS: Cold hardy to 25°F (−4°C) but can be damaged at temperatures near freezing.

Yellow dots is a low-growing perennial whose extended stems root readily as they touch the ground. The leaves are deep green, thick, almost succulent, and separated into three prominent lobes. They are 5 in. (13 cm) long but can extend to 10 in. (25 cm) in favorable circumstances.

Sphagneticola trilobata

The 1-in. (2.5-cm) flowers are held on stalks up to 6 in. (15 cm) tall. Flowers are solitary at the tip of the stalk, and both the rays and the disks are golden yellow.

Yellow dots needs a fertile, but well-drained soil. Maintaining good soil fertility is important to keep the plant from becoming chlorotic.

Like many species of tropical origin that are welcomed into dry gardens, yellow dots will grow larger or smaller in response to how much water is provided. With ample, regular watering it becomes a fast-growing groundcover that can threaten to take over an area in one season. With much more modest watering, once every other week in the deserts, it is a fine splash of deep green, useful as a groundcover in shady areas.

Although frost tender, yellow dots recovers quickly from freeze damage. Prune any damage in the spring after all danger of frost is past. Even in areas where yellow dots does not freeze back, a hard prune in the early spring will help keep it in bounds.

Use yellow dots to fill an area that is in deep shade, such as the entrance to a courtyard or behind a tall wall. The lush green growth and bright yellow flowers light up a dark place beautifully. Because it so dense, it does not blend well with other perennials but can form a good base for shrubs. I also like it as a lush overhang on a low shady wall.

Stachys coccinea

Stachys coccinea
Betony, scarlet hedge nettle

FAMILY: Labiatae.
DISTRIBUTION: In the United States from western Arizona to southwestern New Mexico and western Texas from 1500 to 8000 ft. (460 to 2440 m) elevation. In Mexico from central Baja California to the Cape and on the mainland west to Chihuahua and into south central Mexico.
MATURE SIZE: 12 to 18 in. (30 to 46 cm) tall and spreading up to 24 in. (60 cm) wide.
BLOOMING PERIOD: March to October.
EXPOSURE: Filtered shade in all areas.
HARDINESS: Cold hardy to at least 15°F (−9°C).

Betony is a many stemmed perennial with erect stems that are stout and covered with long, soft hairs. The leaves are gray-green to dark green, ovate to lanceolate, and up to 3 in. (8 cm) long. They usually end in a sharp tip.

Flowers are held in loose whorls of two to three individuals that are widely spaced on the stalk. Each flower is up to 1.25 in. (3 cm) long and tubular with a deep, wide, two-part lip. Although most often red, flower color can range from intense scarlet to pink, occasionally white.

Betony prefers moist, well-drained, fertile, and well-enriched soils. Heavy mulching through the summer is helpful with this species, particularly in the hottest areas.

This sturdy, reliable perennial is ideal for a shady spot that has defied your efforts to plant it with some color. I think it looks best when planted generously and with the plants close together so that they create a massing effect. Hummingbirds are strongly attracted to the flowers.

The selection 'Hot Spot Coral' has coral-red flowers. While white and pink forms are also available, they are generally sold without specific names.

The closely related lamb's ears (*Stachys byzantina*) of herb garden fame is also a charming perennial for dry gardens. Native to southwestern Asia, it has naturalized throughout much of the warm regions of the United States. Lamb's ears is a low-growing plant, rarely over 6 in. (15 cm), and is chiefly grown for its luxurious, white, velvety foliage. The most common selection is 'Countess Helen von Stein' with its large leaves that are over 4 in. (10 cm) long and smothered in dense, long, white hairs. Although it is described as being nonflowering, in fact lamb's ears will flower erratically, with tall, dense spikes crowded with dusky pink-purple flowers. This species is fully at home in the winter sun of the hottest deserts but rarely lasts through the summer. In milder areas it is perennial as long as it grows in well-drained, fertile soil with modest summer rainfall.

Other selections include 'Cotton Boll', which produces flowers heavily covered with hairy bracts that are widely spaced on the stalk; 'Primrose Heron', patented by Sue Gemmell, with golden leaves that turn chartreuse then gray-green; and 'Silver Carpet', which is close to the type for this species with smaller leaves and nonflowering habit.

Symphotrichum praealtum
Rodney's aster, willow aster

Synonym: *Aster praealtus*.
FAMILY: Asteraceae.
DISTRIBUTION: Throughout the United States east of the Rockies and as far east and north as Tennessee and New Jersey and south to central and eastern Texas and the Gulf Coast states.
MATURE SIZE: 6 to 8 in. (15 to 20 cm) tall but up to 3 ft. (0.9 m) tall with the flowering stalks.
BLOOMING PERIOD: September to November.
EXPOSURE: Full sun or filtered shade in all areas, although filtered shade or morning sun is best in the hottest deserts.
HARDINESS: Cold hardy to at least 0°F (−18°C).

Known as willow aster in most of its range, this charming fall-flowering aster acquired the name Rodney's aster in southern Arizona after the late Rodney Engard, horticulturist and onetime director of the Tucson Botanical Garden, introduced it to Arizona gardens without knowing its name. It is a splendid tribute to that remarkable man, and I use the name to honor him.

Rodney's aster is a low-growing species that spreads quickly from rhizomes. The leaves are 1 to 3 in. (2.5 to 8.0 cm) long and smoothly linear with a sharp tip. They are deep green and smooth with the basal leaves congested into a mound.

Symphotrichum praealtum

Flowers are held on long, leafy stalks that begin to grow up during the late summer. By fall, the axillary flowers fill the stalk, turning it from green to purple in a day or two. Individual flowers have purple to lavender rays and yellow disks, and are 1 in. (2.5 cm) or less across.

Rodney's aster will grow in almost any kind of soil. I have known it in fertile, well-drained garden soil. My plants have grown for years in rocky, unamended native soil. It prefers regular watering in the summer and in the low deserts does best with protection from the afternoon sun. After flowering is complete, cut down the old stalk, which will die slowly over the winter anyway. Plants can be lifted and divided anytime in the fall or early spring and transplanted with ease.

This is a superb species to blend into a desert perennial garden not only because it is lovely but also because it is tough and blooms late in the season. Mixed with other late-flowering perennials such as the golden-flowered Mount Lemmon marigold (*Tagetes palmeri*), it makes a spectacular fall show. It can be tall when in flower so put it where there will be plenty of room for the flowering stalks and where it will be easily seen.

Tagetes lucida
Mexican mint marigold, Mexican tarragon

FAMILY: Asteraceae.

DISTRIBUTION: In Mexico from Sonora south to Nuevo León and south into Guatemala in a wide elevation range from 4000 to 13,500 ft. (1200 to 4100 m).

MATURE SIZE: 18 to 30 in. (46 to 76 cm) tall and as wide.

BLOOMING PERIOD: September to November.

EXPOSURE: Full sun in all areas but in the hottest deserts, where filtered shade or morning sun is best.

HARDINESS: Cold hardy to 15°F (−9°C).

Mexican mint marigold is a dense plant with numerous stems rising from a semiwoody base. A strong central root acts as a tuber from which lateral growth emerges.

The deep green leaves are stalkless and crowded up the stems. They end in a strong tip and smell distinctly of anise when crushed.

Flowers are held in small groups at the ends of the stems. Flower heads are less than 1 in. (2.5 cm) wide, and both the rays and the disks are deep golden yellow.

Mexican mint marigold grows best in fertile, well-drained soils. In the hottest deserts it is important to give it some filtered shade and regular summer irrigation.

Cold weather causes the leaves to blacken and eventually to fall off, leaving the stems barren for the winter. Once this happens, prune the plant severely and it will regrow from the base with warmer weather. In warm winter areas it may only diminish in the winter, but it can still be pruned vigorously in the spring to reinvigorate the plant.

Tagetes lucida

During the time I managed plant sales for the Desert Botanical Garden, I met many people who had great stories about the species we offered. I recall one woman who lingered over this species, smiling gently as she touched it. It was a new offering at the time, and as I was nearby I asked her how she knew it. She said that her mother in Mexico used it all the time to calm down her children. Her mother would steep it in hot water and add honey. The tea was supposed to fix anything from a bad date to a case of acne, but for her it recalled the gentle woman who brewed it for her children a long time ago.

For me it has the same effect on the fall garden: a soothing presence just when most things are not blooming well. It is a beacon of the great winter season to come. It is widely regarded as a substitute for tarragon, which is difficult to grow in the deserts. Chefs and other aficionados love to use it with chicken and fish.

Tagetes palmeri

Tagetes palmeri
Mount Lemmon marigold, Copper Canyon daisy

Synonym: *Tagetes lemmonii.*
FAMILY: Asteraceae.
DISTRIBUTION: In the United States in Arizona and New Mexico at elevations between 4000 and 8000 ft. (1200 to 2440 m). In Mexico in the Sierra Madre at similar elevations.
MATURE SIZE: 3 to 6 ft. (0.9 to 1.8 m) tall and as wide.
BLOOMING PERIOD: July to November, with occasional or intermittent bloom anytime.
EXPOSURE: Filtered shade or full sun in all areas but the hottest deserts, where filtered shade or morning sun is best.
HARDINESS: Cold hardy to 5°F (−15°C).

Mount Lemmon marigold is a multibranched perennial whose stems are widely spaced and rise from a semiwoody base. The stems are sturdy and in older plants are almost woody.

The leaves are pale green to deep green, 2 to 3 in. (5 to 8 cm) long, and pinnately compound. These leaves give the plant an overall airy lightweight appearance. The leaves also have an acerbic scent that ranges from pungent to rank, depending on who you ask. You often smell the plant before you see it. I find the sharp aroma both unmistakable and pleasant, but others find it otherwise. Like all scents, it is quite individual whether you find it refreshing or revolting.

The flowers occur on tall, thin stalks up to 6 in. (15 cm) over the foliage. They are 1 in. (2.5 cm) across, and both the rays and the disks are deep golden yellow.

Mount Lemmon marigold prefers fertile, alkaline, well-drained soils. I have known it to grow well in rocky, unamended desert soils and in a luscious, highly amended garden soil. I have grown this species in rocky soils and it did well as long as it had ample shade. To keep it in the best condition and encourage a long flowering season, water it moderately through the summer. In summer rainfall areas it is quite drought tolerant and will grow on nearly natural rainfall. In the hottest deserts it should be watered at least weekly in the summer.

Its habit of fall flowering makes this perennial especially useful in dry gardens. Late-season color can be a challenge in the deserts, and this perennial and its close relative, Mexican mint marigold (*Tagetes lucida*), are among the finest of the golden fall flowers. It blends well with a mixed perennial bed and will carry the blooming season long into the fall. Butterflies live for it, and its late flowering is particularly helpful for insects that are migrating through the region.

A great deal of taxonomic confusion surrounds this species. The name here is the one recognized by most botanists, but others have serious objections to it. Some feel that *Tagetes palmeri* is a species from eastern Mexico and that it is plants of this species that are in cultivation at this time. In this view, *T. lemmonii* is not synonymous but represents a rare species restricted to the canyons of southeastern Arizona and New Mexico which is both smaller and more cold tolerant.

The Lemmons were fabled plant collectors and growers based in California. They sent seed of this species, probably collected in Arizona, to a colleague at Harvard, who then sent it to a friend in England. It was in England that it was "tamed" and sent back to the United States, chiefly Texas, as an ornamental. This is an old refrain in the ornamental history of lots of western natives. Simultaneously, the Lemmons had plants growing in various California nurseries from seed they had collected in many other locales, and those progeny were being distributed around California. Ultimately plants from both of these sources and the progeny between them became the ornamentals many of us know. This tortured history undoubtedly explains why gardeners in various areas find highly irregular results with the plants they buy regarding size, blooming vigor and timing, and cold tolerance.

Tetraneuris scaposa
Angelita daisy, bitterweed

FAMILY: Asteraceae.

DISTRIBUTION: In the United States in Colorado, Kansas, Nebraska, Oklahoma, Texas, and New Mexico. In Mexico in Chihuahua, Coahuila, Nuevo León, Tamaulipas, and San Luis Potosí.

MATURE SIZE: 6 to 18 in. (15 to 46 cm) tall and 6 to 12 in. (15 to 30 cm) wide.

BLOOMING PERIOD: April to October, although in the deserts plants often cease to bloom in the hottest part of summer and resume in fall.

EXPOSURE: Full sun in all areas.

HARDINESS: Cold hardy to 10°F (−12°C), root hardy to well below 0°F (−18°C).

Tetraneuris scaposa

This low-growing perennial has a tight set of basal leaves that form a mound over time. It resembles a green boulder. The leaves are wrapped tightly along the stem and are up to 3 in. (8 in) long, thin, and densely covered with fine, silky hairs. They end in a sharp tip.

Flowers are solitary on tall stalks held 8 to 10 in. (20 to 25 cm) above the leaves. Flowering heads have one row of yellow rays that are cut into three notches at the tips and open out 1 in. (2.5 cm) wide and flat. Disk flowers are golden and mound into a flattened head.

This is one tough little species. Its deep green foliage is deceiving. The species grows well in full sun, rocky soils, and with minimal watering, even in the deserts. To keep it in flower longer and in better condition, water every week to 10 days in the summer in the hottest areas. In milder areas it may grow entirely on natural rainfall except during a protracted dry spell. Good drainage is essential and, in areas with lots of summer rain, adding gravel or raising the plant on a mound can be helpful.

This species was introduced to horticulture in the region as *Tetraneuris acaulis*, the name under which it is still most commonly offered, but the differences between *T. acaulis* and *T. scaposa* are striking if the two plants are seen together. *Tetraneuris scaposa* has a running stem that trails along low to the ground with the leaves tightly clasping the stem up its length. *Tetraneuris acaulis* has a stem that resembles a swollen ball at the base of the plant with the leaves rising out of it. Its leaves are generally hairier than those of *T. scaposa*, but individual plants of both species show much variation on this characteristic.

Angelita daisy is a wonderful ornamental for hot, dry, difficult spots in the garden. Although it spreads somewhat, it is principally a tight, mounding plant. It can look so firm you could imagine walking over it.

Use Angelita daisy to line a path or walkway, fill in a troublesome spot in the hottest part of the garden, or to fall over a small boulder or wall. It blends well with succulents, hard evergreens such as rosemary, or as a low-growing groundcover in hot areas.

Teucrium fruticans
Bush germander

FAMILY: Lamiaceae.
DISTRIBUTION: Western Mediterranean and
    Spain.
MATURE SIZE: 3 to 4 ft. (0.9 to 1.2 m) tall and up
    to 12 in. (30 cm) wide, but 4 to 8 ft. (1.2 to 2.4
    m) tall when grown in wetter regions.
BLOOMING PERIOD: March to May, often with a
    repeat bloom in fall.
EXPOSURE: Full sun or filtered shade throughout
    the area.
HARDINESS: Cold hardy to at least 10°F
    (−12°C).

Teucrium fruticans

Bush germander has numerous silver-colored
stems. The dark gray-green leaves are up to 1.5
in. (4 cm) long, tapered to a tip, and show a silver-
white blush on the underside.

Flowers are oddly shaped with only lower lobes. These are much expanded
and are lavender-blue. They are arranged in loose terminal spikes.

'Azureum' is smaller, almost dwarf form with deeper blue flowers. 'Compactum'
has dark blue flowers but grows to only 3 ft. (0.9 cm) tall and wide.

Grow bush germander in well-drained, even rocky, soils that are somewhat
enriched. Even in the deserts it has good drought tolerance once established;
however, it should be watered in those areas in the summer just enough to keep
it from declining. In areas with regular summer rainfall, good drainage is vital to
keep plants from rotting out.

Bush germander blends well with other dry-growing perennials, especially
other Mediterranean plants such as rosemary and lavender. Its lovely flowers
are highly attractive to native bees, which will then help pollinate the rest of the
garden.

The closely related *Teucrium cossonii* is a short, spreading species that grows
up to 8 in. (20 cm) tall and spreads up to 2 ft. (0.6 m) wide. It has light purple to
rose-colored flowers in the late spring and often again in the fall. This fine, dry-
growing perennial grows like a tight mounding groundcover or fills up a small,
dry corner.

Teucrium ×lucidrys (Mountain States Wholesale Nursery)

Teucrium ×lucidrys
Germander

Synonym: *Teucrium chamaedrys*.
FAMILY: Lamiaceae.
DISTRIBUTION: Europe and southwestern Asia.
MATURE SIZE: 12 to 18 in. (30 to 46 cm) tall and up to 24 in. (60 cm) wide.
BLOOMING PERIOD: March to May and again September to October, but intermittently year-round in many areas.
EXPOSURE: Full sun or filtered shade in all areas.
HARDINESS: Cold hardy to at least 0°F (−18°C).

Germander is a complexly branched perennial with simple, dark green leaves. The leaves are 0.75 in. (2 cm) long, have serrated margins, and end in a sharp tip. Plants are rhizomatous and can make extensive colonies over time.

Flowers are tubular with wide lobes that resemble their near relatives, salvia, although they have no upper, or hooded, lobe. They are crowded into small whorls up the stalk and range in color from dark blue to pink and occasionally white.

Provide good drainage and a fertile soil for best results with germander, growing conditions that most Mediterranean natives prefer. When grown in rocky soils, or perversely, where the soils are too wet or poorly drained, plants will turn yellowish and fade quickly. In the hottest areas, water germander regularly through its cool weather growing season. In these areas, water enough in the summer to keep the plant from declining, but it can rot out with too much water during its dormant season. In milder areas, natural rainfall in the summer is sufficient as long as drainage is outstanding.

'Nana' is a dwarf form and 'Summer Sunshine' is a compact dwarf growing 6 to 8 in. (15 to 20 cm) tall and as wide with variegated foliage and pink flowers. A low-growing form has recently been introduced in the deserts and is called 'Prostrate'.

Germander with its dark leaves and deep blue flowers provides excellent contrast in a mixed planting of perennials. The smaller forms also make good low borders, fillers for dry corners, or groundcovers.

Thymophylla pentachaeta
Golden dyssodia, common dogweed

Synonym: *Dyssodia pentachaeta.*

FAMILY: Asteraceae.

DISTRIBUTION: In the western United States from the Southern California deserts to Utah, southern Arizona, and New Mexico into western Texas at elevations from 3500 to 5500 ft. (1100 to 1670 m). In Mexico from Coahuila to Aquascalientes and south to South America.

MATURE SIZE: 4 to 12 in. (10 to 30 cm) tall and spreading 6 to 8 in. (15 to 20 cm) wide.

BLOOMING PERIOD: March to October, but through winter in the hottest deserts.

EXPOSURE: Full sun even in the deserts.

HARDINESS: Cold hardy to 0°F (−18°C).

Golden dyssodia has numerous small stems that rise from a semiwoody base. The stems are erect and crowded, and the plant has a tight, mounding habit. As they age, stems spread into a low groundcover.

The tiny needlelike leaves are finely divided into 5 to 11 segments while the entire leaf is less than 0.5 in. (1.5 cm) long. Leaves are dark green and strongly fragrant.

Flowers are solitary on thin stalks held barely above the foliage. The flowering head is 0.5 in. (1.5 cm) across. The ray flowers are dark yellow and profuse. The disk flowers are congested into a flattened head and are dark yellow.

Golden dyssodia grows best in well-drained, even rocky soils, and fails quickly in deep clays or poorly drained soils. In the deserts, water every week or two to maintain bloom and vigor through the summer, but water much less often in milder areas. Individual plants are short lived, but golden dyssodia reseeds well, even aggressively in certain areas, so it will appear to be everlasting in the garden. In the early spring or in the fall, prune out any dead or decrepit stems.

The plant is one of the few western perennials that is routinely sold in pony packs and this is a good way to establish a set of plants in the garden. Fall planting is best in the deserts, but where winters are cold, plant it in the early spring. This species also establishes well from seed.

Golden dyssodia is a superb groundcover in hot, dry locations. It extends the blooming season of mixed annual and perennial wildflower plantings. It is so

Thymophylla pentachaeta

small that it does best either in large groupings or in a corner or other confined location where its lovely flowers will be massed to good effect. It grows well in containers and makes an interesting addition to a large potted succulent such as an agave or cactus.

The similar *Thymophylla acerosa* has fewer ray flowers, is slightly shorter, and has an odor of spice rather than the pungent rank odor of *T. pentachaeta*. Plants and seeds of either species are often confused, although *T. pentachaeta* is more common in the trade.

Butterflies are strongly attracted to the nectar of golden dyssodia, making it highly desirable in a butterfly garden. Dainty sulfur butterfly uses golden dyssodia as a larval plant.

Trixis californica

Trixis, American three-fold

Trixis californica

FAMILY: Asteraceae.

DISTRIBUTION: In the United States from southeastern California to western Texas along
rocky slopes and washes from 2000 to 5000 ft.
(600 to 1500 m) elevation. In Mexico in Baja
California as well the lower elevations of
Sonora, Sinaloa, southern Coahuila, San Luis
Potosí, northern Zacatecas, western Durango,
and western Nuevo León.

MATURE SIZE: 3 ft. (0.9 m) tall and as wide.

BLOOMING PERIOD: February to April, but often
in response to summer rains.

EXPOSURE: Full sun even in the deserts.

HARDINESS: Leaves are damaged at 25°F
(−4°C), but the plant recovers rapidly.

Trixis is a profusely branched, shrubby plant with
stiff, brittle, whitish stems. The leaves are bright green, lanceolate or linear, and
up to 2 in. (5 cm) long with or without fine teeth on the margins. The leaves are
sticky and when bruised give off a rank odor.

The flowers are 0.5 in. (1.5 cm), golden yellow, and clustered in groups of 9 to
12 at the ends of stems. When in bud the flowers are encased in long, deep green
bracts that look like a goblet at the ends of the stems. The seed heads become
strawlike after ripening and remain on the plant for a long time.

Once established trixis has great drought tolerance, even in the deserts.
Although it can be watered as infrequently as twice a month in the summer,
more frequent watering will result in more abundant leaves and longer bloom.
Trixis grows in any well-drained soil, even rocky ones. Prune for shape or to
reinvigorate the plant in the spring or early summer, but resist pruning in the fall
to avoid cold damage.

Trixis mixes well with native plantings whether they are perennial, annual
wildflowers, or succulents. The deep green leaves and tidy, rounded form create good contrast when mixed with the spare form of agaves, yuccas, or cacti.
Butterflies flock to the nectar and birds devour the seeds.

Verbena rigida

Verbena rigida
Sandpaper verbena

FAMILY: Verbenaceae.
DISTRIBUTION: Brazil, Paraguay, and Argentina.
Naturalized throughout warm areas of the
United States from Texas to Virginia, including
Florida, as well as parts of California.
MATURE SIZE: 10 to 24 in. (25 to 60 cm) tall and
spreading up to 4 ft. (1.2 m) wide.
BLOOMING PERIOD: April to October. In the des-
erts, heaviest bloom is in the spring, with bloom
tapering off during the hottest months.
EXPOSURE: Full sun in most of the region, as
well as filtered shade in the deserts.
HARDINESS: Cold hardy to at least 15°F (−9°C)
and recovers quickly.

Sandpaper verbena is a multistemmed perennial
with stems that are either erect or prostrate. It gets
its common name from the 2- to 4-in. (5- to 10-cm) leaves that are oblong to lanceolate with serrated margins and fine hairs that make it feel raspy to the touch.
The leaves are deep green and, unlike the leaves of most other verbenas used in
the region, are not deeply lobed.

The tiny flowers are held in 1-in. (2.5-cm) clustered heads on long stalks
above the stems. Each flowering head begins more or less round to flattened but
elongates to a wide thimble shape as flowering continues up the stalk. Flower
color ranges from purple to lavender and rarely white.

In the hottest parts of the region, sandpaper verbena needs weekly watering
in the summer to thrive. It is often unreliable through the summer in these areas
and most often fails when it is grown with a combination of too much sun and
too little water. In all other areas it is an effortless and reliable perennial growing
well on moderate watering only during dry spells.

Neither of the two known varieties is commonly sold. 'Pink Parfait' is an
older variety with pink flowers and a sweet scent. 'Polaris' has silvery leaves and
lavender flowers.

Sandpaper verbena does well in mixed perennial plantings where its summer watering needs can be easily met. The most common form in the region has vivid, dark purple flowers and that color provides a soothing note to a shady bed. This verbena blends well with white- or pink-flowering summer perennials such as lantana, ruellia, and white variegates. It can also be used to great effect in the wells of trees or in areas where a semishady groundcover would be welcomed. Plants can become leggy and overgrown in a season, but a hard prune in early spring revives their form. Butterflies are strongly attracted to this species.

Viguiera parishii
Goldeneye, triangle goldeneye

Synonyms: *Viguiera deltoidea* var. *parishii*, *V. deltoidea*.
FAMILY: Asteraceae.
DISTRIBUTION: In the United States in dry canyons in the desert regions of California, Nevada, and Arizona at elevations between 1000 and 3000 ft. (300 and 900 m). In Mexico in Baja California.
MATURE SIZE: 3 ft. (0.9 m) tall or slightly more in good conditions and spreading 3 to 4 ft. (0.9 to 1.2 m) wide.
BLOOMING PERIOD: March to April and again from October to January, but some individuals bloom year-round.
EXPOSURE: Full sun even in the deserts.
HARDINESS: Young plants can be damaged at 28°F (−2°C), but older plants tolerate temperatures as low as 20°F (−7°C).

Goldeneye is a much-branched perennial with firm stems that are covered with fine hairs. The base of the plant is usually semiwoody.

The leaves are dark green, rough, and triangular. They are variable on the plant, ranging from 1.5 to 4.0 in. (4 to 10 cm) long, but the smaller range is more common.

The flowering head is 1.5 to 2.0 in. (4 to 5 cm) wide and held on a long, branched stalk. Ray flowers are sparse, rarely more than 10, and bright yellow. Disk flowers are yellow and slightly raised in a small mound.

Grow goldeneye in well-drained soils that are not necessarily very fertile. This tough native of the desert can be grown on natural rainfall; however, plants with even intermittent summer watering have a more luxurious form and a lon-

Viguiera parishii

ger blooming season. In areas outside the desert, it can be grown on natural rainfall alone.

The botany of this species is complicated and confusing. A number of natural varieties are recognized, but most of what is sold in the area is this species even though it may still be offered under the old name, *Viguiera deltoidea*. Many of the varieties that are endemic to Baja California exhibit a wider range of both leaf shape and size than the type described here.

This plant needs some room to look its best. Naturally, it has a crisp rounded form, and it is wise to provide enough room for this form to develop. Because it so rugged, it mixes well with naturalized plantings, dry succulent gardens, or areas of the garden that have no regular irrigation. It is so effortless you almost forget you have it until the wonderful flowers erupt. Butterflies crowd to it year-round but especially in the fall, making it a great favorite for butterfly gardens.

Viguiera stenoloba
Skeleton goldeneye

FAMILY: Asteraceae.

DISTRIBUTION: In the United States in the Trans-Pecos, Edwards Plateau, and Rio Grande Valley portions of Texas and in southern New Mexico at elevations from 2000 to 6200 ft. (600 to 1860 m). In Mexico from Chihuahua south to Nuevo León and Tamaulipas.

MATURE SIZE: 1.5 to 4.0 ft. (0.5 to 1.2 m) tall and 3 to 4 ft. (0.9 to 1.2 m) wide.

BLOOMING PERIOD: May to October, often with heaviest bloom in fall.

EXPOSURE: Full sun or filtered shade in all areas.

HARDINESS: Cold hardy to 10°F (−12°C).

Skeleton goldeneye is an intricately branched perennial with numerous stems arising from a semiwoody base. The leaves are linear, deep green and up to 2 in. (5 cm) long. They are divided into fine segments, each of which is marked by

prominent groove down its length and is so narrow that overall the plant looks like a filigree ball.

Flower heads are small, typically 1 in. (2.5 cm)
across, and are held on stalks up to 6 in. (15 cm)
above the foliage. The few golden yellow ray
flowers have an irregular or slightly downturned
appearance. The disk flowers are golden yellow.

Skeleton goldeneye grows best in soils that
have excellent drainage, but it will tolerate almost
any type of soil. When grown in fertile soils it
is greener and has a lush appearance. No matter
where it is grown, skeleton goldeneye needs only
modest supplemental watering. In the deserts it
needs water only once or twice a month in the

Viguiera stenoloba

summer. In milder areas provide supplemental water much less often, if at all.

Plants can be pruned in the early spring to tidy them up or reduce their size.
Cut off spent flowering heads anytime to extend the bloom significantly.

Use skeleton goldeneye in dry perennial gardens or as a softening effect in
dry succulent gardens. It is excellent along walkways or in areas where regular
irrigation is not possible or desirable. Butterflies are strongly attracted to it both
for nectar and as a larval host.

Wedelia texana
Zexmenia, hairy wedelia

Synonyms: *Zexmenia hispida*, *Wedelia hispida*.
Family: Asteraceae.
Distribution: In the United States in Texas along the eastern edges of the
   Trans-Pecos, the Edwards Plateau, and the Rio Grande Plains as well as
   near the Gulf of Mexico. In Mexico from the mountains of Coahuila to
   Tamaulipas, Hidalgo, and the state of México at elevations from 1000 to 6600
   ft. (300 to 2010 m).
Mature size: 3 to 4 ft. (0.9 to 1.2 m) tall and as wide, occasionally more.
Blooming period: April to October, but may continue through December in
   areas with warm winters.
Exposure: Full sun to filtered shade in all areas.
Hardiness: Cold hardy to 0°F (−18°C).

Wedelia texana

Zexmenia is an open, freely branching perennial whose numerous branches arise from a woody base. The plant is often ungainly, especially when grown in too much shade.

The leaves are 1.5 to 2.5 in. (4.0 to 6.4 cm) long and dark green with widely spaced tiny teeth along the margin. The leaves are rough to the touch and end in a distinct spine. They are profuse on the plant, and a well-grown plant looks dense and tight.

Flowering heads are 1 to 2 in. (2.5 to 5.0 cm) wide and made up of 9 to 10 bright orange or yellow rays with disk flowers of the same color. They are held singly on stalks up to 4 in. (10 cm) over the foliage.

Provide zexmenia with fertile, well-drained soils. Even highly enriched garden soil is fine with good drainage. The plant is tolerant of ample summer water and in the deserts should be watered weekly during the hottest temperatures for best results. It tends to sprawl and fall over with time, and a hard prune in the early spring helps keep it upright and tidy. Although very cold hardy, the plant becomes somewhat ragged over the winter, and this spring pruning helps clean up the winter damage as well.

Butterflies are extremely fond of the nectar, and zexmenia makes a splendid addition to the back of a butterfly garden. The long season of bloom, especially the fact that it extends well into the fall, makes it valuable as part of a mixed perennial planting. The lush green leaves provide a cooling note to plantings around patios or pools where the brilliant color can be enjoyed throughout the year.

I don't think this plant has ever quite "caught on," which is a shame. It has a lot going for it: a long blooming season, rugged tolerance to desert or dry garden conditions with only modest amounts of water, resistance to all kinds of pests or diseases, and appeal to numerous species of butterfly.

Zinnia acerosa
Desert zinnia, white zinnia

Zinnia acerosa

FAMILY: Asteraceae.

DISTRIBUTION: In the United States in the deserts and desert grasslands of southern Arizona, southern New Mexico, and the Trans-Pecos region of Texas from 2500 to 5000 ft.(800 to 1500 m) elevation. In Mexico from Sonora to Chihuahua south to Nuevo León and San Luis Potosí.

MATURE SIZE: 6 to 8 in. (15 to 20 cm) tall and 10 in. (25 cm) wide.

BLOOMING PERIOD: March to October.

EXPOSURE: Full sun in all areas.

HARDINESS: Cold hardy to at least 10°F (−12°C).

Desert zinnia is a low, mounding plant that barely resembles its more commonly cultivated cousin *Zinnia elegans*. Stems are thin with numerous branches and, although greenish, are covered with fine hairs giving them a white blush.

The leaves are barely 1 in. (2.5 cm) long and so thin they look needlelike; in fact, the name *acerosa* means needlelike. The leaves are silvery to gray-green and slightly hairy.

The 1-in. (2.5-cm) wide, flat, flowering head is made up of four to six white ray flowers and bright yellow disk flowers. Ray flowers that are finished blooming become tan or dull white and remain on the plant for a long time, making it appear to be in bloom for a longer time.

Desert zinnia grows best in soils with excellent drainage. Rocky sites are ideal and it is wise to resist adding more than a light mulch during the summer to prevent summer root rot problems. Desert zinnia grows slowly in most natural conditions, but you can increase that to a moderate growth rate with some supplemental water.

Established plants should be watered in the hottest parts of the region every other week in the summer and much less often in milder areas. Plants can live through extreme drought but will become deciduous, leafing out fully once moisture is provided.

I once tried desert zinnia in a heavily enriched bed that was also shady, thinking the colors would look good, but it was a quick failure. Even in the deserts, the more sun the better so that both the bloom and the vigor are enhanced.

The similar prairie zinnia (*Zinnia grandiflora*) can be readily distinguished from *Z. acerosa* by its yellow ray flowers and three-ribbed (as opposed to one-ribbed) leaves. The other desert native, *Z. linearis*, also known as *Z. angustifolia*, is rarely seen in horticulture, although it is a fine species for desert gardens.

Desert zinnia makes a great addition to a large complex wildflower planting, where is provides a soothing dash of white, finer leaf texture than most wildflowers, and a sturdy mounding habit. Place it next to boulders or around an interesting stone feature to highlight this delightful species. It is also useful as a border in a more formal planting. Butterflies are attracted to its nectar.

Zinnia grandiflora
Prairie zinnia

FAMILY: Asteraceae.

DISTRIBUTION: In the United States from Colorado to Kansas, south to Texas and west to southern New Mexico and northern and eastern Arizona. In Mexico from Sonora to Chihuahua and Coahuila, south to Durango and Zacatecas at elevations from 2000 to 7000 ft. (600 to 2100 m).

MATURE SIZE: 8 to 12 in. (20 to 30 cm) tall and spreading 10 in. (25 cm) wide, sometimes more.

BLOOMING PERIOD: April to November. In the deserts it blooms profusely in the spring, reduces bloom significantly in the summer, and resumes flowering in the fall. In milder areas it reaches peak bloom in the late summer and fall.

EXPOSURE: Full sun or filtered shade in all areas.

HARDINESS: Cold hardy to below 0°F (−18°C).

Prairie zinnia is a low, spreading plant with long, thin stems that sprawl quickly from the base. The plants are rhizomatous and form dense mounds or mats in congenial circumstances.

The narrowly linear leaves are 1 in. (2.5 cm) long and dark green. They are not as needlelike as the leaves of desert zinnia (*Zinnia acerosa*).

Zinnia grandiflora

Flowering heads are prolific over the plant, often covering the foliage entirely. Each head is 1 in. (2.5 cm) across and made up of four to six bright yellow ray flowers which are slightly downturned. The disk flowers are orange to brown, upright, and of unequal length, making them look shaggy.

Prairie zinnia is more tolerant of heavy or highly enriched soils than is desert zinnia, but it still requires outstanding drainage to avoid root rot during warm weather. In the deserts, water established plants weekly. In the hottest deserts, plants are often short lived and may need to be restored every three or four years. Plants often become dormant when water is scarce but revive when moisture is available.

Trailing plants such as prairie zinnia look good when grown where they can fall over low walls or just barely interrupt your progress on a paved walkway. Try using prairie zinnia to give a hint of randomness in an otherwise tidy perennial planting. Because it spreads so well, prairie zinnia is a good choice for erosion control or filling in a difficult spot in the garden. This species has great charm. It looks like the poster child for an old-fashioned garden.

Butterflies are strongly attracted to prairie zinnia, and in fact to all zinnias. This species is an important food source for adult butterflies as they mate and breed.

CHAPTER 5

Uncommon Perennials

IT HAS HAPPENED TO ALL OF US at one time or another. After pouring over a gardening book, you find an exquisite species that you know is perfect for your garden. You run out to your local nursery, ask for the species, and they have never heard of it. You point out that it is in the book, and they just as adamantly insist that they don't have it and have never heard of it. Persistent gardeners continue to look around only to find it belongs to the obscure club of tantalizing-but-hard-to-find species.

I clearly admit that the species listed below are in this category. The choices of which species to include in this chapter are my own, and they are here because I love them, however much of a challenge they may be to find. These species may be difficult in some areas, but easier in others. Botanical garden sales, gardening events and fairs, as well as a network of good gardening friends, are among the best ways to find and secure unusual or hard-to-locate species.

Ageratina havanensis
White boneset, white mist flower

Synonym: *Eupatorium havanense*.
FAMILY: Asteraceae.
DISTRIBUTION: In the United States in the Edwards Plateau region of Texas, and in Mexico from south central Chihuahua through the mountains of central Coahuila to northeastern San Luis Potosí at elevations from 1700 to 6000 ft. (520 to 1800 m). Also in Cuba and the West Indies.
MATURE SIZE: 2 to 6 ft. (0.6 to 1.8 m) tall and 3 to 4 ft. (0.9 to 1.2 m) wide.
BLOOMING PERIOD: October to November.
EXPOSURE: Filtered shade or morning sun in all areas, full sun only in mild climates.
HARDINESS: Cold hardy to at least 20°F (−7°C).

White boneset is a large, much-branched perennial that in some areas can approach the size of a shrub. It has a semiwoody base and is usually 3 to 4 ft. (0.9 to 1.2 m) tall in the garden. It can be restrained by careful pruning, if necessary.

The leaves are light green, more or less triangular, with slightly serrated or widely toothed margins. The leaves are 1 to 3 in. (2.5 to 8.0 cm) long and end with a sharp tip.

The rayless flowers are held in congested heads and are 1.0 to 1.5 in. (2.5 to 4.0 cm) across. Corollas are white to pale pink and have the extruded stamens that make the entire flowering head look filmy and as if seen through a mist. Flowering heads are profuse on the plant during bloom.

This fall-flowering composite is a must-have for all dry gardens. It takes modest water during the summer and has shown itself so far to prefer only slightly amended, but well-drained soils.

Ageratina havanensis

I find that pinching it back a time or two in the summer makes a full plant with even more bloom. Should a harder pruning be required, shear it early in the spring to increase fullness.

White boneset lights up a darker corner of the garden and blends well with spring-flowering perennials that will not compete with it in the fall. Although used infrequently now, it has proven to be a tough, adaptable species throughout the Southwest.

Asclepias albicans
White-stem milkweed

FAMILY: Asclepiadaceae.

DISTRIBUTION: In the United States in the most arid parts of Southern California and in western Arizona at elevations below 1000 ft. (300 m). In Mexico in northwestern Sonora, western Sinaloa, and Baja California.

MATURE SIZE: 4 to 8 ft. (1.2 to 2.4 m) tall but only 2 to 4 ft. (0.6 to 1.2 m) wide.

BLOOMING PERIOD: March to May.

EXPOSURE: Full sun even in the deserts.

HARDINESS: Cold hardy to at least 20°F (−7°C).

Asclepias albicans (Judy Mielke)

White-stem milkweed is a sturdy plant with 10 to 20 thick, erect, gray-green stems that are covered with a fine white blush as they age. Like its smaller and more slender relative, desert milkweed (*Asclepias subulata*), white-stem milkweed has leaves that are fine, needlelike, and ephemeral, showing up only when there is ample cool-season moisture.

The creamy yellow to white flowers grow in clusters near the ends of the stems. Although individual flowers are tiny, the cluster is 1 to 2 in. (2.5 to 5.0 cm) wide.

This stunning species has chalky, white stems and firm, upright growth habit. It grows best in rocky or otherwise sharply drained soils without excessive supplemental irrigation. Too much water makes plants floppy and reduces the extent of the white blush on the stems.

Use white-stem milkweed in areas that are hot, such as around a pool, or where there is reflective heat, for its drama and striking form. Blend this species with native shrubs, cacti, or succulents to provide height and color in a mixed planting. Plant white-stem milkweed generously in a large area for a sensational massing effect.

I began to grow this species years ago from seed collected along the Colorado River. Like all milkweeds in my experience, this one was easy to grow from seed and I was enchanted by its size and exquisite white form, but it never caught on with most growers and gardeners, with one delightful exception. I still think it is a gorgeous species, providing extraordinarily strong form for areas with extreme conditions, such as commercial areas or along roadsides. It is also useful in home gardens on the edge of the property or other areas that receive minimal care.

Galvezia juncea
Baja bush snapdragon

FAMILY: Scrophulariaceae.
DISTRIBUTION: Endemic to Baja California in
   Mexico.
MATURE SIZE: 3 to 4 ft. (0.9 to 1.2 m) tall and 2 to
   3 ft. (0.6 to 0.9 m) wide.
BLOOMING PERIOD: February to October, but in
   spring and again in fall in the deserts.
EXPOSURE: Full sun in all areas, as well as fil-
   tered shade in the deserts.
HARDINESS: Cold hardy to 25°F (−4°C).

Baja bush snapdragon has numerous thin, green
stems arising from a slightly woody base. These
delicate stems branch repeatedly, and the overall
effect is of a filigreed orb.

Galvezia juncea (Bart O'Brien)

The lanceolate leaves are less than 0.5 in. (1.5
cm) long, narrow, and shed through most of
the year. It is common to see leaves only in the winter growing season, further
enhancing the impact of the stems.

Flowers are narrow, axillary along the stem, and brilliant red. They are typically 1 in. (2.5 cm) long and extremely prolific during the flowering season.

Baja bush snapdragon requires sharp drainage to thrive but will accept up to
weekly watering during the summer, especially in the deserts. Plants grown with
too much water or too much shade are floppy and soft, and may be short lived.

This perennial is currently uncommon in the area, although at one time a few
growers made it available. I think that is a shame, as the plant is immune to most
conditions of the hottest deserts. Although its cold hardiness may prevent its use
in some areas, it hasn't been grown widely enough to know its cold tolerance.
For the adventurous and truly interested gardener, it is one to seek out and try.

Baja bush snapdragon offers excellent contrast with other rugged dry garden
plants like creosote (*Larrea divaricata*), native cacti and agaves, and brittlebush
(*Encelia farinosa*). The green stems are attractive all year, and the lipstick red
flowers are strongly attractive to hummingbirds.

The closely related *Galvezia speciosa* is offered in California. This endemic to
the islands of Santa Catalina, San Clemente, and Guadalupe suffers dramatically
in the hottest desert and is not a reliable choice outside of coastal California.

Glandularia lilacina (Bart O'Brien)

Glandularia lilacina
Lilac verbena

Synonym: *Verbena lilacina*.
FAMILY: Verbenaceae.
DISTRIBUTION: Endemic to Cedros Island off the coast of Baja California.
MATURE SIZE: 2 to 3 ft. (0.6 to 0.9 m) tall and 1 ft. (0.3 m) wide.
BLOOMING PERIOD: February to April, and again in fall in the deserts, but continuing throughout summer in coastal areas.
EXPOSURE: Full sun in all areas but the hottest deserts, where filtered shade is needed.
HARDINESS: Cold hardy to at least 20°F (−7°C).

Lilac verbena is a spreading perennial with deep green leaves 1 to 2 in. (2.5 to 5.0 cm) long. They are deeply divided into wide lobes.

The flowers are deep purple and extremely fragrant. Like all verbena flowers, the tiny individual flowers are held in 1-in. (2.5-cm) heads that stretch out to over 8 in. (20 cm) above the foliage.

This lovely verbena needs sharp drainage and grows well in rocky sites. In the hottest deserts, intermittent summer watering helps keep the plant vigorous. It can suffer from protracted hot spells and, in the hottest areas, filtered shade is advisable. In all other areas it needs minimal supplemental irrigation. Prune this species carefully to preserve the bloom. Late summer or early fall is best, especially if it needs a hard pruning.

Santa Barbara Botanic Garden has released a selection with deep purple flowers, purple stamens, and a white throat called 'De La Mina'. Rancho Santa Ana Botanic Garden has a selection called 'Paseo Rancho' that is much larger and blooms vigorously.

Lilac verbena has a mounded shape when full grown that makes it a splendid choice for a mixed bed or as part of a native wildflower planting. Butterflies are strongly attracted to it, and its highly fragrant flowers make it useful near a patio or seating area. Its tidy shape also makes it a good choice for large decorative pots.

Hertia cheirifolia
Hertia

FAMILY: Asteraceae.
DISTRIBUTION: Algeria and
    Tunisia.
MATURE SIZE: 8 to 12 in. tall (20 to
    30 cm) tall and spreading 3.0 to
    6.5 ft. (0.9 to 2.0 m) wide.
BLOOMING PERIOD: March to May.
EXPOSURE: Full sun to filtered
    shade, with protection from
    afternoon sun in the deserts.
HARDINESS: Cold hardy to at least
    10°F (−12°C).

Hertia cheirifolia

Hertia is a low-growing plant with numerous thick, almost succulent, stems. Over time the base becomes semiwoody.

The 2-in. (5-cm) elliptic to lanceolate leaves are gray-green and thickly succulent. They clasp the stem conspicuously, almost overlapping as they rise up the stem.

Flowers are daisylike with yellow rays and yellow disks and are up to 2 in. (5 cm) across. They are showy because of both their size and their prolific numbers.

Hertia grows best in fertile, well-drained soils with at least weekly watering in the summer in the hottest deserts. It should be kept dry during the winter to avoid rotting problems. Stems can decline over the years, but hard pruning in the early spring reinvigorates the plant.

Some years ago Boyce Thompson Southwest Arboretum in Superior, Arizona, began a series of groundcover trials for the low desert region. Researchers wanted to test not only the selected species' endurance to desert conditions but also the watering requirements. This species was a great performer in those trials, yet despite its hardiness and low water use, it has never caught on with Arizona gardeners. This is regrettable, as it is a worthwhile addition to the paltry number of groundcovers available.

Plant hertia as a vivid groundcover in areas that need its combination of bold leaves and sturdy flowers. It makes a dramatic accent to large plantings or when planted near a large boulder.

Hibiscus denudatus

Hibiscus denudatus
Desert hibiscus

FAMILY: Malvaceae.
DISTRIBUTION: In the United States from Southern California to Arizona, New Mexico, and western Texas, and in Mexico in Baja California, Coahuila, and Durango at elevations below 4300 ft. (1290 m).
MATURE SIZE: 1 to 3 ft. (0.3 to 0.9 m) tall and as wide.
BLOOMING PERIOD: March to May and resuming in August, but sometimes March to October.
EXPOSURE: Full sun in all areas.
HARDINESS: Cold hardy to 5°F (−15°C).

Desert hibiscus is a twiggy, sprawling plant with light gray stems interrupted intermittently by gray-green leaves. The leaves are oblong to triangular and covered with fine hairs. They are drought deciduous and in nature you often see only the stems.

Flowers are 1.5 to 2.0 in. (4 to 5 cm) wide and are solitary in the leaf axils. Their color ranges from pink to pinkish white with a dark pink-red base.

The delicate flowers are entirely misleading about the plant's toughness to desert conditions. This species is found naturally peeking out of rocky fill and thrives in rocky, well-drained soils that are not too fertile. It blooms best and maintains its vigor when watered intermittently through the summer even in the hottest desert. Overwatering will rot out the plant or decrease its life span. In areas with regular summer rainfall, water it only during protracted dry spells.

Because it is so loosely branched, plant desert hibiscus generously to increase the impact of those delightful flowers. Mix it with succulents, native wildflowers, or a dry perennial garden. It can be used as a groundcover if enough individuals are planted. It is a fine choice for areas of the garden that do not receive regular irrigation. It lasts about three years with occasional watering; in less rugged conditions it may live longer.

Justicia adhatoda
Malabar nut, vasaka

FAMILY: Acanthaceae.

DISTRIBUTION: India, Sri Lanka, Malaysia, and Myanmar at elevations below 4300 ft. (1290 m).

MATURE SIZE: 4 to 6 ft. (1.2 to 1.8 m) tall and 3 to 4 ft. (0.9 to 1.2 m) wide.

BLOOMING PERIOD: February to October, with heaviest bloom in spring and intermittent bloom through the rest of the year.

EXPOSURE: Full sun or filtered shade in mild or coastal areas, filtered shade or protected from afternoon sun in the deserts.

Justicia adhatoda

HARDINESS: Leaves are discolored and damaged at 28°F (−2°C), but beyond that cold hardiness is not well documented.

Malabar nut is taller than most perennials in this book, but it is included because it functions more as a loose, semiwoody perennial than as a shrub. It rises from a woody base with a few stems that branch once or twice.

The leaves are up to 6 in. (15 cm) long, thin, and apple green. They are held at wide intervals on the stem, increasing the illusion of being thin and spare.

Flowers are held in congested terminal groups that can be 6 to 8 in. (15 to 20 cm) long. The individual flowers are large, 2 to 3 in. (5 to 8 cm) long, forming a wide tube, and are pure white with purple or rose-colored nectar guides. They are enclosed in pale green bracts that are much smaller than the corolla.

Grow Malabar nut in fertile, well-drained soil. In poorer soils or those without good drainage, plants quickly become chlorotic, lose leaves, and suffer from stress. In the deserts, water Malabar nut weekly in the hottest part of the summer. In milder areas or areas with regular summer rainfall, water much less frequently. In coastal California, Malabar nut can become much larger, but it can be kept at the desired height by watering less frequently. Prune in late winter and again in late spring for shape and to keep the plant tidy.

I came upon this species shortly after we moved to Arizona and could hardly resist its gorgeous white flowers. It grew well for me in our first desert garden, and when I learned that it was from Sri Lanka and other Asian regions, I was astounded; however, many species from the torrid tropics of Asia and the Americas perform well in dry, warm winter areas. Species from these regions, like Malabar nut, are immune to the heat of the hottest deserts but usually need organic matter added to the soil and regular irrigation in the summer. The catch, of course, is the cold, and these plants can be hard to use outside of the mild California coast and the interior nearly frost-free deserts.

Plant Malabar nut in the back of a shady bed or against a shaded wall or courtyard where its exquisite flowering can be appreciated. It blooms early in the spring and again in the fall, both times when there can be a lull in other flowering perennials.

This species is one of the bedrock plants of Indian Ayurvedic medicine. It has been documented as a medicinal plant for over 2000 years.

Justicia runyonii
Runyon's water willow

FAMILY: Acanthaceae.
DISTRIBUTION: In the United States in the Rio Grande Valley of Texas. In Mexico in Coahuila and Tamaulipas.
MATURE SIZE: 2 to 3 ft. (0.6 to 0.9 m) tall and as wide.
BLOOMING PERIOD: April to November in its native habitat, but only in fall when grown in the deserts.
EXPOSURE: Full sun to filtered shade.
HARDINESS: Uncertain, but probably cold hardy to at least 25°F (−4°C).

Runyon's water willow is an intricately branched, upright perennial. The numerous, semiwoody stems hold deep green, ovate to elliptic leaves that are 1.25 to 5.5 in. (3 to 14 cm) long. In the cooler weather of fall the leaves turn a deep, burnished copper red.

Flowers are in widely spaced axillary clusters. The 1-in. (2.5-cm) tubular corolla is surrounded by dense, green bracts for almost half of its length. Color ranges from deep blue to purple.

Runyon's water willow prefers fertile, well-drained soils, although plants in less fertile soils will survive with adequate water and a deep mulch on the roots. This species does not like to dry out completely and should be watered regularly through the summer. Outside of the deserts, or in areas with regular summer rainfall, it should be able to grow on natural rainfall.

Prune it hard in the late winter or early spring to clean out the winter-damaged stems and leaves and to encourage new shoot growth.

Runyon's water willow is not common anywhere in the region, but that is a shame; this easily grown fall-flowering species ought to be incorporated more frequently into our gardens. It reseeds gently in my garden, throwing up one or two seedlings a season. One of these seedlings has a better flower color and larger blooms than its parents, which encourages me in the long-held habit of waiting until a free seedling blooms before I pull it out. It makes for a messier garden but occasionally yields a treasure.

Use Runyon's water willow within any larger perennial planting. It blends well into the background until it is in bloom and looks good with small yuccas, fall-flowering California fuchsia (*Epilobium canum*), and any color of ruellia.

Justicia runyonii

I have heard, but cannot confirm, that it gets woody with age, but my plants show no sign of this and they have been there for more than five years. Both butterflies and hummingbirds favor this species.

Justicia sonorae
Sonoran water willow

FAMILY: Acanthaceae.
DISTRIBUTION: In the United States in Arizona and into adjacent Mexico.
MATURE SIZE: 3 ft. (0.9 m) tall and as wide.
BLOOMING PERIOD: February to April.
EXPOSURE: Filtered sun or morning sun in all areas, although full sun is possible in mild areas.
HARDINESS: Cold hardy to at least 25°F (−4°C).

Sonoran water willow is an uncommon member of a wide-ranging genus. The thin stems are interrupted at wide intervals by the dark green, linear leaves. The leaves are both sparse and deciduous so the plant often has a green, twiggy appearance.

Justicia sonorae

Flowers are tubular, in axillary clusters, and the corolla is a deep, intense blue to reddish purple with white nectar guides and greatly extended lower lobes. The pattern of the white resembles a feather that fell on the interior of the flower. The bracts are light green and linear and barely cover the corolla.

Sonoran water willow accepts a wide range of cultural conditions, from fertile, well-drained soils to rocky, native soils. Watering every other week in the summer in the hottest deserts encourages a greener, lush appearance, but plants will survive on much less.

Because of its twiggy look, it is a good choice to plant near or even within a denser plant that blooms in a different season, much like you would let a vine climb a tree. Such pairings can give the illusion of a multicolored or longer season of bloom than either species individually. Sonoran water willow reseeds in the wetter areas of the garden, and I allow my plants to find their own way, often with exciting results.

This is one of a large group of species that does well in the basins of trees. The watering schedule, particularly for fruit, is just about right, and the plants sprawl just enough to cover the area well.

Macrosiphonia brachysiphon
Rock trumpet

FAMILY: Apocynaceae.

DISTRIBUTION: In the United States from southeastern Arizona west into extreme southern New Mexico and western Texas. In Mexico in Sonora and Chihuahua.

MATURE SIZE: 6 to 24 in. (15 to 60 cm) tall and as wide.

BLOOMING PERIOD: July to September.

EXPOSURE: Full sun in all areas, as well as filtered shade in the hottest deserts.

HARDINESS: Cold hardy to at least 20°F (−7°C).

Rock trumpet is a low, dense plant with numerous intertwined stems. Stems are often reddish in color and are covered with fine hairs.

Macrosiphonia brachysiphon

Leaves are elliptic or almost round at the base and come to a sharp tip. They are small, rarely over 0.5 in. (1.5 cm) long, deep green above and paler on the underside, and often covered with fine hairs. The margins of the leaves are wavy in most individuals.

Flowers are formed by a long, thin corolla tube that is up to 3 in. (8 cm) long. They have much-expanded lobes that are folded back and resemble an origami bird. They are pure white and extremely fragrant.

Rock trumpet is one of the mysteries of the horticultural world to me. This exquisite perennial grows readily in dry alkaline soils on minimal watering and puts out gorgeous, beautifully aromatic flowers. It blooms in the late summer when good bloom can be hard to find, yet it is difficult to locate and remains uncommon in horticulture in the region.

A closely related species in the Hill Country and western Texas, known as plateau rock trumpet (*Macrosiphonia languinosa* var. *macrosiphon*, formerly *M. macrosiphon*), is equally lovely and difficult to find. Both species are worth seeking out for a dry perennial garden where night flowering would be appreciated. Their sweet fragrance punctuates humid summer nights and would blend with other night-flowering species like four o'clock (*Mirabilis jalapa*) and sacred datura (*Datura wrightii*) to form a memorable night garden.

Menodora longiflora
Showy menodora

FAMILY: Oleaceae.

DISTRIBUTION: In the United States in southeastern New Mexico and the Edwards Plateau region of Texas, and in Mexico in eastern Chihuahua, Coahuila, Nuevo León, and Puebla at elevations from 2500 to 7000 ft. (800 to 2100 m).

Menodora longiflora

MATURE SIZE: 6 to 18 in. (15 to 46 cm) tall and as wide.

BLOOMING PERIOD: June to October.

EXPOSURE: Full sun even in the deserts.

HARDINESS: Cold hardy to at least 20°F (−7°C).

Showy menodora has a woody base with several erect stems. The stems and the leaves may be either smooth or covered in fine hairs.

Leaves are similarly variable, oblong lanceolate or elliptic, with smooth margins. The leaves are 0.5 to 1.25 in. (1.5 to 3.0 cm) long and prolific on the stems, often dying from drought toward the base.

Flowers are in short, congested terminal clusters. The 1-in. (2.5-cm) tubular corolla is bright yellow. Flowers are prolific after summer rains or when the plant receives deep irrigation.

I have grown this species for a long time. It was originally part of a set that I sold years ago, but I find its scarcity in the marketplace puzzling. It is without doubt one of the toughest and most drought tolerant perennials I have ever grown. It will accept any kind of well-drained soil, but rots quickly in poorly drained ones. It requires intermittent summer watering, even in the deserts, and I find it does best with irregular hand watering rather than the consistency of a drip system.

Showy menodora reseeds just enough to keep a steady supply of plants around, although my original plant has been in the ground for over 10 years. In colder parts of the region it is deciduous, coming back after the weather warms in the spring. In the warmer areas it is never entirely leafless but is more or less dormant during the winter. In the late winter or early spring, most of the leaves are dried and withered, and that is a good time to strip it of these useless leaves and prune it back for shape

Twin pod (*Menodora scabra*) is a closely related species, native to the deserts of the region, with a twiggy appearance owing to the extremely narrowed leaves and numerous fine branches. Flowers are similar to those of showy menodora but much smaller, usually only 0.5 in. (1.5 cm) or less in length, and with a more open, funnel shape. Another related species, *M. heterophylla*, native to the Rio Grande Valley region of Texas and south into Mexico, should also be considered for use as a well-adapted ornamental for the region. It looks similar to showy menodora, but its flowers are beautifully reddish when in bud.

Showy menodora blends wonderfully with native gardens, dry succulent plantings, or any area that receives irregular irrigation. It blooms intermittently throughout the summer and, when used generously or in mass, makes a welcome relief to the relative dearth of bloom in such gardens in the summer.

Pavonia hastata
Pink pavonia

FAMILY: Malvaceae.

DISTRIBUTION: Australia from New South Wales and Queensland. In Brazil, Argentina, and Paraguay. Introduced and naturalized into the Australian states of Victoria and South Australia as well as the U.S. states of Florida and Georgia.

MATURE SIZE: 3 to 4 ft. (0.9 to 1.2 m) tall and as wide.

BLOOMING PERIOD: May to November.

EXPOSURE: Full sun or filtered shade throughout the region.

HARDINESS: Cold hardy to 20°F (−7°C).

Pink pavonia has numerous complicated stems arising from a semiwoody base. Leaves are 2 to 4 in. (5 to 10 cm) long and strongly arrow shaped, with the two lower lobes much wider than the central one. The apple green leaves have serrated margins.

The flowers are solitary but prolific during the season and have the odd habit of being able to pollinate themselves while still in the bud. Despite the common name, the flowers are white with a magenta or deep purple throat and about 1.5 in. (4 cm) across.

Pink pavonia is an effortless perennial for dry gardens. Grow it in well-drained, fertile soil with weekly watering in the summer. It can grow with less water but will not flower as well and will be drought deciduous. No matter how it is grown, it is deciduous in the winter.

The spreading growth habit is much improved by gentle tip pruning early in the spring. Nip out the tips once or twice during spring so that the plant will become fuller and denser.

This species has never become popular in the region and has even appeared to have fallen out of production. That is a shame, as this heat-tolerant perennial

Pavonia hastata

is well suited for the region and satis-
fies the continuous need for drought-
tolerant perennials that bloom through
the summer.

Although pink pavonia occurs
in Australia, it also occurs in South
America. This odd distribution has
caused quite a controversy in Australia
over the origins of the species. Many
Australian botanists insist it is an introduced species. Other botanists affirm
that records of the species date back to
long before European settlements on the
continent and therefore it must be native. I have no opinion, but it is certainly widely
distributed in Australia at this time.

Poliomintha incana
Hoary rosemary mint

FAMILY: Lamiaceae.
DISTRIBUTION: In the United States from southeastern California and south-
   ern Utah, through northern Arizona, New Mexico, and western Texas at
   elevations from 3500 to 6000 ft. (1100 to 1800 m). In Mexico in Sonora and
   Chihuahua.
MATURE SIZE: 3 to 4 ft. (0.9 to 1.2 m) tall and 4 to 6 ft. (1.2 to 1.8 m) wide.
BLOOMING PERIOD: May to September.
EXPOSURE: Full sun in all areas but the deserts, where filtered shade or morn-
   ing sun is best.
HARDINESS: Cold hardy to 10°F (−12°C) or more.

Hoary rosemary mint is an upright, multibranched perennial arising from a
woody base. The leaves are gray-green with a silver to white blush of fine hairs.
They are linear and thin. The flowers are up to 0.5 in. (1.5 cm) long, axillary, and
sky blue.

   This perennial is less common than its cousin, Mexican oregano (*Poliomintha
maderensis*), but I am fond of it in my garden. The silver-white leaves make a
charming contrast with deeper greens or plants that are dark green.

A rigorous species, hoary rosemary mint grows in any kind of soil as long as it is extremely well drained, even sandy. In the deserts it tolerates a modest amount of water. In my yard I water it when I think about it, or place it near the well of a tree and that seems to be sufficient.

The flowers are small and, while beautiful, are not the plant's most stunning feature. I grow it and recommend it for its gentle foliage and sturdy nature. The leaves are fragrant with a crisp aroma that reminds me of a combination of juniper and oregano. Use this plant where you might be apt to brush against it to release the cleansing fragrance.

Poliomintha incana

Salazaria mexicana
Bladder sage, paperbag bush

FAMILY: Lamiaceae.

DISTRIBUTION: In the United States in western Texas, southern New Mexico, Arizona, Utah, and Nevada, and southeastern California at elevations from 1000 to 3000 ft. (300 to 900 m). In Mexico in central Baja California as well as northeastern Chihuahua and Coahuila.

MATURE SIZE: 3 to 4 ft. (0.9 to 1.2 m) tall and as wide.

BLOOMING PERIOD: March to May, occasionally June.

EXPOSURE: Full sun even in the deserts, where filtered shade is also tolerated.

HARDINESS: Cold hardy to 5°F (−15°C).

Bladder sage is a rounded plant with intricate branching. It has few leaves on its thin, wiry branches. Branches commonly end in a sharp tip, giving the plant a spiny, filigree look. Leaves are present only during the cool weather growing season, and they are less than 1 in. (2.5 cm) long and leathery.

Flowers are profuse on the plant, rising from nodes up the stem. The flower is covered with fine whitish hairs and is a deep, intense purple to indigo. Magenta forms are found in nature, as well. The common names refer to the odd, inflated pod formed by the folded calyx around the seed. The pod is more or less round, pale tan to whitish, and persistent for months.

Salazaria mexicana

Bladder sage grows well in native, unamended soils, rocky soils, and even in sandy soils. Excellent drainage is important; this desert native will rot in poorly drained or tight soils. Once established, it can grow on natural rainfall with only intermittent watering in the summer to assure its vigor. When watered somewhat more regularly it loses fewer stems over the summer but is otherwise not much changed.

The Mojave Desert is full of interesting species. This one has caught my eye for a long time, although it remains obscure in most nurseries in the region. It is an excellent choice to blend into a native planting, in wildflower beds, or in areas of the garden that will not receive regular or consistent watering. Use it to provide contrast in dry succulent gardens, as well.

Stemodia lanata
Woolly stemodia

Synonym: *Stemodia tomentosa*.
FAMILY: Scrophulariaceae.
DISTRIBUTION: In the United States in far southern and western Texas along the Rio Grande and into adjacent Mexico.
MATURE SIZE: 4 to 6 in. (10 to 15 cm) tall and spreading to 3 ft. (0.9 m) wide.
BLOOMING PERIOD: April to August.
EXPOSURE: Full sun in all areas but the hottest deserts, where filtered shade is needed.
HARDINESS: Cold hardy to at least 20°F (−7°C).

Woolly stemodia is a low-growing perennial whose extended stems make it a good choice for a groundcover in a dry garden. The stems are thin and delicate, rising from a single base, and are whitish in color.

The leaves are small, rarely over 1 in. (2.5 cm) long. They are elliptic or almost round and gray-green. They are covered profusely with fine, silvery hairs.

The flowers are tiny, less than 0.25 in. (0.7 cm) long. Held in the axils of the leaves, they are blue-purple to purple and have a striking white throat, which you can see if you can get close enough to the flower.

The plant appreciates well-drained soils, and it thrives in rocky situations. In the hottest deserts it should be watered weekly in the summer, but in all other areas it can be grown with much less supplemental watering. It is dormant, often deciduous, in the winter, and watering should be sharply reduced at that time.

Woolly stemodia makes a delicate groundcover particularly when com-

Stemodia lanata

bined with smaller perennials, bulbs, or other small succulents. It is especially effective around larger rocks or where it can cascade over a wall or large container. If you grow it in a hanging basket, you can get close enough to appreciate the tiny snapdragon-like flowers.

Although not well-known in the deserts, this species has a following in Texas, particularly among native plant enthusiasts. My own experiments with it in the Phoenix area have been promising, and I would urge a wider audience for this lovely ground-hugging perennial.

Thymus capitatus
Conehead thyme

Synonym: *Cordiothymus capitatus*.
FAMILY: Lamiaceae.
DISTRIBUTION: Israel and other eastern Mediterranean countries.
MATURE SIZE: 3 ft. (0.9 m) tall and as wide.
BLOOMING PERIOD: Late spring and early summer.
EXPOSURE: Full sun even in the deserts.
HARDINESS: Cold hardy to at least 25°F (−4°C).

Many plants are described as being mounding, but this species is so tightly compressed and tidy that it looks like a rock that you could walk over. Hundreds of whitish stems arise from a woody base.

Thymus capitatus

Leaves are tiny, deep green, and needlelike with a sharp tip. They have a pungent but pleasing fragrance when crushed and are edible.

Flowers are also tiny and tubular with flared lobes. They are held in small clustered heads on the ends of the stems and can be so profuse that they coat the plant. They range in color from pale lavender-pink to blue.

Like rosemary, conehead thyme can become much more in a dry garden than simply a delightful culinary herb, and like its Mediterranean cousin, it wants to grow on the dry side with superb drainage. Conehead thyme will grow in alkaline, well-drained soils and is not particular about soil fertility. It accepts generous watering in the winter but requires minimal watering through the summer. Plants may lose some of their leaves and become sparer in the summer but green up beautifully once the weather cools and they resume growing. In the hottest deserts, water enough to keep the plant from declining, but in summer rainfall areas no summer irrigation may be needed.

I first came upon conehead thyme through my friend Sarah, who thought I would like it. I thought of it as an amusing experiment and at one time had one in almost every perennial bed in the garden. All the plants thrived, but the most exquisite one is growing in a rocky, unamended bed with full sun. It rapidly became one of my favorite ornamental perennials, particularly for hot, dry areas or those that do not receive consistent watering.

Conehead thyme is an excellent plant for a formal or a tidy planting. It is the essence of elegant form in the garden. It is durable enough to be mixed with hardy succulents and full-sun agaves or yuccas in a dry succulent garden. It is also a good species to anchor a planting of winter-flowering bulbs because of its need to be reasonably dry during the summer.

The leaves are delicious as a seasoning and are a vital component of the Middle Eastern spice blend za'tar. Bees find the species irresistible and so do many butterflies.

Tithonia fruticosa
Mexican sunflower, mirasol

Tithonia fruticosa

FAMILY: Asteraceae.

DISTRIBUTION: In Mexico in southern Sonora, Chihuahua, Durango, and Sinaloa at 800 to 4000 ft. (240 to 1200 m) elevation.

MATURE SIZE: 4 to 12 ft. (1.2 to 3.7 m) tall and 4 to 6 ft. (1.2 to 1.8 m) wide.

BLOOMING PERIOD: March to May, again from August to October in the hottest deserts, throughout the summer elsewhere.

EXPOSURE: Full sun or filtered shade throughout the region, although filtered sun is best in the deserts.

HARDINESS: Leaves suffer minor damage at 30°F (−1°C), but the plant recovers quickly.

Mexican sunflower is a large, sometimes floppy plant, with dozens of rounded, hollow, hairy stems. The stems tend to fall over with the weight of flowering. Although the plant falls outside the size parameters of most of the perennials in this book, it is too outstanding to leave out. Despite its size, it is a soft-looking plant and is actually herbaceous, not woody.

The gray-green leaves are 4 to 10 in. (10 to 25 cm) long, held on long petioles that are hairy and flattened against the stem. The underside of the leaf is whiter and rougher than the upper side.

The 3- to 4-in. (8- to 10-cm) flowering heads occur as either terminal and solitary on the stem or in groups of three or four. Ray flowers are yellow, broad, and showy. Disk flowers are a deep gold.

Lust plays a great role in gardening, and many gardeners find themselves hot after the newest plant, on the trail of the finest cultivar, prettiest flower, or the most unusual offering they can find. This is what happened to me with Mexican sunflower. I first saw it many years ago growing and blooming spectacularly at the nursery of good friends in Tucson. I thought about it a lot but did very little for a long time. Then I got some seeds, and typical of the cantankerous sunflower family, they failed to germinate. I thought about it some more until finally

I found a plant at a botanical garden sale. By that time I was crazed to have it and try it in my own garden. I first planted it in a location with rocky, native soil that received hot, reflected sun in the summer. It sulked spectacularly and nearly died twice. I then moved it to a place with ample morning sun and richer soil, and it turned into the star of one of the perennial beds.

Prune mirasol hard in the late winter or early spring after all danger of frost is past to clear out any winter damage and rejuvenate the plant for the spring. Prune lightly throughout the year, ending in midsummer, to keep it tidy and to encourage repeat flowering. This type of pruning will also keep the plant from becoming overly large or floppy.

Because of its size, Mexican sunflower needs to be given room and used in the back of a large, mixed planting. It is highly attractive to butterflies and would blend into a butterfly garden well. The large and showy flowers make good cut flowers.

Tradescantia sillamontana
White velvet, white gossamer

FAMILY: Commelinaceae.
DISTRIBUTION: Northeastern Mexico.
MATURE SIZE: 6 to 8 in. (15 to 20 cm) tall and spreading up to 30 in. (76 cm) wide.
BLOOMING PERIOD: Late spring through the summer, although summer bloom is intermittent.
EXPOSURE: Light shade or filtered shade in all areas.
HARDINESS: Cold hardy to 32°F (0°C).

Stems are erect when new but relax to spread horizontally quickly. They are thick, somewhat hollow, and covered with fine, long, white hairs.

Leaves are entire, 2 in. (5 cm) long, with a sharp tip. They are coated with fine, long, white hairs that are usually so dense that you cannot see the underlying gray-green color of the leaf.

Flowers are nearly buried within large fan-shaped bracts that are less than 1 in. (2.5 cm) across. Colors range from pink to light purple.

Because of its trailing nature, white velvet looks outstanding in a hanging basket. In areas where it can be grown in the ground, it becomes a charming groundcover. It grows best in fertile soil that is well-drained.

I have included this species because it is one of the few members of this genus from the arid regions of the Southwest and Mexico that is sold with its true name. Many other plants are offered from time to time, and it is difficult to find their proper names. I have grown a number of these anonymous tradescantias and have found that they are an undervalued, and virtually unknown, group that is outstanding in dry shade.

This species and nearly all other well-adapted members of the genus suffer when overwatered. Good drainage is critical in either beds or areas

Tradescantia sillamontana (Scott Ogden)

that receive consistent watering. In the hottest deserts, most plants are dormant or semidormant in the summer, and watering should be only enough to keep them from declining. Winter-dormant species are even more uncommon in the region.

My first introduction to this delightful genus was when I was a college student trying to key out the plants that grew in a small state park near my home. A number of species occurred, and the differences were small, but they were all tall, upright habitués of wet, nearly boggy, areas in central Texas.

Now I have the same confusion when I try to find out the names of the dry-land tradescantias that have come to me from friends over the years. Members of this motley horde are all similar to the plant described here in their culture. They are all low, spreading plants with thick, succulent, often hollow, stems.

The first and still most vigorous species I received came as a cutting from Ron Gass, owner of Mountain States Wholesale Nursery in Glendale, Arizona. I was a bit skeptical but put it in a shady spot and more or less forgot about it. It has thrived with its slick, shiny green to reddish leaves, and I love the fact that it blooms white.

More tradescantias have arrived from friends over the years—a minute one with dusky, purple foliage and tiny lavender to rose flowers, while yet another has deep green leaves and dark purple flowers. I have come to believe that any trailing tradescantia is worth a try, even if we don't yet know what to call it.

Viguiera lanata

Viguiera lanata
Woolly leaf sunflower

FAMILY: Asteraceae.
DISTRIBUTION: In Mexico in the Vizcaino peninsula of Baja California and in Cedros Island off the coast.
MATURE SIZE: Up to 3 to 4 ft. (0.9 to 1.2 m) tall and as wide.
BLOOMING PERIOD: November to April, with occasional summer flowering.
EXPOSURE: Full sun or filtered shade in all areas.
HARDINESS: Cold hardy to at least 25°F (−4°C).

This unusual member of the genus is a much-branched, rounded perennial that arises from a slightly woody base. The stems are numerous and so thick that the plant appears impenetrable.

The leaves are lanceolate with an acute tip and, although gray-green, are so smothered with fine, white hairs that they look white and furry. The leaves occur in a cluster at the nodes with the largest ones prominent but with two to four pairs of smaller leaves crammed in the node. The effect is that of a bouquet and creates the dense look of the plant.

Flowers are solitary on numerous branched stalks held high over the foliage. The 2- to 4-in. (5- to 10-cm) flowering heads have ray flowers of an unusual, iridescent yellow with a darker base. The disk flowers are bright yellow.

Like most California desert and northern Baja natives, this species is sensitive to overwatering in the summer unless drainage is superb. Grow woolly leaf sunflower in sharply drained, alkaline soils and provide just enough water to prevent wilting or leaf drop in the summer. In milder areas it may need no supplemental water in the summer.

Everyone who grows plants knows that you begin to get a "feel" for what will do well in your area or your garden. When I first saw this plant, my "feel" was that it would be another failed California experiment; there had after all been so many. I have brought home dozens of plants from California sales, friends, and botanic gardens—always with the cheerful optimism so inherent in gardening. Most of them failed: it is too hot in summer, it is too humid when it is hot, it is too cold for them—you name it. Those gnarly California trials have been a true test of gardening patience. But this species was irresistible and it has proved to be one of the best migrants.

We found it and purchased it from the Rancho Santa Ana Botanic Garden, that fountain of good California desert natives, but it is also available from some California native nurseries. It is a beautiful plant year-round owing to its brilliant, almost glowing, white foliage and its tidy, rounded habit. Put it where the foliage will be as interesting and congenial as the flowers—at the end of walkway, as you round a turn in the garden—but definitely reserve it for a well-drained, rocky, and low-water location.

It is included here because it is so gorgeous and so incredibly easy in the desert regions. I doubt that it has been used much outside of a few aficionados in California, but it should become a common choice in any dry, hot garden.

Xylorhiza tortifolia var. *tortifolia*
Mojave aster, Mojave woody aster

Synonym: *Machaeranthera tortifolia*.
FAMILY: Asteraceae.
DISTRIBUTION: In the United States in southeastern California, southern Nevada, southwestern Utah, and western Arizona.
MATURE SIZE: 2 to 3 ft. (0.6 to 0.9 m) tall and as wide.
BLOOMING PERIOD: March to May.
EXPOSURE: Full sun in all regions.
HARDINESS: Cold hardy to at least 15°F (−9°C).

Mojave aster is a multibranched perennial with light green, herbaceous stems in the upper part of the plant and woody stems below. The leaves are 1 to 2 in. (2.5 to 5.0 cm) long and about 0.5 in. (1.5 cm) wide. They are gray-green, sturdy, and leathery, with minute gray hairs on the surface. The margins are marked by small teeth and there is a definite spine at the tip.

Flowering heads are solitary on stalks held up to 4 to 6 in. (10 to 15 cm) high above the foliage and are 2 to 4 in. (5 to 10 cm) across. Ray flowers are light lavender, almost white, thin, and numerous. Disk flowers are yellow.

Xylorhiza tortifolia (Judy Mielke)

Species that naturally range in the Mojave Desert are some of the most xeric in our gardening repertoire, but they can also be some of the most challenging. It is essential to grow them in well-drained soil in hot, dry locations for best results. In areas that receive more than 15 in. (380 mm) of rain a year, it is important to keep them as dry as you can and provide sharp drainage.

Watering twice a month through the summer in the deserts will encourage a second flowering in the fall and keep the plants from going entirely dormant. In regions with summer rainfall, natural rainfall may be more than sufficient. It is important not to treat this perennial too nicely.

Because of its extreme hardiness to desert conditions, Mojave aster is an excellent choice in a largely native planting or a dry succulent garden. Use it to give some soft color in the spring to a wildflower planting or to calm down a hot spot in the garden.

Another closely related species, Takota daisy (*Xylorhiza tanacetifolia*, formerly *Machaeranthera tanacetifolia*), is less reliable in the hottest parts of the region. It is, however, an excellent choice in dry, but less severe areas such as El Paso or central Texas. Takota daisy, too, appreciates growing on the dry side but handles humid conditions with more ease. The flowers are much the same, although darker in color, and the leaves are greener and split into a fernlike appearance. Takota daisy is often grown as an annual in cold winter regions, and many gardeners believe that it is truly a biennial.

I have tried some of the other desert native members of this genus, particularly *Xylorhiza cognata*, a rare endemic from the desperate Mecca Hills of Southern California. It did well for a number of years in plantings both at the Desert Botanical Garden and in private homes, but eventually it gave out, probably just from old age, and is undoubtedly unobtainable now.

GLOSSARY

acute. Ending in a sharp point.

alternate. Arranged in two ranks along a stem.

annual. A plant that completes its life cycle in one year.

axil. The angle between the upper surface of a leaf and the stem to which it is attached.

axillary. Arising from an axil.

basal. Arising at ground level directly from the rhizome or on a very short, sometimes buried stem.

biennial. A plant that completes its life cycle in two years.

bract. A modified leaf usually beneath or surrounding the flower.

caliche. A lens or shelf of calcium carbonate that forms in arid regions and is essentially impenetrable.

calyx. A collective term for all the sepals in a flower.

corolla. A collective term for the petals in a flower.

cultivar. A hybrid form created intentionally or arising spontaneously in a garden or other cultivation.

deciduous. Shedding all leaves seasonally and more or less all at one time.

dieback. A condition in woody plants in which peripheral parts are killed.

disk flower. A small tubular flower at the center of a composite head.

dormant. Of a plant that is not actively growing.

drought deciduous. Shedding leaves in response to low water availability.

elliptic. Shaped like an ellipse.

endemic. Native and restricted to a particular place.

entire. Of a leaf margin that is not toothed, lobed, or indented.

evergreen. Retaining leaves in all seasons or losing leaves gradually.

exserted. Projecting beyond a corolla.

fascicle. A cluster of leaves appearing to arise from a common point.

herbaceous. A plant whose stems and branches are not woody.

incised. Deeply and irregularly dissected.

inflorescence. The complete arrangement of flowers and flowering parts on a flower stalk.

involucre. Whorl of leaves or bracts beneath a flower.

lanceolate. Shaped like a lance, and tapering to the tip and broader below.

lateral. On or to the side.

lobe. A segment of a leaf separated by a cleft and usually rounded.

naturalized. To become established in an area, growing as if native to that area.

nectar guide. A contrasting color on a petal that guides a pollinator to nectar at the base of the flower.

node. The point on a stem where a leaf, flower, or branch is attached.

oblanceolate. Shaped like a lance, but tapering to the bottom and broader above.

oblate. Spherical with flattened ends.

obovate. Egg shaped with the lower half narrower than the upper half.

opposite. Attached to a stem at the same point but on opposite sides, as of leaves.

ovate. Egg shaped with the lower half broader than the upper half.

palmately lobed. Having lobes that radiate from one point, like a hand.

panicle. An inflorescence with flowers at the ends of stalks that branch from the main axis, similar to a candelabra.

pappus. A tuft of delicate bracts beneath a flower.

pedicel. A stalk that unites a flower and a stem or branch.

perennial. A plant that lives out its life cycle over more than one year, or is neither succulent nor woody, is not a bulb, and usually grows less than 4 ft. (1.2 m) tall.

petiole. A stalk which unites a leaf and a stem or branch.

pinna, pinnae. In a pinnately compound leaf, the structure that holds the leaflets and is attached to the main axis of the leaf.

pinnately compound. Having leaves divided into leaflets and pinnae.

pistil. The female part of a flower, made up of a style, stigma, and ovary.

pod. A general term for a dry fruit.

pubescent. Having short hairs.

raceme. An inflorescence with flowers on short stalks that are attached to the unbranched main axis.

ray flower. One of several small flowers surrounding the disk flowers in a composite head.

receptacle. The end of stem often flat and from which the floral parts arise.

rhizome. A horizontal, usually underground stem that often spreads away from the main body of the plant.

semideciduous. Shedding some of its leaves annually.

semidormant. Of a plant in a slower-than-normal growth cycle, where leaves may be present but buds are dormant.

serrated. Having sawlike teeth.

solitary. Having a single flower.

spatulate. Shaped like a spatula.

spike. An inflorescence with stemless flowers attached directly to the unbranched main axis.

spur. A projection.

stamen. The male part of a flower, made up of a filament and anthers.

stigma. The pollen-receiving structure at the tip of the pistil.

succulent. Having specialized water-storing tissue in leaves, stems, flowers, or roots.

terminal. Growing or appearing at the end of a stem, branch, or stalk.

whorl. An arrangement of three or more flowers or leaves that radiate from a single point along a stalk.

xeric. Being dry, usually extremely so.

BIBLIOGRAPHY

Arizona Native Plant Society. 1991a. *Desert Wildflowers*. Tucson, Arizona: Arizona Native Plant Society.

Arizona Native Plant Society. 1991b. *Desert Groundcovers and Vines*. Tucson, Arizona: Arizona Native Plant Society.

Arizona Native Plant Society. 1996. *Desert Butterfly Gardening*. Tucson, Arizona: Arizona Native Plant Society and Sonoran Arthropod Studies Institute.

Arizona Native Plant Society. 1997. *Desert Bird Gardening*. Tucson, Arizona: Arizona Native Plant Society and Tucson Audubon Society.

Bailey, Liberty Hyde. 1947. *The Standard Cyclopedia of Horticulture*. New York: Macmillan Company.

Bradley, Fern Marshall, ed. 1996. *Gardening with Perennials*. Emmaus, Pennsylvania: Rodale Press.

Brenzel, Kathleen N., ed. 2001. *Sunset Western Garden Book*. Menlo Park, California: Sunset Publishing Corporation.

Brickell, Christopher, and Judith D. Zuk, eds. 1996. *The American Horticultural Society A–Z Encyclopedia of Garden Plants*. New York: DK Publishing.

Busco, Janice, and Nancy R. Morin. 2003. *Native Plants for High-Elevation Western Gardens*. Golden, Colorado: Fulcrum Publishing in partnership with The Arboretum at Flagstaff.

Clebsch, Betsy. 1997. *A Book of Salvias: Sages for Every Garden*. Portland, Oregon: Timber Press.

Correll, D. S., and M. C. Johnston. 1979. *Manual of the Vascular Plants of Texas*. Dallas, Texas: University of Texas at Dallas.

Coyle, Jeanette, and Norman C. Roberts. 1975. *A Field Guide to the Common and Interesting Plants of Baja California*. La Jolla, California: Natural History Publishing Company.

Cromell, Cathy, ed. 2001. *Desert Landscaping for Beginners*. Phoenix, Arizona: Arizona Master Gardener Press.

Cromell, Cathy, Jo Miller, and Lucy K. Bradley. 2003. *Earth-Friendly Desert Gardening*. Phoenix, Arizona: Arizona Master Gardener Press.

DiSabato-Aust, Tracy. 1998. *The Well-Tended Perennial Garden: Planting and Pruning Techniques*. Portland, Oregon: Timber Press.

Duffield, Mary Rose, and Warren Jones. 2001. *Plants for Dry Climates.* Cambridge, Massachusetts: Perseus Publishing.

Eck, Joe. 1996. *Elements of Garden Design.* New York: Henry Holt and Company.

Enquist, Marshall. 1987. *Wildflowers of the Texas Hill Country.* Austin, Texas: Lone Star Botanical.

Felger, Richard Stephen. 2000. *Flora of the Gran Desierto and Rio Colorado of Northwestern Mexico.* Tucson, Arizona: University of Arizona Press.

Gentry, Howard Scott. 1998. *Rio Mayo Plants: The Tropical Deciduous Forest and Environs of Northwest Mexico.* Revised and edited by Paul S. Martin, David Yetman, Mark Fishbein, Phil Jenkins, Thomas R. van Devender, and Rebecca K. Wilson. Tucson, Arizona: University of Arizona.

Haehle, Robert G., and Joan Brookwell. 2004. *Native Florida Plants.* New York: Taylor Trade Publishing.

Hartlage, Richard W. 1999. "Making the Hard Choices." *Pacific Horticulture* 60 (1): 1–2.

Heflin, Jean. 1997. *Penstemons: The Beautiful Beardtongues of New Mexico.* Albuquerque, Mexico: Jackrabbit Press.

Henrickson, James, and Marshall C. Johnston. 1997. *A Flora of the Chihuahuan Desert Region.* Unpublished manuscript.

Hickman, James C., ed. 1993. *The Jepson Manual: Higher Plants of California.* Berkeley, California: University of California Press.

Irish, Mary. 2000. *Gardening in the Desert.* Tucson, Arizona: University of Arizona Press.

Irish, Mary. 2003a. *Arizona Gardener's Guide.* Nashville, Tennessee: Cool Springs Press.

Irish, Mary. 2003b. *Month by Month Gardening in the Desert Southwest.* Nashville, Tennessee: Cool Springs Press.

Johnson, Eric, and Scott Millard. 1993. *How to Grow the Wildflowers.* Tucson, Arizona: Ironwood Press.

Jones, Fred B. 1975. *Flora of the Texas Coastal Bend.* Corpus Christi, Texas: Mission Press.

Jones, Warren, and Charles Sacamano. 2000. *Landscape Plants for Dry Regions.* Tucson, Arizona: Fisher Books.

Kearney, Thoms H., and Robert H. Peebles. 1960. *Arizona Flora.* Berkeley, California: University of California Press.

Martin, William C., and Charles R. Hutchins. 1980. *A Flora of New Mexico*. Vaduz, Germany: J. Cramer.

Mason, Charles T., and P. B. Mason. 1987. *A Handbook of Mexican Roadside Flora*. Tucson, Arizona: University of Arizona Press.

Mielke, Judy. 1993. *Native Plants for Southwestern Landscapes*. Austin, Texas: University of Texas Press.

Miller, George O. 1991. *Landscaping with Native Plants of Texas and the Southwest*. Stillwater, Minnesota: Voyageur Press.

Munz, Philip A., and David Keck. 1968. *A California Flora*. Berkeley, California: University of California Press.

Nelson, Kim. 2003. *A Desert Gardener's Companion*. Tucson, Arizona: Rio Nuevo Press.

Nokes, Jill. 2001. *How to Grow Native Plants of Texas and the Southwest*. Austin, Texas: University of Texas Press.

Ogden, Scott. 1992. *Gardening Success with Difficult Soils*. Dallas, Texas: Taylor Publishing Company.

Perry, Bob. 1992. *Landscape Plants for Western Regions*. Claremont, California: Land Design Publishing.

Phillips, Judith. 1987. *Southwestern Landscaping with Native Plants*. Santa Fe, New Mexico: Museum of New Mexico Press.

Phillips, Judith. 1998. *New Mexico Gardener's Guide*. Nashville, Tennessee: Cool Springs Press.

Richardson, Alfred. 1995. *Plants of the Rio Grande Delta*. Austin, Texas: University of Texas Press.

Ryan, Julie. 1998. *Perennial Gardens for Texas*. Austin, Texas: University of Texas Press.

Shreve, Forrest, and Ira L. Wiggins. 1964. *Vegetation and Flora of the Sonoran Desert*. Stanford, California: Stanford University Press.

Sutton, John. 1999. *The Gardener's Guide to Growing Salvias*. Portland, Oregon: Timber Press.

Turner, Raymond M., Janice E. Bowers, and Tony L. Burgess. 1995. *Sonoran Desert Plants: An Ecological Atlas*. Tucson, Arizona: University of Arizona Press.

Warnock, Barton H. 1970. *Wildflowers of the Big Bend Country, Texas*. Alpine, Texas: Sul Ross State University.

Warnock, Barton H. 1974. *Wildflowers of the Guadalupe Mountains and the Sand Dune Country, Texas*. Alpine, Texas: Sul Ross State University.

Warnock, Barton H. 1977. *Wildflowers of the Davis Mountains and Marathon Basin, Texas*. Alpine, Texas: Sul Ross State University.

Wasowski, Sally. 1988. *Native Texas Plants: Landscaping Region by Region*. Austin, Texas: Texas Monthly Press.

Wasowski, Sally, and Julie Ryan. 1985. *Landscaping with Native Texas Plants*. Austin, Texas: Texas Monthly Press.

Watkins, John V., and Thomas J. Sheehan. 1975. *Florida Landscape Plants: Native and Exotic*. Gainesville, Florida: University Presses of Florida.

Welch, William C. 1989. *Perennial Garden Color: Perennials, Cottage Gardens, Old Roses, and Companion Plants*. New York: Taylor Trade Publishing.

Web Sites

I found the Internet a superb resource for information that would have taken years to ferret out in more conventional resources. I also found it a full of information that was odd, misleading, wrong, and suspicious. The Web sites listed here were reliable and consistent sources of solid information, and there are many more I am sure. In addition, many nursery Web sites contain information about the plants sold.

http://aggie-horticulture.tamu.edu—Texas A&M University horticultural resources.

http://gecko.gc.maricopa.edu/glendalelibrary—Glendale Xeriscape Botanical Garden at the Glendale Public Library in Glendale, Arizona.

http://museum.utep.edu/chih/gardens/gardens.htm—Chihuahuan Desert Garden at the University of Texas at El Paso.

http://nmrareplants.unm.edu—New Mexico Rare Plant Technical Council.

http://ucjeps.berkeley.edu—Jepson Herbarium of the University of California at Berkley.

http://uvalde.tamu.edu/herbarium—Native Plants of South Texas database of the Texas A&M Research and Extension Center.

http://www.ag.arizona.edu—Arizona County Extension Services. Individual counties accessed by adding "/" and the county name at the end of the URL.

http://www.cahe.nmsu.edu—New Mexico County Extension Services.

http://www.cnplx.info—California Native Plant Link Exchange, a collection of Web sites about California native plants.

http://www.cnps.org—California Native Plant Society.

http://www.desertmuseum.org—Arizona-Sonora Desert Museum in Tucson, Arizona.

http://www.desert-tropicals.com—A commercial site on garden plants of Arizona.

http://www.floridata.com—A commercial garden site on Florida ornamental plants.

http://www.itis.usda.gov—Integrated Taxonomic Information System of the United States Department of Agriculture.

http://www.mediterraneangardensociety.org—Mediterranean Garden Society.

http://www.mobot.org—Missouri Botanic Garden, with access to its TROPICOS database.

http://www.nargs.org—North American Rock Garden Society.

http://www.nazflora.org—A commercial site on native plants of northern Arizona.

http://www.npsot.org—Texas Native Plant Society.

http://www.plants.usda.gov/cgi_bin—Plants Database of the United States Department of Agriculture.

http://www.plantzafrica.com—South African Native Biodiversity Institute.

http://www.rhs.org.uk—Royal Horticultural Society.

http://www.sp2000.org—Species 2000, an international federation of database organizations to create and maintain a worldwide taxonomic database.

INDEX

Numbers in brackets refer to main entry pages. *Italic* numbers refer to photo pages.